The ABC's of AutoCAD

The ABC's of AutoCAD®

Alan R. Miller

San Francisco • Paris • Düsseldorf • London

Cover design by Thomas Ingalls + Associates
Cover photography by Michael Lamotte
Book design by Jeffrey James Giese

AutoCAD is a trademark of Autodesk, Inc.
IBM PC, IBM PC/AT, and **PC-DOS** are trademarks of International Business Machines Corportion.
Hewlett-Packard, NP, and **LaserJet** are trademarks of the Hewlett-Packard Corp.
Intel, 8086, 8088, 8087, 80286, 80287, and **80386** are trademarks of Intel Corp.
MS-DOS is a trademark of Microsoft Corporation.

SYBEX is a registered trademark of SYBEX, Inc.

SYBEX is not affiliated with any manufacturer.

Every effort has been made to supply complete and accurate information. However, SYBEX assumes no responsibility for its use, nor for any infringements of patents or other rights of third parties which would result.

Copyright ©1988 SYBEX Inc., 2021 Challenger Drive #100, Alameda, CA 94501. World rights reserved. No part of this publication may be stored in a retrieval system, transmitted, or reproduced in any way, including but not limited to photocopy, photograph, magnetic or other record, without the prior agreement and written permission of the publisher.

Library of Congress Card Number: 88-42629
ISBN 0-89588-498-4
Manufactured in the United States of America
10 9 8 7 6 5 4

Acknowledgments

I am sincerely grateful to Cheryl Holzaepfel, developmental editor of the manuscript, to Suzy Anger for her skillful copy editing, and to Jeff Giese for his technical review of the exercises. Other SYBEX staff members who made contributions are Jocelyn Reynolds, word processing; Aidan Wylde, typesetting; Ingrid Owen, chapter design and layout; and Kristen Iverson, proofreading. Thanks also to Robert Thomas Associates for preparing the index.

Contents at a Glance

Introduction		*xv*
Chapter 1:	Using Your Computer for Technical Drawing	*1*
Chapter 2:	Getting Down to Work with AutoCAD	*9*
Chapter 3:	Drawing and Selecting Shapes	*41*
Chapter 4:	Changing an Existing Drawing	*57*
Chapter 5:	Making More Elaborate Changes	*81*
Chapter 6:	Creating a Three-View Mechanical Drawing	*123*
Chapter 7:	Printing the Drawing	*155*
Chapter 8:	Some Shortcuts and Enhancements	*171*
Chapter 9:	Inserting Labels, Notes, and Legends	*213*
Chapter 10:	Adding the Dimensions to Your Drawings	*237*
Chapter 11:	Drawing in Three Dimensions	*281*
Appendix A:	Installing AutoCAD	*325*
Appendix B:	AutoCAD Commands	*349*
Index		*352*

Table of Contents

Introduction — xv

How to Use this Book — xv
Conventions Used in this Book — xvi

1 Using Your Computer for Technical Drawing — 1

Technical Drawing Conventions Used in this Book — 1
Computer Basics — 2
    The Hardware — 2
    The Software — 3
    The Keyboard — 4
How to Type Information at the Keyboard — 5
How to Correct Your Mistakes — 6

2 Getting Down to Work with AutoCAD — 9

How to Start AutoCAD — 9
How to Give Commands to AutoCAD — 12
    Responding to AutoCAD Prompts — 13
    The Mouse and Its Buttons — 13
How to Work with the Drawing Editor — 13
    The Drawing Cursor and the Coordinate Readout — 14
How to Use Cartesian and Polar Notation — 15
How to Change the Drawing Limits — 18
How to Use AutoCAD's Grid System — 20
    Positioning the Cursor Precisely with the Snap Mode — 21

Changing the Grid Spacing	22
How to Set the Number of Displayed Digits	23
How to Draw a Line with the Line Command	24
Drawing an Attached Line Segment	27
How to Draw an Angled Line	28
How to Erase a Line with the U Command	30
How to Use U and Redo After a Command is Completed	32
How to Get Help from AutoCAD	33
Getting Help for a Particular Command	34
How to Draw a Circle with the Circle Command	35
How to Save Your Work	37

3 Drawing and Selecting Shapes   41

How to Select by Pointing	41
How to Select Previously Selected Items	45
How to Select Previously Drawn Items	45
How to Select with a Regular Window	46
How to Remove Objects from the Selection Set	49
How to Add Objects to the Selection Set	50
How to Select with a Crossing Window	51
How to Undo the Previous Command	53
How to Complete a Drawing with the End Command	54

4 Changing an Existing Drawing   57

How to Create a Copy of a File	57
How to Align Lines Horizontally or Vertically	60
How to Enlarge Drawings with the Zoom Command	61
How to Duplicate Lines with the Copy Command	62

How to Establish the Displacement	63
How to Rotate an Object	63
How to Make Precise Connections with the Osnap Options	65
Displaying the Osnap Menu	65
How to Move Objects in a Drawing	67
How to Use the Trim Command	68
Trimming Lines	69
Trimming a Circle	72
Trimming the Trim Boundary	73
The Trim Command Compared to the Erase Command	76

5 Making More Elaborate Changes — 81

How to Set up the Drawing Area	81
How to Draw Two Connected Circles	84
How to Draw Tangent Lines with the Tan Command	86
How to Rotate the Drawing	90
How to Move an Object with the Stretch Command	92
How to Enlarge an Object with the Zoom Command	94
How to Use the Mark Option to Undo Your Work	96
How to Use the Break Command	97
Erasing Part of a Circle	98
The Trim Command Compared to the Break Command	101
How to Draw Concentric Circles	104
How to Draw Tangent Circles	104
How to Make Multiple Copies with the Array Command	106
Duplicating a Pattern	106
How to Draw an Arc	107
How to Draw a Wedge	112
Replicating an Object with the Mirror Command	113

6 Creating a Three-View Mechanical Drawing — 123

How to Draw Borders with the P-Line Command — 124
How to Make a Border Template — 127
How to Draw Rectangles — 128
    Drawing a Rectangle — 128
    Drawing a Square with the Polygon Command — 131
How to Use the Explode Command — 133
How to Modify a Drawing with Circles and Arcs — 138
How to Use AutoCAD's Standard Line Types — 145
How to Draw Hidden Lines — 146
    Changing the Line Type to Hidden — 149
    Changing the Scale of the Line Type — 151

7 Printing the Drawing — 155

How to Print a Drawing — 155
How to Widen Lines with the P-Edit Command — 159
    Changing Lines to Polylines — 159
How to Make a Larger Printer Plot — 166

8 Some Shortcuts and Enhancements — 171

How to Insert a Standard Border — 171
How to Draw the Top View — 173
    Drawing the Three Circles — 173
    Converting a Circle to an Arc — 177
    Connecting Two Circles — 178
    Extending Lines with the Extend Command — 179

Trimming the Circle Opening	181
Replicating the Circle Opening	182
How to Draw the Front View	188
Drawing the Center Line	188
Drawing the Left Side of the Front View	190
Adding Detail with Interior Lines	191
Drawing the Right Side of the Front View	192
How to Add Section Lines Using Hatching Patterns	194
Erasing Hatching	197
How to Break Lines with the Break Command	197
How to Add More Hatching	202
How to Widen the Object Lines	203

9 Inserting Labels, Notes, and Legends   213

How to Define the Legend Border	214
How to Use AutoCAD Typefaces	215
Changing the Typeface	216
Selecting the Typeface from the Screen	217
How to Write Text in the Legend Border	219
How to Speed Up Text Regeneration	221
Using the QText Command	221
Speeding Up Text Regeneration with the Layer Command	223
How to Reset the Text Height	226
How to Create the Legend for the Flange	227
Drawing the Legend Border	228
Setting the Variable Text Height	229
Writing Text in a Separate Layer	230
Changing to a Different Layer	232

Fixing the Text Height	233

10 Adding the Dimensions to Your Drawing   237

Principles of Dimensioning	237
Continuing with the Bracket Drawing	238
How to Dimension Using the One-Point Method	239
Specifying a Vertical Dimension	240
Specifying a Horizontal Dimension	241
Adding Center Lines	243
How to Use Other Dimensioning Techniques	245
Dynamic Zooming to the Top View	245
Establishing the Center Line Form	246
How to Dimension a Radius	247
How to Dimension a Diameter	249
How to Dimension with the Leader Command	250
Extending the Center Line	253
Converting a Line to a Center-Line Style	253
How to Dimension the Right View	254
Adding a Center Line to the Slot	255
Dimensioning the Slot	255
Dimensioning the Corner	257
Extending the Vertical Center Line	258
Converting to a Center-Line Style	259
How to Dimension the Flange	260
Specifying a Vertical Dimension for the Front View	261
Specifying a Horizontal Dimension for the Front View	262
Dimensioning the Top View	263
Changing the Circle to a Center Line	270

11 Drawing in Three Dimensions — 281

How to Set Up an Isometric Drawing	282
How to Identify the Three Isometric Views	284
How to Draw an Isometric View of a Cube	285
How to Draw an Isometric Circle	288
How to Erase Parts of an Ellipse	291
How to Draw the Isometric View of the Bracket	295
Drawing the Rectangular Parts	295
Drawing the Ellipses	298
Copying the Two Ellipses	302
Connecting the Ellipses	305
Drawing the Bracket Corners	310
Trimming the Openings	314
Replicating the Three Ellipses	316
Adding Connecting Lines to the Ellipses	317
Trimming the New Ellipses	318

A Installing AutoCAD — 325

Working with Floppy Disks	325
Handling Disks	325
Inserting a Disk into the Disk Drive	326
Required and Recommended Equipment to Run AutoCAD	326
How to Configure Your Computer for AutoCAD	327
How to Set the Prompt	328
How to Set the Number of Files and Buffers	329
How to Set Up the AUTOEXEC.BAT File	330
How to Set Up Mouse-Driver Software	332
How to Reset the Computer	333

How to Set Up the AutoCAD Subdirectory	333
How to Copy AutoCAD to Your Hard Disk	334
Configuring AutoCAD for Your Computer	336
Copying the Driver Routines to Another Floppy Disk	336
Temporarily Storing the Driver Routines on the Hard Disk	337
Configuring AutoCAD for Your Hardware	339
How to Erase the Hard-Disk Drivers	345

B   AutoCAD Commands   349

Index   352

Introduction

If you've never used AutoCAD before and want to start now, this book is for you. If you've been frustrated while trying to learn AutoCAD from other books, this book is for you. If you already know how to use AutoCAD, but need to help someone else get started, this book is for them. (It will save you time.)

This book will teach you how to use AutoCAD on your IBM or IBM-compatible computer. You do not need any previous experience with AutoCAD or with the operation of your computer because all the terminology and basic procedures are explained with the beginner in mind. Even if you already have some experience with AutoCAD, you will find useful tips throughout the book that will show you how to use AutoCAD more effectively.

You may have looked through the manual that came with AutoCAD. Though it is a comprehensive and useful reference, most new AutoCAD users find they need a more convenient tool while learning the program. That is the aim of this book—to supplement the manual, not replace it. As a hands-on introduction, this book contains numbered, easy-to-follow exercises that will get you drawing with AutoCAD immediately. Let's take a closer look.

How to Use this Book

If you've just bought AutoCAD and haven't installed it on your computer, begin with Appendix A. It will give you all the information you need to set up AutoCAD on your computer, and will even give you tips on how to configure the program to suit your computing needs. The first chapter shows you some computer basics. In Chapter 2, you'll learn how to start AutoCAD and how to communicate with it. Then you'll set up the drawing area and draw several lines and a circle. You'll use these shapes in Chapter 3 to learn how to select objects you want to change. This important concept is needed for many commands such as those that erase, move, copy, rotate, and mirror objects.

Then in Chapters 4 and 5 you'll discover some exciting and useful features that will enable you to make both simple and complex changes to your drawings.

In Chapter 6 you'll create a complete three-view drawing with hidden and center lines. You print the drawing in Chapter 7.

The next few chapters introduce you to features that will enhance your drawings and make your tasks easier. You'll create another complete drawing, adding hatching and labels. The concept of layers in AutoCAD is discussed, and you will learn how to add the dimensions to your drawing. An isometric view of the bracket is drawn in Chapter 11, and a list of AutoCAD commands is given in Appendix B.

Conventions Used in this Book

While you're using this book, you'll be asked to type information, you'll see messages from AutoCAD, and you'll be given instructions by me. So that you can differentiate between these types of information, we've devised a few rules, as follows:

- Explanatory information appears in standard paragraphs.
- When you are to do something on your computer, I will give you instructions in numbered steps:

    1.

    2.

    3.

    etc.

- When you are to type something in from the keyboard, you'll see the information you are to type in colored type:

    acad

- AutoCAD will give you messages or ask you for information. These messages and questions will also be in colored type, like this:

    AutoCAD message

1

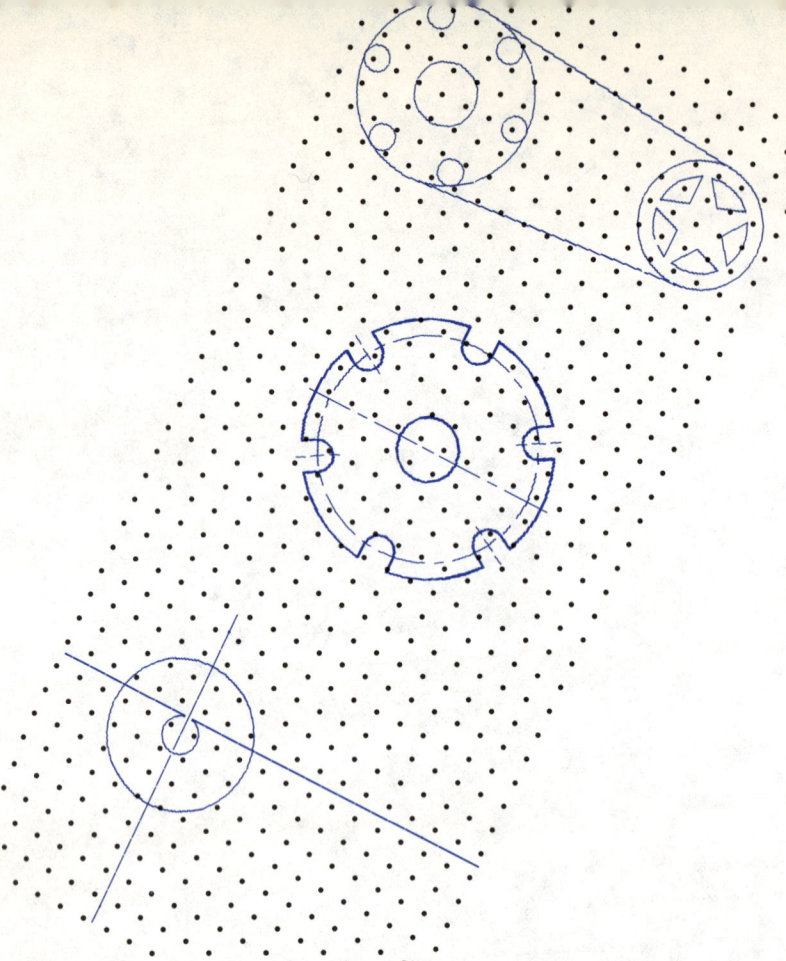

Using Your Computer for Technical Drawing

Featuring:
Technical drawing conventions
Computer basics

For many years, technical drawings were produced on paper using a pencil or a pen. The paper was mounted on a smooth board and the lines were guided with tools such as the T square, triangle, divider, and compass. Hand-guided lettering machines produced legible writing. The development of drafting machines improved the precision and speed of the drawing, although pen and pencil were still used. However, all these methods have a major disadvantage: extensive changes to a drawing require much effort. If a change is required, a line must be erased and a new one is drawn.

A major advance occurred with the invention of the computer-driven plotter. This made it possible to revise a drawing stored in a computer. Unfortunately, both the plotter and the computer that drove the plotter were expensive to buy and expensive to operate. Several recent developments have changed that—powerful microcomputers, plotters, and computer-aided design (CAD) programs that are fast, easy to use, and inexpensive.

Before we look at AutoCAD in the next chapters, let us consider some of the important drawing conventions that we will use.

Technical Drawing Conventions Used in this Book

In this book we will follow the conventions of engineering rather than architectural drawing. Nevertheless, the details of using a computer for CAD will be similar for both disciplines.

An engineering drawing usually shows a front view, a right view, and a top view all on the same sheet. An auxiliary view may also be given. (In Chapter 6 we will draw the front, right, and top view of a bracket.)

An important concept in an engineering drawing is that the right view is on the right side of the front view, and the top view is above (on top of) the front view. Furthermore, the top view is the one seen when looking down on the top of the object, while the front view is seen when looking at the front. This method of presenting information is known as *orthographic projection* because each view is drawn as we would see it when viewed perpendicular to the corresponding surface of the object.

Computer Basics

Your computer has two parts that work together. The *hardware* is the physical part of the computer and includes the keyboard, video screen, disks, mouse, printer, and plotter. The *software* is the intangible aspect of the computer. It includes the programs and data that tell the computer what to do. We can compare the hardware to a piano and the software to the music written for the piano.

The Hardware

The hardware is contained in several parts. Let us look at some of these parts in more detail.

The *system unit* contains most of the computer. It has the disk drives; the input and output (I/O) ports; and the electronic circuits such as the central processing unit (CPU), the main memory, and the math coprocessor.

Your *video screen*, or monitor, shows you what is happening. One knob on the screen sets the contrast and another sets the brightness. There may also be an on/off switch. It is a good idea to turn the brightness as low as possible. This makes the images sharper and lessens the chance that the screen will be damaged.

Most of the computer memory is lost each time the computer is turned off. Therefore, copies of programs and data must be stored on a more permanent medium such as a magnetic *disk*. When using AutoCAD, you should be familiar with two types of disk: floppy and hard. All personal computers have at least one floppy disk. When the computer needs information stored on a disk, it copies or *loads* the information from the disk into its main memory. In effect, the computer temporarily memorizes the information.

There are two sizes of floppy disk—$5^1/_4$ inches wide (called a 5-inch disk) and $3^1/_2$ inches wide. The disk is protected by an outer plastic envelope. When the disk is in use, it rotates within this envelope.

There is another important piece of hardware you should have for successful computer operation: a *surge suppressor*. You can use Auto-CAD without this equipment, but you will find that it is well worth the extra cost. The electricity supplied to your computer may contain high frequencies generated by other electrical appliances nearby. These higher frequencies may cause errors in the operation of your computer. A more serious problem is high voltage caused by lightning or by turning a heavy appliance on or off. This can subject your computer to a voltage that is too high and can burn out components of your computer.

Both these problems can be prevented with a surge suppressor. You plug the surge suppressor into the electrical outlet and then you plug your computer and its accessories into the surge suppressor. Suppressors range in cost from $10 to $100. You can obtain a very good one for around $55 from an electronic supply or computer store.

The Software

A computer needs a set of instructions, called a *program*, to make it operate properly. The program is installed in the main memory of the computer. Once installed, the program directs the computer to perform specific operations. Computer programs and any data needed by the program are called *software*. Software can be divided into three basic categories: system software, applications software, and data files.

System software includes the *disk operating system* (DOS) and utility programs. The operating system runs the computer while the utility programs do special tasks such as preparing and copying disks.

DOS manages the resources of the computer. It reads your commands from the keyboard, displays information on the video screen, printer, and plotter, and executes applications programs for you. In addition, the operating system does such chores as managing the disk space and the main memory space of the computer.

You use *applications software* to perform specific tasks. Word processing programs, spreadsheet programs, and AutoCAD are examples of applications software.

Collections of characters and numbers—for example the names and addresses for a mailing list and a drawing you create with AutoCAD—are known as *data files*. Data files are created by you and manipulated by computer programs.

The Keyboard

Instructions you type at the keyboard are sent to the system unit and placed into main memory. One type of keyboard is shown in Figure 1.1. The keyboard has regular alphabetic and numeric keys similar to those found on a typewriter. The key marked Enter, Return, or ⏎ serves the same purpose as the typewriter carriage return key: it marks the end of a line. In this book, we call it the Enter key. Another useful key is Backspace. This key is labeled with either the word *Backspace* or a left-pointing arrow. If it does have an arrow, be careful not to confuse it with the other key that has a left-pointing arrow and a 4 on it. That is one of the cursor-movement keys.

Figure 1.1: Standard IBM keyboard

The keys marked Shift or ⇧ are like the shift keys on a typewriter. The shift-lock key is labeled CapsLock. It works just like the shift-lock on a typewriter except it only works for letters. It also has an interesting feature. If you press a shift key when the CapsLock is engaged, you temporarily return the keyboard to lowercase.

The computer keyboard has two other important keys: Ctrl, for control and Alt, for alternate. When these keys are pressed, they change the meaning of the other keys. The Tab key, next to the letter Q, is marked with the ⇆ symbol. Finally, there is a key marked Esc for escape. This key allows you to interrupt, or escape, from the current task. It is found on either the right side or the left side of your keyboard.

Function Keys

The computer keyboard also has keys labeled F1 through F10 or F12 on the left end or at the top of the keyboard. These are called *function keys*. The meanings of these keys change because any program can redefine them. We will frequently use several of these keys with AutoCAD.

Numeric Keys

The right side of the keyboard has a grouping of keys called the *number pad* that duplicates the regular number keys (0–9) across the top of the keyboard. These keys do double duty; you can either use them as numbers, or you can use them to move around on the video screen. The keys show arrows pointing up, down, left, and right. There are also keys labeled Home, PgUp, End, PgDn, Ins, and Del that you can use if you don't have a mouse. (We won't use these keys.) The key labeled NumLock selects which of these two meanings you want. If you press NumLock and then the number keys, you will see numbers on the screen. If you press NumLock again and then press the number keys, you will move on the screen. The regular shift keys can also be used to quickly change from one of these meanings to the other. That is, if the pad is set to numbers, you can move on the screen by holding one of the shift keys. Some keyboards have two sets of keys on the right side: one set of keys to move around the screen and one set for typing numbers.

How to Type Information at the Keyboard

In this section you'll use a few keys on your keyboard, so start your computer and turn on your video screen. If you need help getting started, read Appendix A. Notice that there is a blinking symbol next to the C> prompt on the video screen. This is the *cursor*. It shows where the next character you type will appear. Press the Enter key and notice that the DOS prompt appears again on the next line. Do this several times and notice how the computer simply repeats the prompt on the next line.

The Enter key is used to send a command to DOS. However, in this instance, no command was given. Therefore, DOS simply repeats the prompt. You have also seen that it is necessary to press the Enter key at the end of each *command line*. This tells DOS to execute the line, that is, to do what the command says. But there is an exception.

Certain commands are given by pressing two keys at once: the key marked Ctrl (the control key) and another key. When you give such a command, only a single character, known as a *control character*, is sent from the keyboard to the computer. In this book, control characters are represented by the symbol ^ followed by the corresponding letter.

Because control characters are a special type of command, you do not press the Enter key after the control character has been typed. Rather, DOS begins executing the command as soon as the pair of keys is pressed.

For example, while holding the Ctrl key, press the I key twice. The cursor moves to the right because this is the tab character. Now while holding the Ctrl key, press the H key twice. The cursor moves back to the original position because this is the backspace character. It does not matter if the CapsLock is engaged when you type a control character. In other words, a lowercase ^h is the same as an uppercase ^H. The set of control characters includes the letters (^A through ^Z) and other characters such as ^@ and ^[. However, not all control characters are used by DOS. A different set of control characters is used by AutoCAD. For example, ^C terminates the current AutoCAD command.

How to Correct Your Mistakes

Whether you are giving a command to DOS or to AutoCAD, you can correct a typing error if you have not pressed the Enter key. Simply press the Backspace key (or ^H which, as you have seen, is the same thing). Then the cursor backs up and the most recently typed character is erased from the screen.

You can erase an entire line by pressing the Esc key when in DOS, or ^X when running AutoCAD.

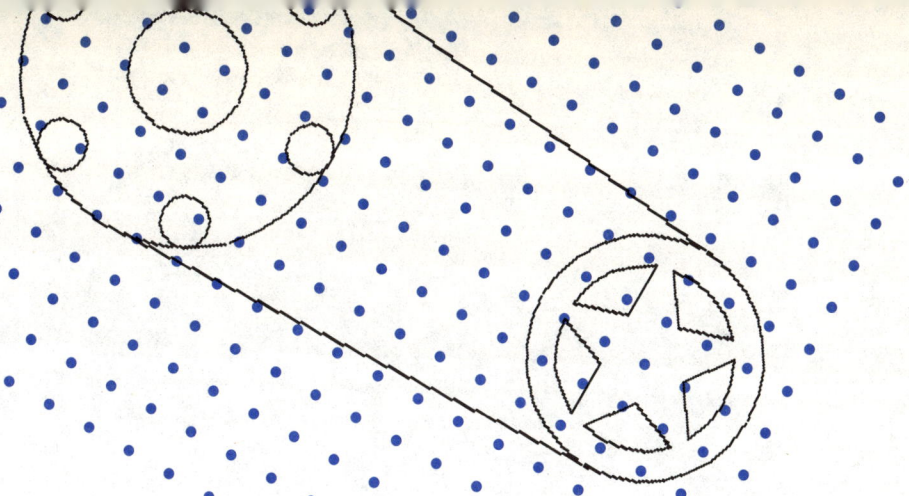

2

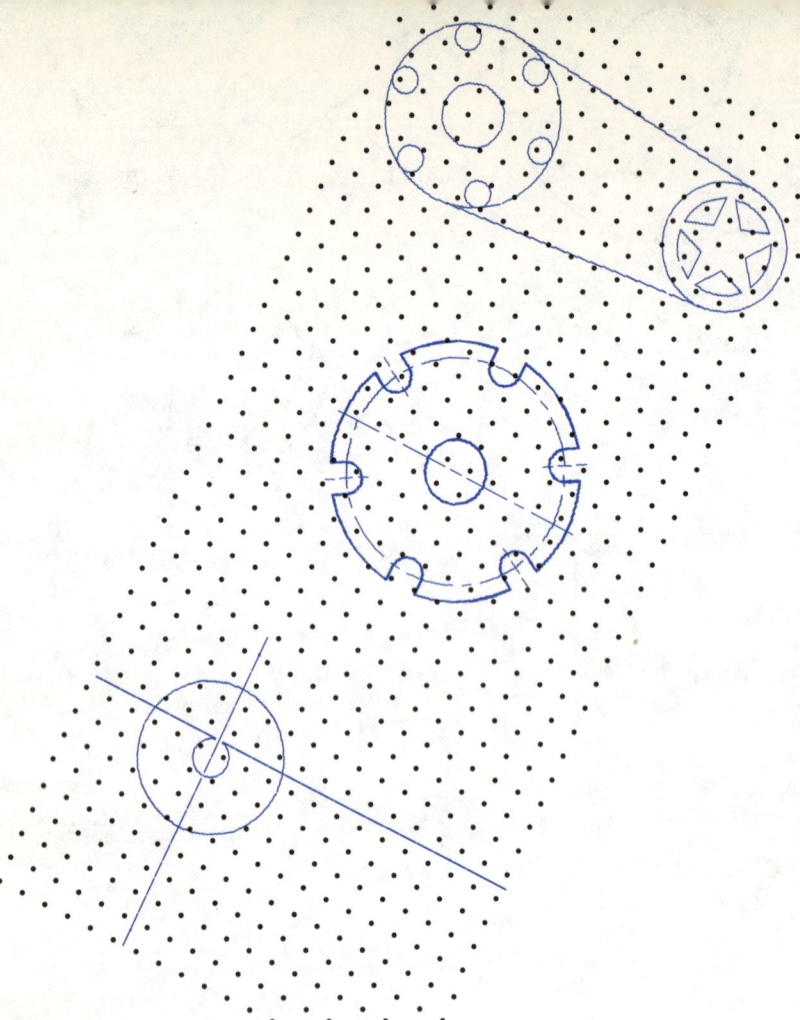

Getting Down to Work with AutoCAD

Featuring:
- Starting AutoCAD
- Working with the drawing editor
- Drawing lines and circles
- Correcting mistakes
- Saving your work
- Getting help from AutoCAD

Now that you're familiar with your computer, let's take a closer look at AutoCAD. In this chapter you will start AutoCAD, learn how to give commands, set up the drawing area, use the drawing cursor, and draw some straight lines and a circle. You'll use this drawing in the next chapter to learn additional AutoCAD features.

AutoCAD commands introduced in this chapter are

- Status to check the status of your drawing screen
- Limits to change the drawing size
- Snap to precisely locate a position
- Grid to display an array of dots
- Units to change the way numbers are displayed
- Line to draw a line
- Ortho to force orthogonal alignment
- U to undo the previous command
- Redo to reverse the U command
- Circle to draw a circle
- Save to save an intermediate version of a drawing

We begin by starting AutoCAD.

How to Start AutoCAD

Because running AutoCAD from a floppy disk is so awkward, let us assume that your computer runs from a hard disk. Before you start the computer from the hard disk, make sure you do not have a floppy disk in the floppy drive or the computer will not be able to start from the hard disk. If the hard disk is properly set up, the computer will read a copy of DOS from the hard disk.

If your video screen has an on/off switch, turn it on. Also turn on your printer and plotter. Then turn your computer on. You will see the DOS prompt C> on the video screen. DOS displays this symbol to show that it is ready to accept your next command. The letter C in the prompt also identifies the name of the current drive.

1. Change to the AutoCAD directory by typing

    cd acad

    and pressing Enter.

2. Start AutoCAD with the command

    acad

    and press Enter.

3. If you see the AutoCAD greeting for new users (Figure 2.1), press Enter.

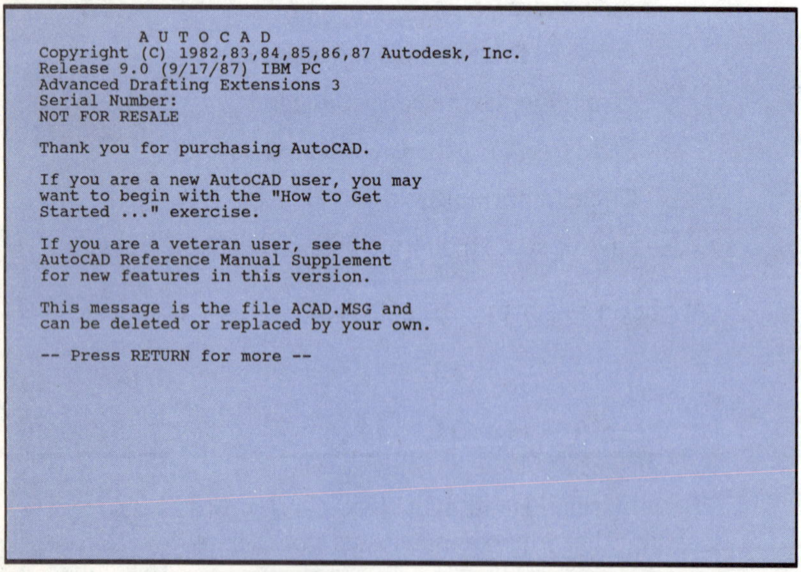

```
           A U T O C A D
Copyright (C) 1982,83,84,85,86,87 Autodesk, Inc.
Release 9.0 (9/17/87)  IBM PC
Advanced Drafting Extensions 3
Serial Number:
NOT FOR RESALE

Thank you for purchasing AutoCAD.

If you are a new AutoCAD user, you may
want to begin with the "How to Get
Started ..." exercise.

If you are a veteran user, see the
AutoCAD Reference Manual Supplement
for new features in this version.

This message is the file ACAD.MSG and
can be deleted or replaced by your own.

-- Press RETURN for more --
```

Figure 2.1: The AutoCAD greeting

4. The Main menu shown in Figure 2.2 appears next. Since we are starting our first file, choose option 1 by pressing the 1 key (the one above the Q key, not the one on the number pad at the right side of the keyboard), and then press the Enter key. AutoCAD asks for a file name with this prompt:

    Enter NAME of drawing:

Getting Down to Work with AutoCAD **11**

```
                A U T O C A D
Copyright (C) 1982,83,84,85,86,87 Autodesk, Inc.
Release 9.0 (9/17/87) IBM PC
Advanced Drafting Extensions 3
Serial Number:
NOT FOR RESALE

Main Menu

    0.  Exit AutoCAD
    1.  Begin a NEW drawing
    2.  Edit an EXISTING drawing
    3.  Plot a drawing
    4.  Printer Plot a drawing

    5.  Configure AutoCAD
    6.  File Utilities
    7.  Compile shape/font description file
    8.  Convert old drawing file

Enter selection:
```

Figure 2.2: The AutoCAD Main menu

5. We'll call our file FIRST. Type

   first

   and press Enter. If AutoCAD was already running when you sat down to the computer, type

   first =

   and press Enter. Adding the equal sign to the end of the name resets certain features, such as the drawing size, that may have been changed by the previous user. Of course, it does no harm to include the equal sign. If AutoCAD responds with the message

   *** * Warning! Drawing FIRST already exists.
   Do you want to replace it with the new drawing? <N>**

   This means that there is already a drawing with that name. Type

   y

   and press Enter to replace the existing version of your drawing with your new one.

You will now see the drawing editor screen (Figure 2.3). Look at the bottom of the screen to see if the line

Mouse driver has not been installed

appears. If this message appears, you must leave AutoCAD and install the mouse driver before continuing. (See Appendix A for instructions on installing the mouse driver. Skip to the last section of this chapter to learn how to leave AutoCAD.)

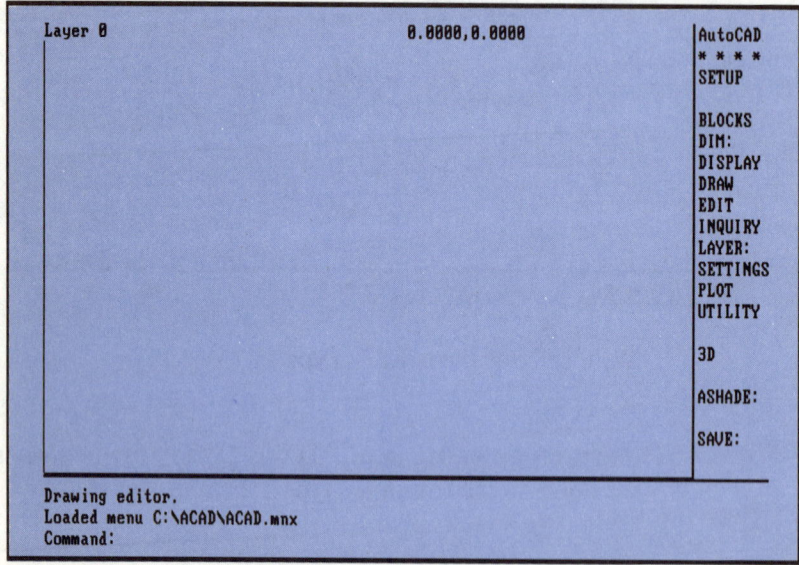

Figure 2.3: The AutoCAD drawing editor screen

Good. AutoCAD is now ready to use. Let's take a moment to look at how you communicate with AutoCAD.

How to Give Commands to AutoCAD

As you use AutoCAD, you will need to give instructions, or *commands*. You can give commands to AutoCAD in one of two ways: typing them at the keyboard or selecting them from a screen menu and pressing a mouse button. When you type a command, you must press the Enter key at the end of the line to start the command. When you select a command from the screen menu, you press the left button on the mouse to start the command.

You will find that typing commands is much faster than selecting them from the menu, especially if you are a good typist. Furthermore, for many commands you need only type one word while you must select a series of items from a sequence of the screen menus. However, sometimes you may want to select commands from one of the menus, especially if you are not sure which command you want to use.

Responding to AutoCAD Prompts

When AutoCAD wants you to respond, there will be a prompt on the bottom line of the screen. The common prompt is

Command:

You can respond by typing a command at the keyboard and pressing Enter. Alternatively, you can move the cursor to the menu on the right edge of the screen. When the desired item is highlighted, press the left mouse button.

The Mouse and Its Buttons

You tell AutoCAD where you want to draw by moving the mouse. The mouse has two or three buttons, which you press to select options. The left button is frequently used to choose a location or to select one word from a group of words in a menu. Consequently, this button is called the *pick* button. The second (or middle) mouse button is equivalent to the Enter key. You will frequently use this button to complete one stage of a command.

How to Work with the Drawing Editor

The drawing editor screen is divided into three areas. The right side of the screen shows a menu of commands from which you can select. You'll learn more about this menu later. In this chapter, you will type your commands from the keyboard because it is faster. Additional information is shown on the top line of the screen. We will consider items in this line shortly. The remainder of the screen is used for your drawing.

*T*he Drawing Cursor and the Coordinate Readout

To draw an object, you move your mouse and the *drawing cursor,* a pair of crossed lines, moves on the screen accordingly. The drawing cursor tells AutoCAD where you want to draw. When you start a new AutoCAD drawing, this cursor is hidden in the lower-left corner of the drawing area.

The cursor on screen moves with your mouse. As you move the mouse left or right, the cursor moves correspondingly left or right. Similarly, if you move the mouse away from or toward yourself, the cursor moves either upward or downward on the screen.

All positions on the drawing screen are referenced to the origin located at the lower-left corner of the drawing. Horizontal distances are measured to the right, in the X direction; vertical distances are measured upward in the Y direction. The coordinates of a point (a pair of numbers) give the X and Y positions separated by a comma. The value of the origin is 0,0. Thus the coordinate location 4,3 is located 4 units to the right and 3 units upward from the origin. The units can represent inches, feet, meters, or any other unit.

To see how cursor movement affects the coordinate readout, try this exercise.

1. Look at the top line of the screen, just to the right of the center. Two numbers, separated by a comma, are displayed. These numbers are initially zero.

2. Press the F6 function key to turn on the coordinate display.

3. Move your mouse upward and to the right until the drawing cursor appears (Figure 2.4). Notice that the coordinate readout changes as you move the cursor. The numbers give the X and Y coordinates of the crossed lines of the cursor.

Getting Down to Work with AutoCAD   15

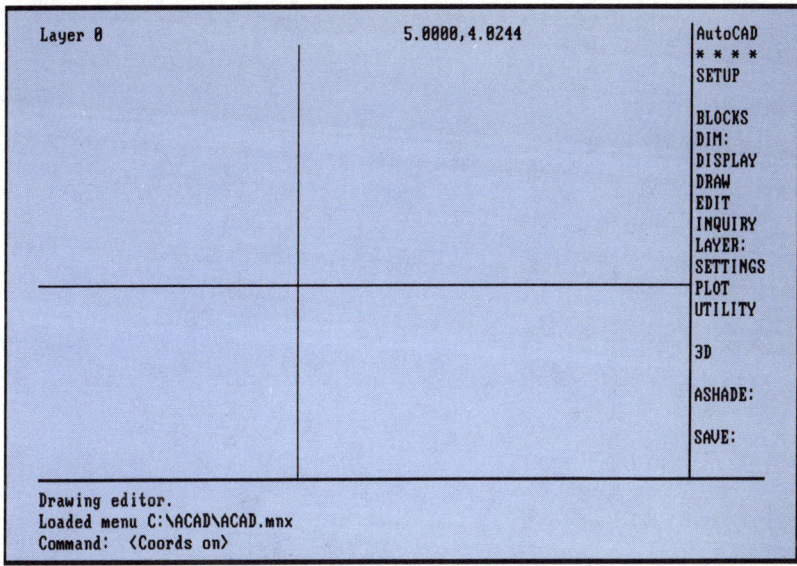

Figure 2.4: The AutoCAD drawing cursor is two crossed lines

How to Use Cartesian and Polar Notation

Before we set up the drawing area, let us consider cartesian and polar notations. A *cartesian* or rectangular coordinate system is established to locate items precisely on the drawing. There is a horizontal or X-axis and a vertical or Y-axis. The two axes are *orthogonal* or perpendicular for orthographic projection. Each point on the drawing is referenced to the coordinate system by a pair of numbers which give the X and Y distances. The intersection of the X and Y axes is the origin of the coordinate system and the coordinate position there is 0, 0. The horizontal X numbers increase to the right and the vertical Y numbers increase vertically upward.

As an example, consider the two points, A and B, shown in Figure 2.5. The coordinate position of point A is 2, 1 because it is located at an X distance of 2 and a Y distance of 1 from the origin. The coordinate position of point B is 6, 4 because it is located at an X distance of 6 and a Y distance of 4 from the origin.

We define a straight line by the coordinates of its two end points. For example, we might draw a line from point A at coordinate

16   The ABC's of AutoCAD

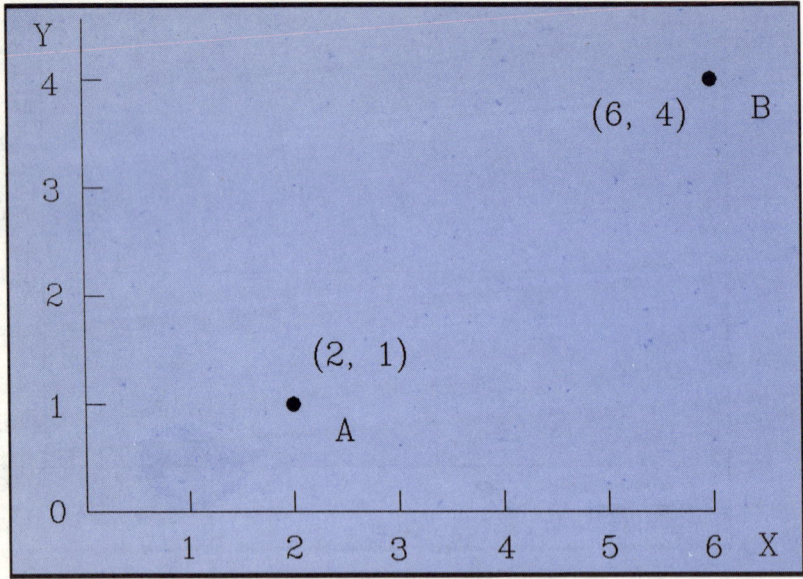

Figure 2.5: Two points in the rectangular coordinate system

location 2, 1 to point B at coordinate position 6, 4 as shown in Figure 2.6. This is called an absolute cartesian reference because both ends are referenced absolutely to the coordinate system. Sometimes, however, it will be more convenient to give the coordinates of the second point relative to the first point, rather than to the coordinate origin. In the present example, the second point has the relative coordinates 4, 3 because the X distance between the points (6-2) is 4 and Y distance between the points (4-1) is 3.

A variation of the relative reference system is known as *polar notation*. With this method, you give a relative radial distance and an angle from the horizontal. For the present example, the length of the line is 5. Therefore, the second point has a relative polar location of 5 at the angle 37 degrees as shown in Figure 2.7. This polar coordinate is written as 5 <37.

Thus, with polar notation, the direction to the right (the east or 3 o'clock orientation) is an angle of zero, while straight up (the north or 12 o'clock orientation), in the direction of the Y axis, is an angle of 90 degrees. The direction to the left is 180 degrees while the direction downward is both 270 degrees and −90 degrees.

Getting Down to Work with AutoCAD   17

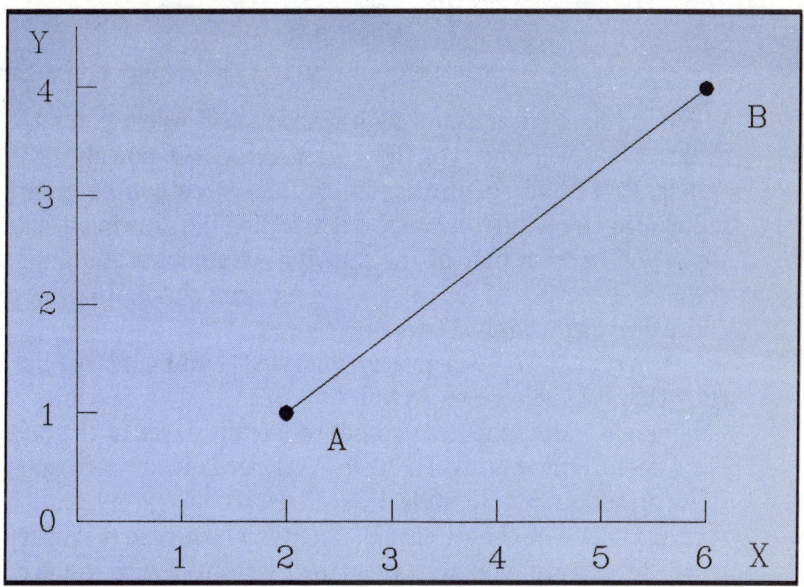

Figure 2.6: Cartesian coordinates of a straight line

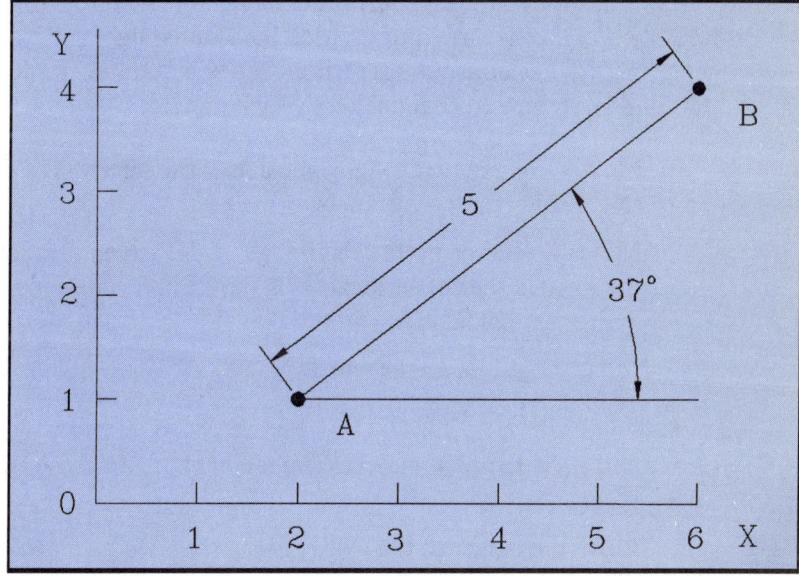

Figure 2.7: Polar coordinates of a straight line

How to Change the Drawing Limits

When you create a technical drawing with a pencil, you must select a scale. However, when you draw with AutoCAD, you always draw in full scale. The image displayed on the screen can be enlarged or reduced to any desired size without affecting the drawing itself. Then, when you make a plot of the drawing, you choose the appropriate scale to fit the size of the paper. You also can choose to print out the entire drawing or only a part of it.

In this section you will give an AutoCAD command that automatically changes the screen. As you have seen, only a few lines of your commands and AutoCAD's responses are displayed at the bottom of the screen. However, when AutoCAD needs to display many lines of information, it automatically switches to the *text screen*. Then the drawing area is no longer visible. After you have read the information on the text screen, you must press the F1 key to return to the drawing editor screen.

The size of the drawing area is established by AutoCAD variables known as the horizontal and vertical *drawing limits*. AutoCAD automatically sets the size at 12 units wide by 9 units high, but you can change these dimensions. In this section, you will examine the drawing limits and learn how to change them. Try it now.

1. Move the cursor to the far right side of the screen. The cursor shape changes to a rectangle.

2. Move the cursor up the right edge of the screen. Notice that the word at the cursor location is shown in reverse video or in a different color.

3. Move the cursor to the word

    INQUIRY

    and press the pick button. The menu changes to the Inquiry menu.

4. Move the cursor to the word

    STATUS:

    and press the pick button.

Getting Down to Work with AutoCAD 19

This command does two things. First, it automatically switches to the text screen. Then it displays information about your drawing screen and about your computer. (Notice that you had to pick two items from the screen menu: INQUIRY first and STATUS: second. Alternatively, you only have to type the one word—status—from the keyboard to do the same thing.)

The screen looks like that in Figure 2.8. The second and third lines give the limits of your drawing area. The values in this example are

Limits are X: 0.0000 12.0000
Y: 0.0000 9.0000

They show that the drawing size has a width of 12 units (in the X direction) and a height of 9 units (in the Y direction). That is, the lower-left corner, the coordinate origin, is at location 0,0 and the upper-right corner is at coordinate location 12,9. The limits shown on your screen will be these default values if you placed an equal sign at the end of the file name when you started your drawing. Of course, you will want to enlarge the limits when drawing large items.

```
      0 entities in FIRST
   Limits are        X:      0.0000     12.0000   (Off)
                     Y:      0.0000      9.0000
   Drawing uses      *Nothing*
   Display shows     X:      0.0000     13.1826
                     Y:      0.0000      9.4984
   Insertion base is X:      0.0000  Y:  0.0000  Z:   0.0000
   Snap resolution is X:     1.0000  Y:  1.0000
   Grid spacing is   X:      0.0000  Y:  0.0000

   Current layer:    0
   Current color:    BYLAYER -- 7 (white)
   Current linetype: BYLAYER -- CONTINUOUS
   Current elevation:     0.0000  thickness:    0.0000
   Axis off  Fill on  Grid off  Ortho off  Qtext off  Snap off  Tablet off
   Object snap modes: None
   Free RAM:   7512 bytes      Free disk: 2197504 bytes
   I/O page space: 143K bytes

   Command:
```

Figure 2.8: The Status command from the Inquiry menu shows information about the drawing screen

Now let's change these limits.

5. Type the command

   limits

   and press Enter. AutoCAD responds with

   ON/OFF<Lower left corner><0.0000,0.0000>:

   showing the current coordinates for the lower-left corner (AutoCAD encloses current values in angle brackets).

6. Press the Enter key to accept the current value. AutoCAD then shows the current coordinates for the upper-right corner and waits for you to enter new values.

7. Type

   13, 10

   and press Enter to change the upper-right corner.

8. Press F1 to change back to the drawing screen.

How to Use AutoCAD's Grid System

In the previous section you saw how to establish the coordinate origin and the size of the drawing area. On the drawing screen, each part of your drawing is precisely referenced to the origin through a rectangular grid system. *Grid points* are dots that appear at regular intervals in both the horizontal and vertical directions. The grid points are like mile markers on a highway because they help you locate certain positions. The grid points have a default spacing of one unit, but you can easily change the spacing to something else. The grid only appears on the video screen. It does not show on a printout of your drawing.

In this section you'll turn on the grid system and learn how to move the cursor from one point to another.

1. Press the F7 function key to turn on the grid system. An array of dots appears on the drawing screen. (The grid is visible on the figures of this chapter). F7 is a *toggle key;* each time you press it, it changes the display of the grid—off if it is on, and on if it is off.

2. Try to position the cursor precisely at the coordinate location

   4.0000, 3.0000

   As you move the cursor, notice that it is difficult to position it at exactly that location. In the next section you will learn to position the cursor precisely.

3. Now move one grid point to the right and notice that the first number, the horizontal reading, has changed by 1 because the grid spacing is one unit.

*P*ositioning the Cursor Precisely with the Snap Mode

You saw in the previous section that it is difficult to precisely position the cursor. To help you with this task, AutoCAD can lock the cursor onto the grid system. Then, when you draw an object, the cursor can stop only at the grid points. This feature is known as *Snap* mode because as you move the cursor, it does not move smoothly; rather, it jumps or snaps from one grid point to another.

Let's see how Snap mode works.

1. Move the mouse; notice that the cursor moves smoothly on the screen.

2. Move the cursor near the coordinate position

   4.0000, 3.0000

   but do not try to position it exactly.

3. Press F9 to turn on Snap mode. The word *Snap* appears on the top line of the screen. Notice that the cursor snaps to the nearest grid point. The coordinate readout at the top of the screen will now show precisely

   4.0000, 3.0000

4. Now, move the cursor to the right. Notice that this time it jumps or snaps from one grid point to the next.

The default snap spacing is 1 but you can change it to something else. For example, the drawings you will create later in this book use measurements that are multiples of 0.5. Therefore, if you set up the snap spacing to 0.5, you will be able to draw rapidly but precisely.

5. To change the snap spacing, type

    snap

    and press Enter. AutoCAD responds with the prompt

    Snap spacing on ON/OFF/Aspect/Rotate/ Style <1.0>:

    to show you what options you can select. The value given in angle brackets (1.0) is the current spacing.

6. Type

    0.5

    and press Enter to change the snap spacing to 0.5. Notice that the grid is now denser. There are four times as many points because the spacing was reduced in both directions.

Good. Now go on to change the grid setting so it matches the snap spacing.

Changing the Grid Spacing

As you have seen, the cursor is automatically positioned to the snap points. On the other hand, the grid spacing is only used to help you find your way. Nevertheless, it is usually convenient to set the grid spacing to the snap spacing.

1. Type the command

    grid

    and press Enter. AutoCAD responds with

    Grid spacing(X) or ON/OFF/Snap/Aspect <0>:

    Notice that options given for the Snap and Grid commands have a mixture of upper- and lowercase letters. This is a general AutoCAD style. When you type an option, you can abbreviate it to just the uppercase letters given in the response.

2. Type

   s

   for Snap and press Enter to set the grid spacing to the snap spacing (0.5 now). (Of course, you can spell out the word *Snap* if you want.)

3. Move the cursor to coordinate position

   4.0000, 3.0000

   Then move it right to the next grid point. Notice that the coordinate location is

   4.5000, 3.0000

   showing that the grid spacing is 0.5.

How to Set the Number of Displayed Digits

AutoCAD maintains an accuracy of 14 decimal digits, although it normally displays numbers with four digits past the decimal point. However, you can easily change the number of displayed digits with the Units command to suit your need for precision. (You will normally want to make the display match the snap spacing.) Try it now.

1. Give the command

   units

   and press Enter. The screen shifts to Text mode and shows a list of options. You can choose to display numbers in one of five styles:

   1. Scientific (with an exponent)
   2. Decimal

3. Engineering (feet and decimal inches)
4. Architectural (feet and fractional inches)
5. Fractional

2. Press the Enter key to accept the current display of decimal numbers (item 2 on the screen).

3. At the next prompt:

   Number of digits to right of decimal point:

   Type

   1

   and press Enter. Now AutoCAD will display numbers with only one digit past the decimal point rather than the four we have been seeing.

4. To skip over the remaining questions, press ^C. This cancels the current AutoCAD command.

5. Press F1 to switch back to the graphics screen.

6. Move the cursor; notice that the coordinate readout on the top line now shows only one digit past the decimal point.

Congratulations. Your drawing area is set up and you're ready to use AutoCAD for drawing. In the following sections, you will draw and erase straight lines and draw a circle.

How to Draw a Line with the Line Command

In this section you learn how to draw straight lines with the Line command. You also learn how to use the Ortho command to make your lines automatically align with the horizontal and vertical axes.

1. If the grid is off, turn it on by pressing F7.
2. Check the top line of the screen. If the word *Snap* does not appear, press F9 to turn Snap mode on.

3. Type the command

   line

   and press the Enter key to start the Line command.

4. Move the mouse upward and to the right. Watch the coordinate readout (on the top line) change as the cursor snaps from one grid point to the next. (If the coordinate display does not change as you move the cursor, press F6 to turn on this feature.)

5. Move the cursor until it is located at the coordinate position of

   4.0, 3.5

   This is a rectangular reference. It shows a position of 4.0 units to the right and 3.5 units upward from the lower-left corner of the drawing area. You can verify this by counting the grid points, which appear at intervals of 0.5.

6. To start drawing a line from the cursor position, press the pick, or left, mouse button. Alternatively, you can press the space bar or the Enter key. A plus symbol appears at the cursor position to mark the start of the line. The coordinate display resets to zero.

7. Move the cursor upward and to the right. You are drawing a line on the screen as you move the cursor—one end is attached to the point you selected, the other end is fastened to the cursor (Figure 2.9). As you move the cursor, watch the coordinate display on the top line. It is now displaying your position in polar coordinates relative to the starting point. Move the cursor until the coordinate display shows

   4.3 <21

   This notation describes a line length of 4.3 units oriented at a 21-degree angle.

Notice that this angled line is not smooth. It has zigzags or steps along its length. Since lines on the video screen are created from a sequence of dots that are arranged in horizontal and vertical patterns, only horizontal and vertical lines will be smooth.

Sometimes you want to draw a line that is angled. Other times you want a line that is exactly horizontal or vertical. Let us see how to

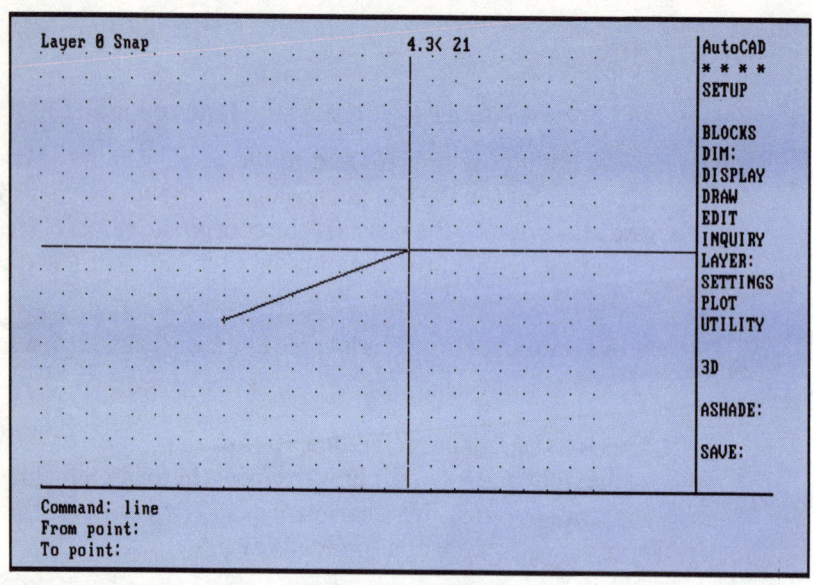

Figure 2.9: Drawing a line with the Line command

draw a horizontal line. Then we will draw a vertical line. Finally, we will draw several angled lines.

8. Press the F8 function key to turn on *Ortho* mode. The word *Ortho* appears on the top line when it is on. This forces new lines to be oriented *orthogonally*, that is, either vertically or horizontally (whichever is closer to the cursor). Now, the new line you drew will connect with only one line of your cursor rather than at the intersection of both lines. In the example shown in Figure 2.10, the closest line was horizontal, so the new line was oriented in that way. Notice that the zigzags have disappeared. If your line is oriented vertically, move the cursor downward until the line becomes horizontal, as in Figure 2.10. The coordinate readout shows the position of the end of the line rather than the cursor.

9. Now move the cursor to the right until the coordinate readout shows

    6.0 <0

Getting Down to Work with AutoCAD 27

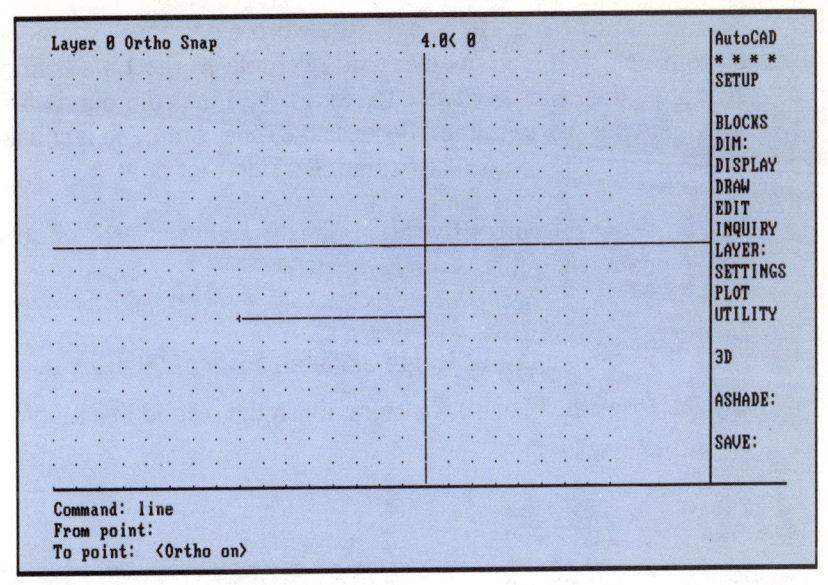

Figure 2.10: New line with Ortho mode on

This position is a polar reference to the line, not to your cursor. It shows that your line has a length of 6.0 units and is oriented at an angle of zero degrees.

10. Press the pick button to establish the first line segment. Notice that the coordinate display resets to the cursor position.

Good. You've just drawn your first line with AutoCAD. Now let's draw a second line attached to the first.

Drawing an Attached Line Segment

In the previous section you drew a line with the Line command. Notice that the bottom line of the screen shows

To point:

rather than

Command:

to show that the Line command is still active, even though you established, or fixed, the line. (If the word *Command:* shows on the bottom line, you have inadvertently completed the Line command. Just press the Enter key twice to restart the Line command and connect up to the previous line.) Because the Line command is still active, you can add a line to your first line. Let's do that now.

1. Move the cursor five grid points straight upward. The coordinate readout is

    2.5 <90

    to show a line of length 2.5 at an angle of 90 degrees.

2. Press the pick button to establish the second line segment.

How to Draw an Angled Line

Now let's draw four more line segments that are angled rather than vertical or horizontal. However, you must turn the Ortho mode off to do this.

1. Press F8 to turn off Ortho mode. The word *Ortho* disappears from the top line of the screen.

2. Move the cursor five grid points to the left and four grid points upward to draw a third line. The coordinate display reads

    3.2 <141

    This shows a line length of 3.2 units oriented at an angle of 141 degrees (Figure 2.11).

3. Press the pick button to establish the third line.

Now you will need to turn off Snap mode so you can position the cursor between grid points for the next line.

4. Press F9 to turn off Snap mode. Notice that the word *Snap* disappears from the top line.

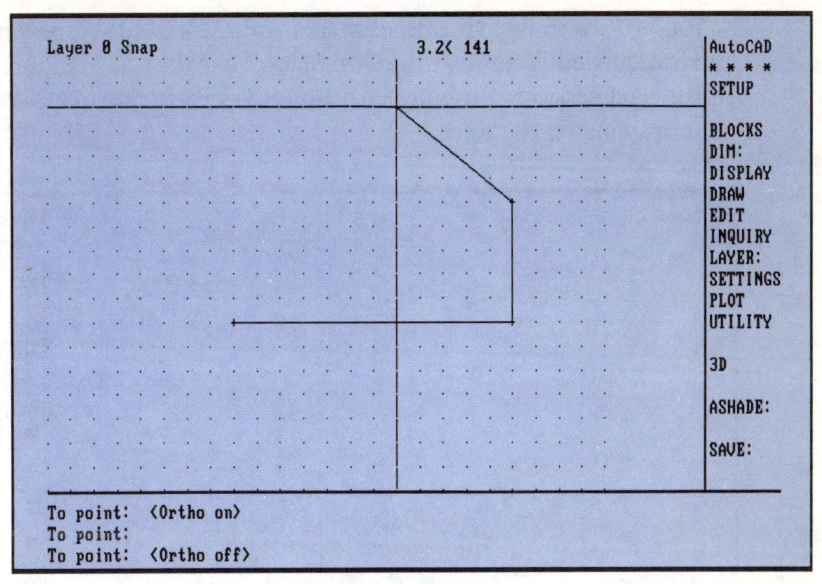

Figure 2.11: The third line segment is drawn

5. Move the cursor downward and to the left until the coordinate position is approximately

    4.6 <202

6. Press the pick button to establish the fourth line.

7. Move the cursor downward and to the left again until the coordinate position shows approximately

    5.0 <246

    Press the pick button to establish the fifth line.

8. Move the cursor downward and to the right until the coordinate position shows approximately

    7.1 <356

    Press the pick button to fix the sixth line.

9. Move the cursor off the drawing area to the far right and into the menu area. Notice that the prompt *To point:* appears on the bottom line of the screen. AutoCAD is waiting for you to draw another line segment.

You've now drawn six line segments—one horizontal, one vertical, and four angled. Your drawing should look like the one in Figure 2.12. In the next session you will learn how to correct mistakes, so keep your drawing on the screen.

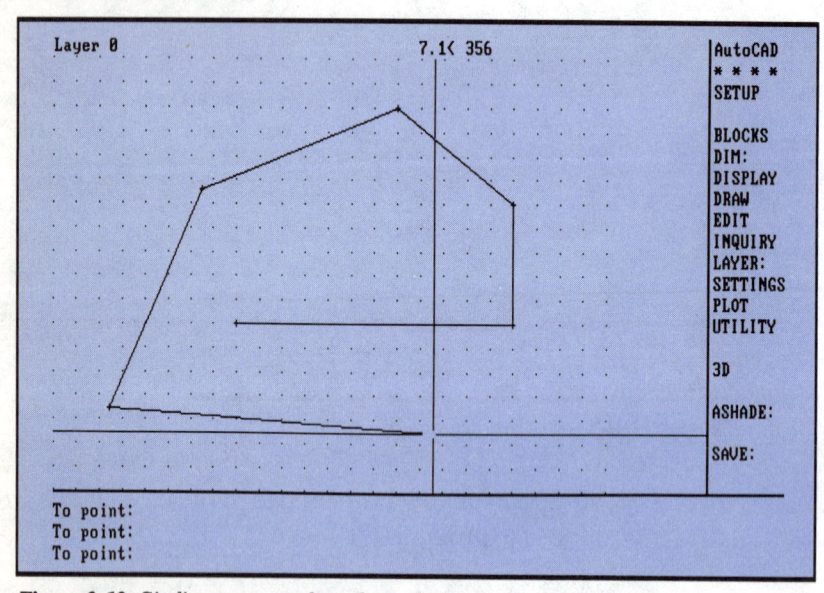

Figure 2.12: Six line segments have been drawn

How to Erase a Line with the U Command

Because AutoCAD keeps track of all the commands you have given, you can easily undo your work, step by step. The Undo and U commands are used for this purpose.

The U command is not simply an abbreviated spelling of the Undo command; it is a different, though similar, command. The U command only restores the most recent command, while the Undo command can restore more than one command. (Of course, you can give the U command more than once to undo more than one command.)

The U command works at two levels. If you have completed a command, it can instantly undo all changes that were made with that command. On the other hand, if you are in the middle of the Line command, as you are now, the U command can erase the previously drawn line segments one at a time.

As you have seen, you can determine whether you have completed a command or are still in the middle of a command by looking for the word *Command:* on the bottom line of the screen. If that word is displayed, you have finished a command and AutoCAD is waiting for another. If the command is still active, you will see the words *To point:* on the bottom line of the screen. Since the Line command is still active, let's use the U command to erase the two most recently drawn lines.

1. Type the letter

    u

    and press Enter. The last line you drew disappears.

2. Type

    u

    again and press Enter. The next line disappears.

Notice that plus signs still mark the end points of the erased lines. These marks make it easy to redraw erased lines, but they will not be printed with your drawing.

You can remove a line with the U command and then continue to add more lines without ending the Line command. Let's do that.

1. Move the cursor back onto the drawing area. Notice that a line connects your cursor to the last line of your drawing, indicating that the Line command is still active.

2. Redraw the second line you erased by moving to the left plus mark. The coordinate position shows

    5.0 <246

3. Press the pick button to reestablish the fifth line.

When you have finished working with a command, you must complete the command before you go to your next task. Here's how.

1. Press the Enter key, or the second mouse button, to complete the Line command. You can also give the ^C command.

On the bottom line of the screen, the word *Command:* shows that the Line command has been completed. Notice that no line segment is attached to your cursor. AutoCAD now waits for your next command.

2. Press F7 to turn off the grid and erase the plus marks from the screen.

3. Press F7 again to turn the grid back on.

How to Use U and Redo after a Command is Completed

In the previous exercise you erased the two most recently drawn line segments one at a time by giving the U command. You were able to erase one line segment at a time because the Line command was still active. After the Line command has been completed, however, the U command works differently.

If you give the U command after completing another command, the last command is undone. That is, the drawing is returned to the state it was in prior to the last command you gave.

1. Type the command

    u

    and press the Enter key. Now all the lines you created with the last Line command are removed at one time rather than individually. This is because you gave the U command after completing the last command. The drawing area is blank. If you accidentally give the U command, however, all is not lost.

2. Type the command

    redo

    and press the Enter key. All the lines erased by the U command reappear. That is, the Redo command reverses the effect of the U command.

Remember that U and Redo can be applied to any command, not just to the Line command.

How to Get Help from AutoCAD

So far in this chapter, you have learned to use several AutoCAD commands. However, there are more than one hundred commands and many of them have several variations. With so many different commands, it is easy to become confused. Therefore, AutoCAD provides the Help command to give you details about a particular command. Help also lists the names of all the commands in case you have forgotten the spelling of a particular one. Furthermore, AutoCAD will automatically start the Help command if you give an incorrect command. Let us see how Help works.

1. Check that the word *Command:* appears on the bottom line of the screen. If not, press ^c.

2. Type

   help

   and press Enter. (You can also type a question mark instead of spelling out the word *help*.) AutoCAD responds with the prompt:

   Command name (RETURN for list):

3. Press the Enter key again and you will see a list of the AutoCAD commands arranged in alphabetical order (Figure 2.13).

Notice that several commands in the list are followed by the symbols +1, +2, or +3. This notation shows commands that are only available if you have accessories called ADE-1, ADE-2, and ADE-3. (Since most AutoCAD programs include these accessories, these exercises will use commands with these symbols.) Also notice that several commands begin with an apostrophe. These commands can be run while another command is active.

4. Turn on your printer and press ^PrtSc to obtain a printed listing of the commands shown on the screen. If all the commands do not fit on the screen, press Enter to see the next screen. Press ^PrtSc again to obtain a listing of this screen.

```
AutoCAD Command List  (+n = ADE-n feature, ' = transparent command)
APERTURE +2   BREAK +1      DIM/DIM1 +1   END          HIDE +3
ARC           CHAMFER +1    DIST          ERASE        ID
AREA          CHANGE        DIVIDE +3     EXPLODE +3   IGESIN +3
ARRAY         CIRCLE        DONUT +3      EXTEND +3    IGESOUT +3
ATTDEF +2     COLOR         DOUGHNUT +3   FILES        INSERT
ATTDISP +2    COPY          DRAGMODE +2   FILL         ISOPLANE +2
ATTEDIT +2    DBLIST        DTEXT +3      FILLET +1    LAYER
ATTEXT +2     DDATTE +3     DXBIN +3      FILMROLL +3  LIMITS
AXIS +1       'DDEMODES +3  DXFIN         'GRAPHSCR    LINE
BASE          'DDLMODES +3  DXFOUT        GRID         LINETYPE
BLIPMODE      'DDRMODES +3  ELEV +3       HATCH +1     LIST
BLOCK         DELAY         ELLIPSE +3    'HELP / '?   LOAD

Press RETURN for further help.
```

Figure 2.13: AutoCAD help screen

5. Press

   ^ c

   to complete the Help command.

6. Press F1 to switch back to the drawing screen.

Getting Help for a Particular Command

You have just learned how to get help in general. However, sometimes you need help about a particular command after you have started that command. You can start the Help command while you are in the middle of another command by prefacing *Help* with an apostrophe. Let us see how to do that.

1. Check that the word *Command:* appears on the bottom line of the screen. Press ^ c if it does not.

2. Give the command

   line

   and press Enter to start the Line command.

3. Check that the bottom line of the screen shows the words *To point:* rather than *Command:*.

4. Type

   'help

   (or '?) and press Enter. The screen presents information about the Line command. The last line tells you to

   Press RETURN to resume the LINE command

5. Press the F1 key first, to return to the drawing screen.

6. Press Enter to return to the Line command.

7. Press

   ^ C

   to complete the Line command.

How to Draw a Circle with the Circle Command

In this section you will add a circle to the lines you drew previously. In the previous section you drew a straight line by typing the Line command and then marking the two ends with the mouse pick button. To draw a circle, you give the Circle command and then mark two points. You can specify a circle in several ways. However, we begin with the default method: marking the center and then the radius.

1. If the word *Ortho* appears on the top line of the screen, press F8 to turn Ortho mode off.

2. If the word *Snap* does not appear on the top line of the screen, press F9 to turn Snap mode on.

3. Be sure that the word *Command:* appears at the bottom of the screen, showing that you have completed the most recent command. If not, type the command

   ^ C

4. Now type the command

   circle

   and press Enter.

5. Move the cursor toward the center of the screen, to the coordinate position

    7.0, 4.0

6. Press the pick button. This establishes the center of the circle at the cursor location. A plus symbol marks the center.

7. Establish the circle size by moving the cursor three grid points to the right and three upward. The further you move outward from the center, the larger the size of the circle. The edge or perimeter of the circle goes through your cursor position. Your drawing should now look like Figure 2.14.

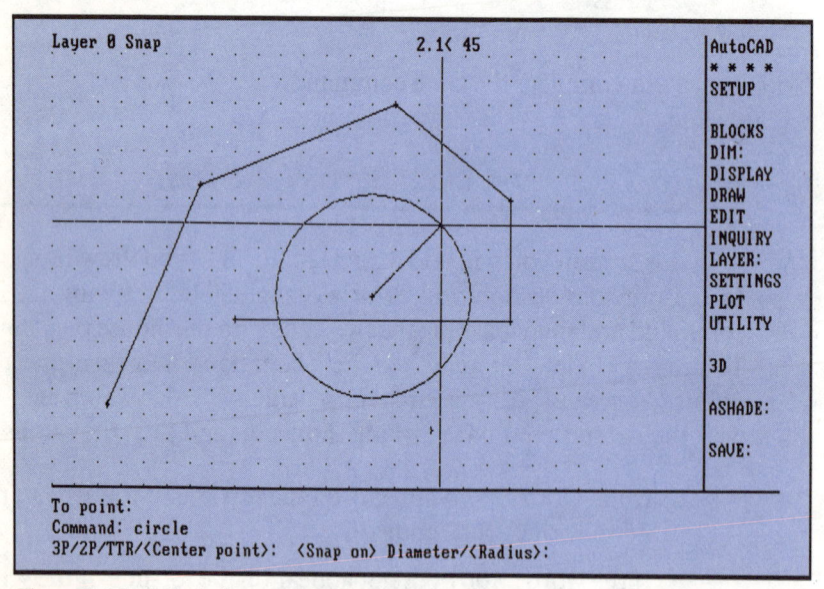

Figure 2.14: A circle drawn with the Circle command

8. When the coordinate display shows

    2.1 <45

    press the pick button to fix the circle size. Notice that the word *Command:* appears on the bottom line of the screen to show that the Circle command has been completed.

9. Press F9 to turn off Snap mode.

How to Save Your Work

Now that you've worked so carefully to create your drawing, spend the next few moments learning how to protect it from accidental erasure. If the electricity should fail at this point, you would lose all your work because it has not been saved on a disk. To avoid such a loss, you should save your work with the AutoCAD Save command every 10 or 15 minutes. Then you cannot lose more than 10 or 15 minutes worth of work. Let's do that now.

1. Type the command

    save

    and press Enter. AutoCAD responds with the line:

    File name <first>:

    (The name enclosed in angle brackets is the one you chose at the beginning. AutoCAD will use this name if you do not give a different one.)

2. Press Enter to accept the name *FIRST*.

Alternatively, you can type something else to save your drawing with a different name or on a different disk. Then you will have a backup copy of your work.

Remember to repeat these two steps every 10 to 15 minutes. If you want to take a break, you can leave your drawing on the screen. You will need it to continue with the work in the next chapter. Or, you can shut off the computer if you want to quit for a longer time.

3

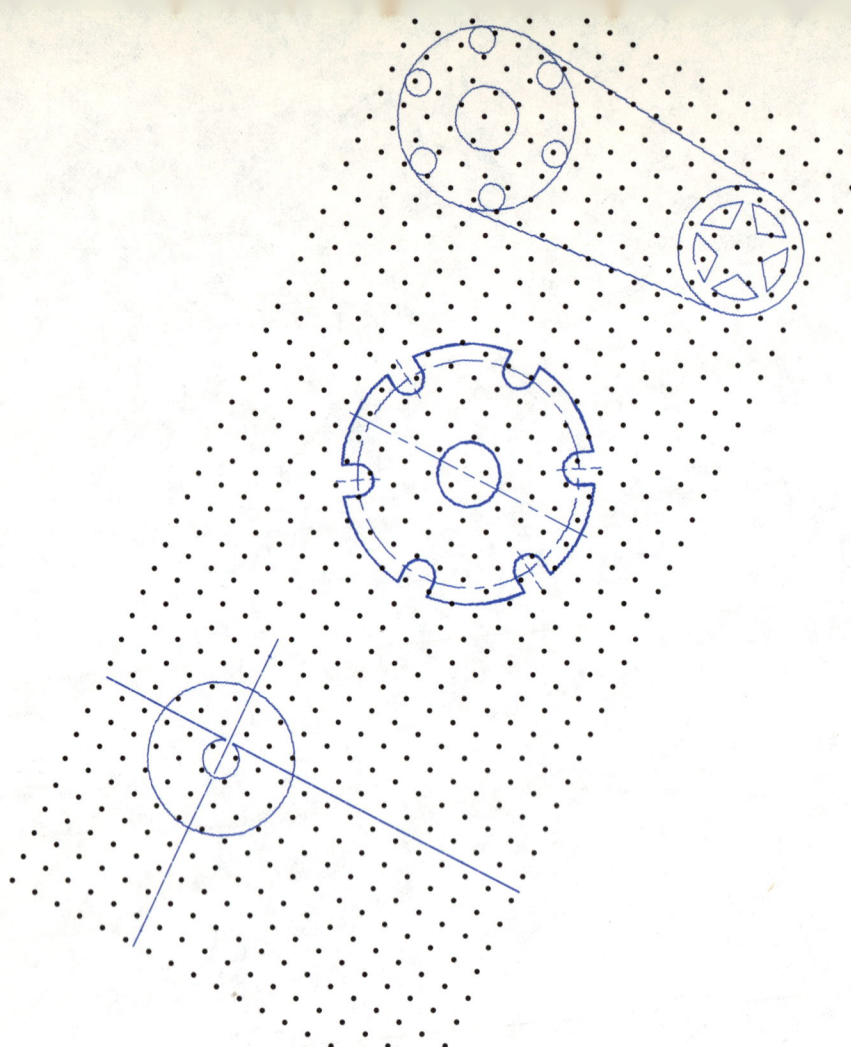

Drawing and Selecting Shapes

Featuring:
- Recalling a file
- Selection by pointing
- Selection with the Regular window
- Selection with a Crossing window

Many AutoCAD commands, such as those that move, copy, or erase objects, require you to select those objects with which you want to work.

You select an object such as a line or circle by pointing to it with the cursor and then pressing the pick button. Alternatively, you can select several items at a time by drawing a box or window around them.

Object selection is an operation you must master if you are to be proficient with AutoCAD. There are several ways to select items in AutoCAD—you'll learn how to use each one, so you can choose the method best suited to your task. Fortunately, item selection is nearly identical for most of the commands. In this chapter, we'll explore item selection using the AutoCAD Move command.

To learn selecting, you'll use the drawing you made in Chapter 2. Your drawing screen should have five connected lines and a circle, as shown in Figure 2.10. If not, please go back to the previous chapter and draw these items.

AutoCAD commands introduced in this chapter are

- Move to move an object
- Previous to select the previously selected object
- Last to select the last item drawn
- Window to select a group of items
- Remove to remove an object from a selection set
- Add to select an object
- Erase to erase an object
- Crossing to select objects with the Crossing window
- End to complete and save the drawing

How to Select by Pointing

Let us begin with the simplest method of selection—pointing with the cursor. During the AutoCAD selection process, the cursor shape changes from crossed lines (the drawing cursor) to a small box, known as the *selection cursor* or *selection box*. To select by pointing, you place the box-shaped cursor over a line that is a part of the object you want to select. In this exercise, you will select a horizontal and a vertical line. You will use the first part of the AutoCAD Move command to demonstrate the different selection methods. However, the techniques will apply to many other AutoCAD commands, too. Let's try this method. First you'll recall the FIRST drawing.

1. If AutoCAD is not running, give the DOS command

    acad

    and press enter to start it up.

2. Type

    2

    at the Main menu and press the Enter key.

3. Type

    first

    to recall your drawing to the screen.

4. Move the cursor (the pair of crossed lines) into the drawing area if it is not already there.

5. Type the command

    move

    and press Enter. The cursor shape changes to a small box. AutoCAD now requires you to select the object you want to move. The bottom line on the screen reads

    Select objects:

6. Move the selection box over the line that crosses the circle. Choose a place well away from the intersection points of the line and the circle.

7. Press the pick button or the Enter key to select the horizontal line for the Move command. Notice that the line becomes spotty (Figure 3.1). This is how AutoCAD lets you know what has been selected. The other objects on the screen do not

change appearance because you have not selected them. The bottom line again reads:

Select objects:

AutoCAD waits for you to select another item to be added to the first object you selected. Also notice that the following message appears on the next-to-last line:

1 selected, 1 found

This means that AutoCAD accepted the item you selected. (On the other hand, if this line reads *1 selected, 0 found,* it means that AutoCAD did not find an object at the point you selected. Perhaps you did not position the selection box carefully. Try to select the item again.)

8. Choose a second item by moving the selection box over the vertical line at the right end of the line you just selected. It is important that you do not place the cursor near the intersection of two lines. Otherwise, AutoCAD will not know which line you want.

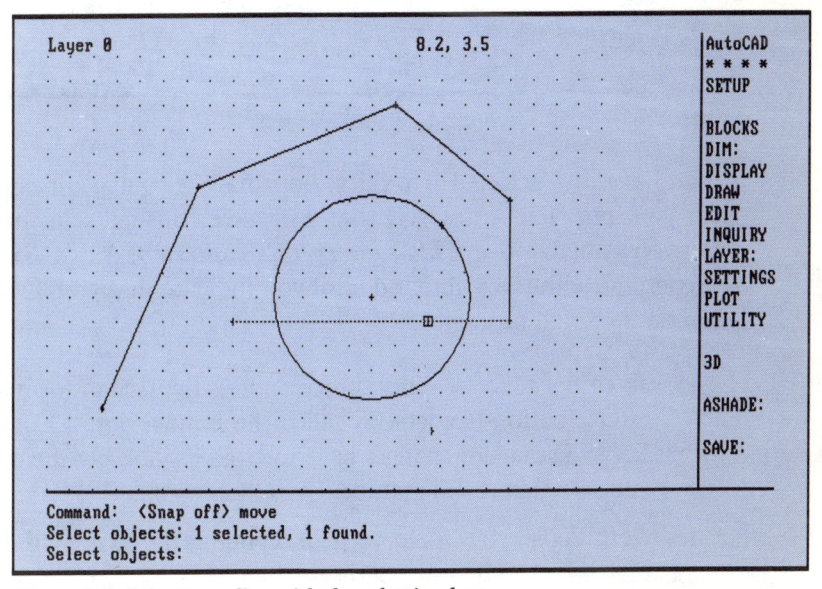

Figure 3.1: Selecting a line with the selection box

9. Press the pick button. The second line also becomes spotty (Figure 3.2). The words

    1 selected, 1 found

    appear on the next-to-last line to tell you that AutoCAD found another object.

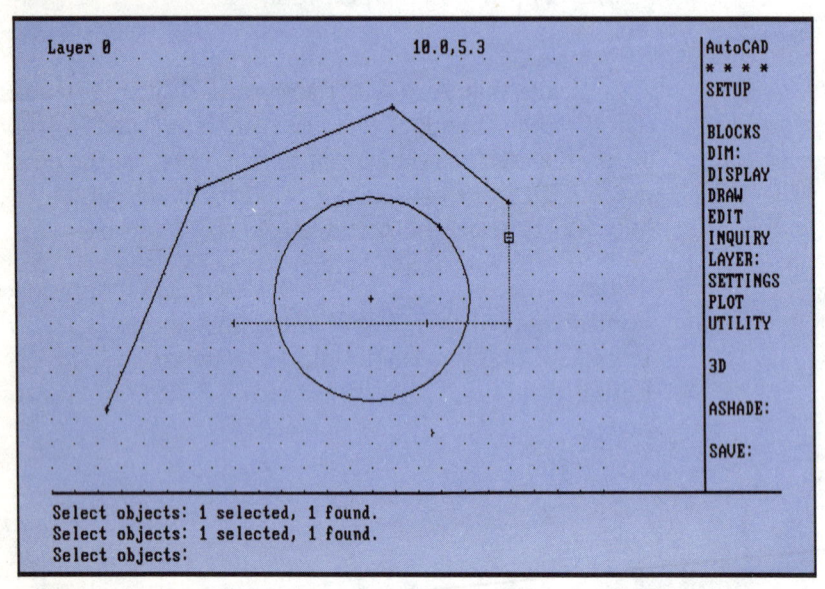

Figure 3.2: Selecting a second line

You have now selected two lines; both have a spotty appearance. Next you must tell AutoCAD that you have finished selecting the items you want to move. *This is a very important step.* AutoCAD cannot continue with the command until you indicate that you have finished the selection process.

10. To complete the selection process, press the *second* (or middle) mouse button (sometimes called the Return button) or press Enter. The cursor changes back to crossed lines, but the objects you selected are still marked.

11. At this point you would normally continue the command. However, we are only studying the selection process. Therefore, press

^ C to terminate the command. The two lines return to normal. The bottom line of the screen shows the word

Command:

How to Select Previously Selected Items

You will frequently want to perform a sequence of operations on the same group of items. Therefore, you will need to select the same set of objects more than once. To help with this, AutoCAD provides a command that lets you select items you have previously selected—the Previous, or P, command. For example, if you want to move a set of objects and then make copies of them, you have to make two selections of the same group, once for the Move command and once for the Copy command. Let's try this.

1. Restart the Move command by pressing the second mouse button or the Enter key.
2. When the prompt

   Select objects:

   appears on the bottom line, type the command:

   p

   for Previous and press Enter. The two lines you selected in the previous Move command are marked again. In this example, we selected items from a previous Move command for another Move command. This technique is very general. It will work for any combination of commands that requires a selection of items.

How to Select Previously Drawn Items

The AutoCAD Last command is a variant of the Previous command. It selects the most recently *drawn* item rather than the most recently *selected* item. Let's see how this works by selecting another item.

1. Type the command:

    L

    for Last and press Enter. Now the circle becomes spotty showing that it too is selected. This object was selected because it was the last or most-recently drawn object.

2. Press ^C to interrupt the Move command. All objects return to normal and the cursor shape changes to crossed lines.

Good. You've learned three ways to select items. Let us explore another approach to selection.

How to Select with a Regular Window

In a previous section you selected two items by pointing to each one in turn. However, this method is cumbersome when you want to select many items in a group. Let's learn another method—selection by window. With this method you can select a group of objects by surrounding them with a window. There are two types of windows—Regular and Crossing. The Regular window selects all items that are wholly within the window border. The Crossing window selects those objects that are crossed by the window border as well as those objects that lie completely within the border. We'll learn to use the Crossing window later in this chapter. Let us try the Regular window first.

1. Move the cursor into the drawing area if it is not already there.
2. Type the command

    move

    and press Enter. As before, the cursor changes from crossed lines to a small box and the bottom line reads

    Select objects:

3. Type the letter

    w

    for Window and press Enter. The cursor shape changes back

Drawing and Selecting Shapes **47**

from a small box to crossed lines. The message

First corner:

appears on the bottom line of the screen. You are going to mark the first of two diagonally opposite corners of the rectangular window. You can choose any one of the four corners first and then choose the diagonally opposite corner.

4. To select the first corner, move the cursor to the lower-right corner of the screen to the grid position

   10.8, 1.3

   Press the pick button to mark one corner of the window. The crossed lines of the cursor disappear and the words

   Other corner:

   are shown on the bottom line.

5. Move the cursor upward and to the left. You'll see a box begin to grow on the screen. One corner is fixed at the point you selected. The diagonally opposite corner automatically follows your cursor.

6. Move the cursor until the box completely encloses all but the far-left line (Figure 3.3). As shown in the figure, the second coordinate position is

   2.3, 8.3

   (If the window does not enclose the desired object because you have selected the wrong starting point, press ^C to cancel the Move command and begin again at step 2.)

7. When the upper-left corner is correctly positioned, press the pick button or the Enter key to fix the window size. The selected lines and the circle become spotty and the window disappears (Figure 3.4). The bottom of the screen shows the two lines:

   5 found
   Select objects:

48 The ABC's of AutoCAD

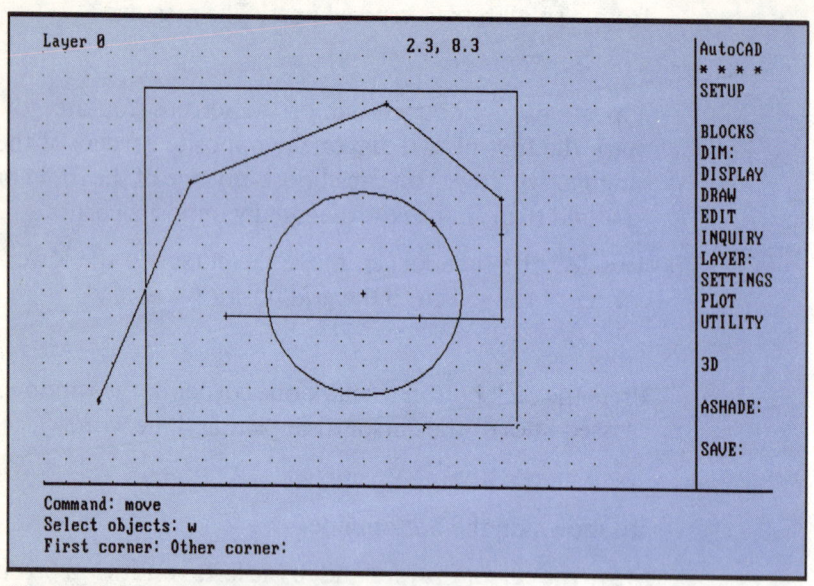

CH. 3

Figure 3.3: Selecting objects with a Regular window

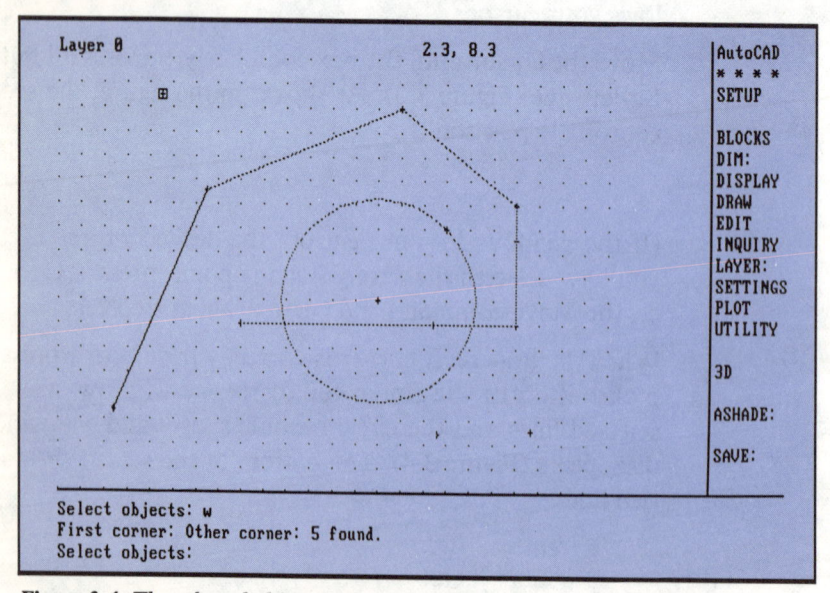

Figure 3.4: The selected objects appear spotty

AutoCAD announces that it has located five objects and that it is waiting for you to select additional items. The cursor shape has returned to a small box. You can now select additional items by pointing to them as you did previously. You can also remove some of the selected objects. Let's see how.

How to Remove Objects from the Selection Set

Sometimes you want to select almost all the items in a group rather than the entire group. In this case it's easier to select all the items with a Regular window, then remove selected items from the window with the Remove command. Remove causes the selection process to work in reverse. You can also use the Remove option when you have selected an object in error. Let us explore this command by continuing with the previous selection.

The circle and all but one of the lines on the drawing screen should be selected as shown by their spotty appearance (Figure 3.4). If not, please return to the previous section and select these objects. On the bottom line of the screen, the words

Select objects:

show that the Move command is current and that AutoCAD is ready for you to select more items.

1. Type the command

   r

   for Remove and press Enter. AutoCAD shows

   Remove objects:

   on the bottom line of the screen. Next you will remove two items from the set of selected objects.

2. Move the selection box to the edge of the circle and press the pick button. The circle returns to normal. The bottom line shows:

   1 selected, 1 found, 1 removed

3. Now move the selection box to the horizontal line that crosses the circle and press the pick button again. This line also returns to normal (Figure 3.5). AutoCAD responds with

1 selected, 1 found, 1 removed

```
Layer 0                          6.3, 3.5                    AutoCAD
                                                             * * * *
                                                             SETUP

                                                             BLOCKS
                                                             DIM:
                                                             DISPLAY
                                                             DRAW
                                                             EDIT
                                                             INQUIRY
                                                             LAYER:
                                                             SETTINGS
                                                             PLOT
                                                             UTILITY

                                                             3D

                                                             ASHADE:

                                                             SAVE:

Remove objects: 1 selected, 1 found, 1 removed.
Remove objects: 1 selected, 1 found, 1 removed.
Remove objects:
```

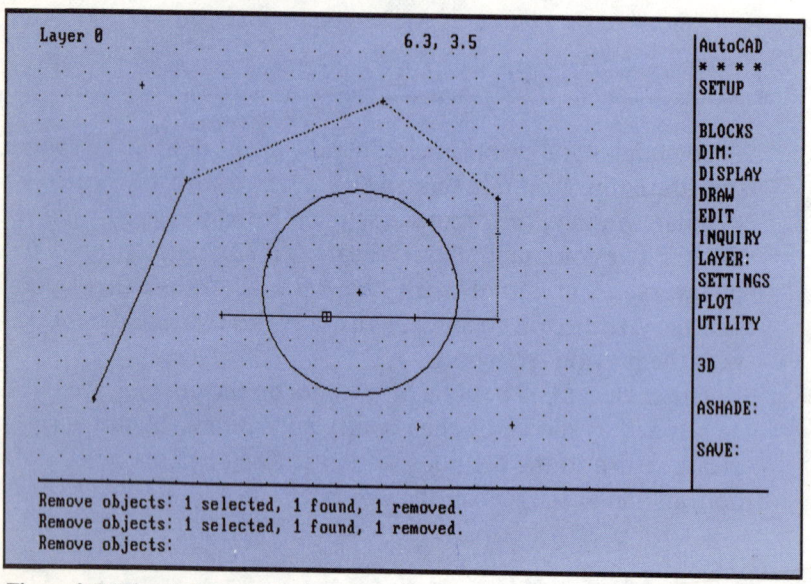

Figure 3.5: The circle and one line are removed from the set of selected objects

How to Add Objects to the Selection Set

The Add command is the reverse of the Remove command. Let us add another line to the set of selected objects.

1. Type the command:

    a

    for Add and press Enter. The bottom line shows

    Select objects:

    as AutoCAD changes back to Selection mode.

2. Move the selection box over the far-left line. Press the pick

button. This line becomes spotty to show that you have included it in the set of selected items.

3. Press the second mouse button or the Enter key to complete the selection process.

4. Press ^C to interrupt the Move command. All objects return to normal.

Now let's look at the last type of selection—the Crossing window.

How to Select with a Crossing Window

Sometimes you want to select a group of items with a window but it is inconvenient or impossible to draw a window around all the items. The Regular window we used in the previous section requires that all parts of selected items be entirely within the window boundary. Any item crossed by the window edge is not selected.

A Crossing window allows you to select objects in a different way. This window selects not only those items that are completely enclosed by the window boundary, but also any object that is crossed by the window edge. The window is drawn exactly as before. Let us use this window to select the circle and all the lines except for the one crossing the circle. Then we'll remove the circle from that selected set, and erase the other objects with the Erase command.

1. Move the cursor into the drawing area if it is not already there.

2. Type the command

   erase

   and press Enter. As with the Move command, the cursor changes to a small box and the bottom line reads

   Select objects:

3. To choose a Crossing window, type the letter

   c

   and press Enter. As with the Regular window, the cursor

changes from a small box to crossed lines. The prompt

First corner:

appears on the bottom line.

4. Move the cursor to the right side of the screen, stopping at coordinate location

   11.0, 5.0

   Press the pick button to fix one corner of the window. The crossed lines of the cursor disappear.

5. Move the cursor upward and to the left and watch the window grow larger. Stop at the plus symbol marking the previous location of the window corner. This is the coordinate position

   2.3, 8.3

   The window should cross or enclose all objects except the line through the circle (Figure 3.6).

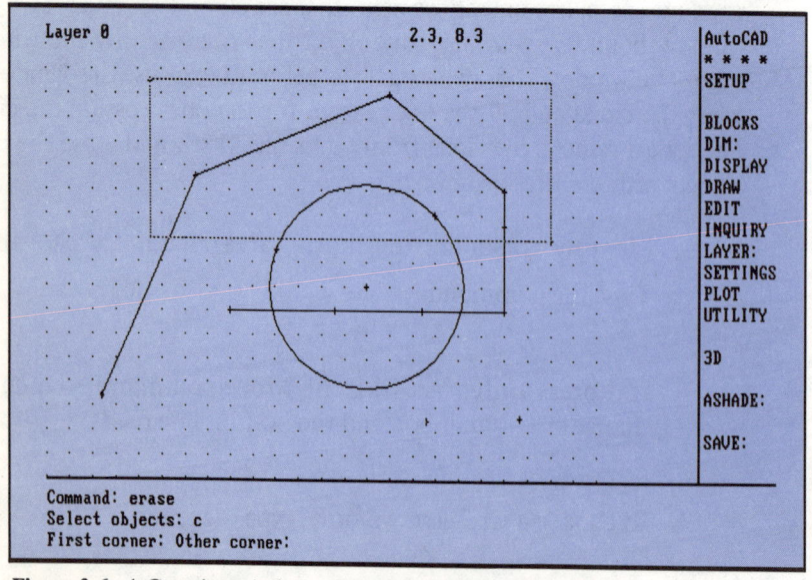

Figure 3.6: A Crossing window selects four lines and the circle

6. Press the pick button to fix the window size. The circle and all the lines except the one not selected become spotty, even those that penetrate the window boundary. AutoCAD waits for you to select additional items. As before, the cursor has returned to a small box.

7. Type the letter

    r

    for Remove and press Enter.

8. Move the selection box to the edge of the circle and press the pick button. The circle returns to normal because it is removed from the selection set.

9. Press the second mouse button or the Enter key to complete selection and erase all but the circle and the one line.

How to Undo the Previous Command

Previously, we used the U command to erase the most recently drawn line or circle, but U is in fact a general command that can be used to undo any previous command. Therefore, let's use that command to undo the most recent command (Erase).

1. Type the command

    u

    and press Enter. The erased lines are instantly restored.

2. Type

    redo

    and press Enter. The lines are erased again. Thus you can alternately give the U and Redo commands to switch between the last two versions.

Good. You've learned several ways to select objects with AutoCAD. Continue to the next section to learn how to complete your work.

How to Complete a Drawing with the End Command

In the previous chapter you gave the Save command to save an intermediate version of your program. However, when you have completed your work you use the End command. This command does two things—it saves a copy of your work and it returns you to the main AutoCAD menu. Let us do that now.

1. Type the command

    end

    and press Enter. AutoCAD returns to the Main menu and saves your work with the file name you chose.

2. Type

    0

    (zero) and press Enter to leave AutoCAD and return to the DOS prompt.

4

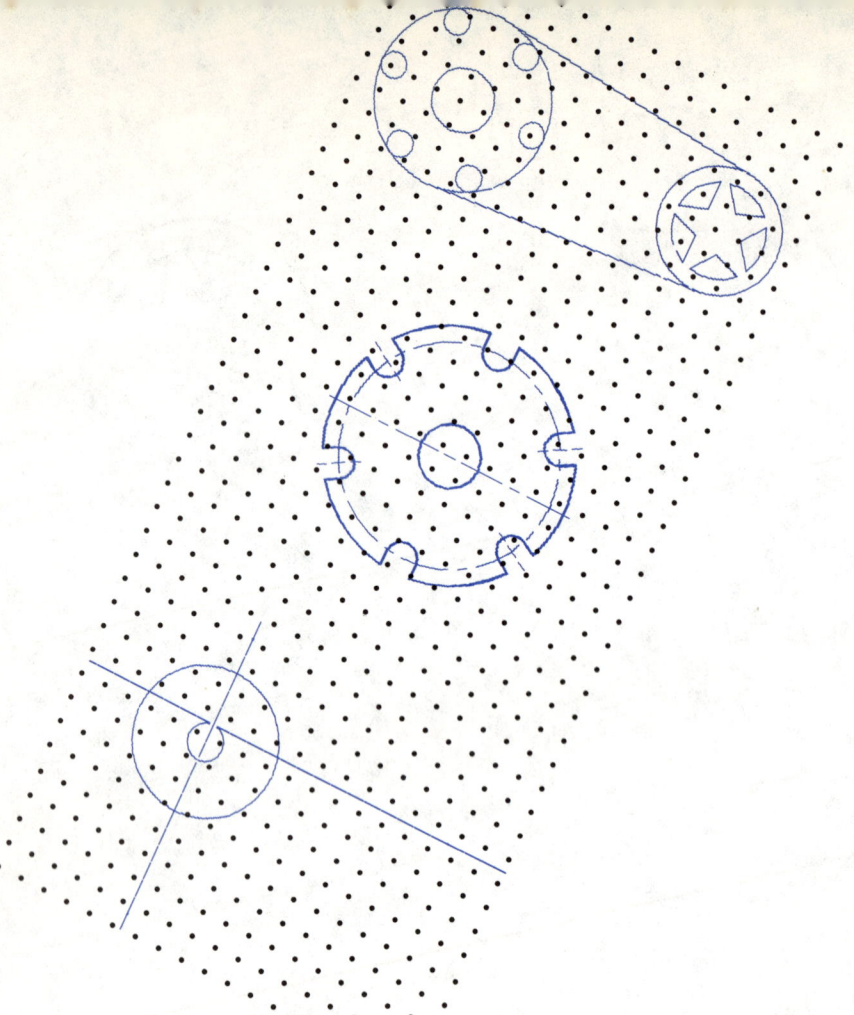

Changing an Existing Drawing

Featuring:
    Duplicating objects
    Enlarging the view
    Rotating objects
    Moving objects

Changing an Existing Drawing 57

In the previous chapters you started AutoCAD, drew lines and a circle, learned several important commands for selecting items you want to change, and learned how to save your work on disk. Now that you understand the important concept of selecting items you want to change, let us continue with your drawing of the circle and line.

First you will add a line to the drawing with the Ortho mode off, which will make the line appear zigzagged, or stepped. To correct this, you will use the Change command to straighten it. You will enlarge the view with the Zoom command. Then you will duplicate the two lines with the Copy command, turn them with the Rotate command, and move them with the Move command. You will then have a drawing of a circle with four lines, two horizontal and two vertical. Finally, you will remove parts of the drawing with the Trim command.

New AutoCAD commands introduced in this chapter are

- Change to alter an object
- Zoom to enlarge the screen image of an object
- Copy to duplicate an object
- Center to select the center of a circle
- Quad to select one quadrant of a circle
- Rotate to turn an object
- Trim to remove part of an object

How to Create a Copy of a File

Let's make a copy of your drawing so that we can make changes to it without losing the original.

1. If AutoCAD is not running, give the DOS command

    acad

    and press the Enter key to start it up.

2. Type

    1

at the Main menu and press the Enter key to create a new drawing.

3. Type the command

    second = first

    and press Enter. This starts the drawing editor, begins a new file named second.dwg, and adds the objects contained in the file first.dwg. You will see the line and circle on the drawing screen.

Let us begin by drawing a second horizontal line across the circle. We are going to draw a line with Ortho mode off and deliberately slant the line a bit away from the horizontal. Then we will make the line level with the Change command. Of course, if you had originally drawn the line with Ortho mode on, the line would be horizontal. However, the idea is to learn how to use one feature of the Change command.

1. If the word *Ortho* appears on the top line of the screen, press F8 to turn Ortho mode off.
2. If the word *Snap* appears on the top line of the screen, press F9 to turn Snap mode off.
3. If the grid is displayed, press F7 to turn it off.
4. Move the mouse and look at the coordinate readout on the top line of the screen. If the coordinates do not change with cursor movement, press the F6 key to turn on the coordinate display.
5. Type the command

    line

    and press Enter.
6. Move the cursor to the left side of the circle above the line. The coordinate position is

    4.0, 4.6

7. Press the pick button to establish the beginning of the line.

8. Move the cursor to the right and upward a little. Cross the right edge of the circle and stop where the coordinate readout shows

    6.1 <1

    (You learned previously that this is a polar reference. It shows a line of 6.1 units oriented at the angle of 1 degree.) Notice that the new line has steps or zigzags as do all lines that are not horizontal or vertical.

9. Press the pick button to fix the second line. Notice that the bottom line of the screen shows the words

    To point:

    showing that the Line command is still active.

10. Press the second mouse button or the Enter key to complete the Line command. Notice now that the word

    Command:

    appears on the bottom line of the screen. Your drawing should look like that in Figure 4.1.

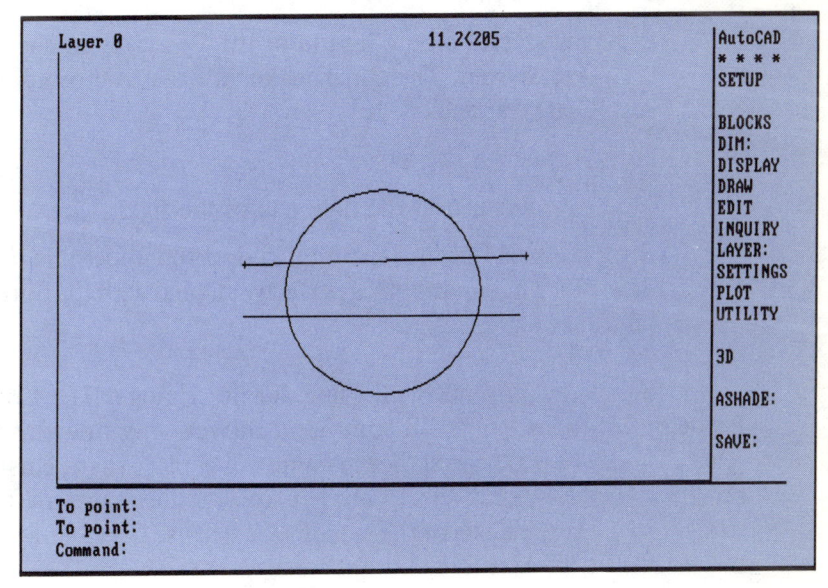

Figure 4.1: *A circle and two lines*

How to Align Lines Horizontally or Vertically

In the previous section, you drew a line with the Ortho mode turned off, and therefore, the line is not horizontal. What if you decide that you want to change it to a horizontal line? In this section you will learn how to change the orientation of this line so that it will align with the coordinate system.

1. Press F8 to turn on Ortho mode. Check that the word *Ortho* appears on the top line.
2. Type the command

    change

    and press Enter. The cursor changes to a selection box.
3. Type

    L

    (for Last) and press Enter to select the last item drawn. The zigzag line becomes spotty.
4. Press the second mouse button or the Enter key to complete the selection step. The cursor changes back to crossed lines. AutoCAD responds with

    Properties/<Change point>:
5. Move the cursor near the right end of the zigzag line.
6. Press the pick button. The right end of the upper line moves downward until it becomes perfectly aligned with the horizontal axis (Figure 4.2).

Notice that the left end of this line did not change. The Change Point option of the Change command moves only one end of a selected line. The end nearest the cursor moves as close to the cursor as possible. However, since Ortho mode is on, the line can only move straight to the vertical line of the cursor. (We will use the Change command later to do other things.)

Changing an Existing Drawing 61

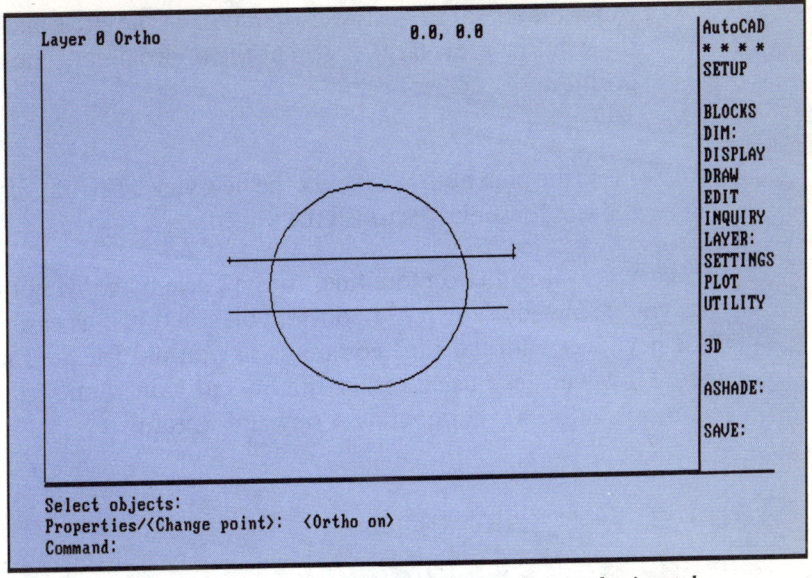

Figure 4.2: The Change command makes upper line become horizontal

How to Enlarge Drawings with the Zoom Command

In this section you will enlarge the view of the drawing with the Zoom command. It will then be easier to see what is happening. Auto-CAD always keeps track of items in full scale. However, you can display your drawing on the screen using any convenient scale.

1. Give the command

    zoom

    and press the space bar.

2. Type

    w

    for Window and press Enter.

3. Move the cursor to the upper-left part of the circle, to the coordinate position

    3.2, 7.8

    Press the pick button to start a window.

4. Move the cursor to the lower-right part of the circle and watch the window grow larger. Stop at the approximate coordinate position

   11.2, 0.4

5. Press the pick button to select the new view. The image within the window enlarges to fill the screen.

Next you will add two more lines to the circle by copying the two lines you've already drawn. Of course, you could just as easily draw these new lines with the Line command as you did for the first two lines. However, let's use another method to gain familiarity with two more AutoCAD commands: Copy and Rotate.

How to Duplicate Lines with the Copy Command

As the name implies, the Copy command makes a copy of an object or group of objects on your drawing. The Copy command is like the Move command except that the original version stays in place. With the Move command, a new version of a group of items is created at a different location. Then the original version is erased. With the Copy command, the original is not erased. You select the items to be copied by methods you learned in the previous chapters—pointing to individual items or selecting with a window. With both the Copy and Move commands, you must designate a displacement, that is, how far and in what direction to move.

1. Give the command

   copy

   and press the Enter key. The cursor changes to the selection box.

2. Move the selection box over the upper line, away from the circle, and press the pick button. The line becomes spotty. (You could also have typed L for last item drawn.)

3. Move the selection box down over the lower line and press the pick button again. That line becomes spotty too.

4. Press the second mouse button or the Enter key to complete the selection process. The words

   <Base position or displacement>/multiple:

   appear on the bottom line of the screen.

How to Establish the Displacement

Now you must tell AutoCAD how far you want to move the marked objects and in what direction you want to move them. This is known as the displacement. You can do this in one of two ways. You can enter the horizontal and vertical displacement from the keyboard or you can select two points with the cursor. Then the marked items will move the distance between the two points and in the corresponding direction. Let us use the second method.

1. Move the cursor to the center of the circle and press the pick button. This establishes the first point of the displacement. The words

   Second point of displacement:

   appear on the bottom line.

2. Move the cursor straight up to the top edge of the circle. Notice that images of the two marked lines move on the screen along with your cursor. Spotty images remain at the original locations.

3. Press the pick button to fix these items in the new position (Figure 4.3).

How to Rotate an Object

Now we will rotate the upper lines from the horizontal to the vertical position.

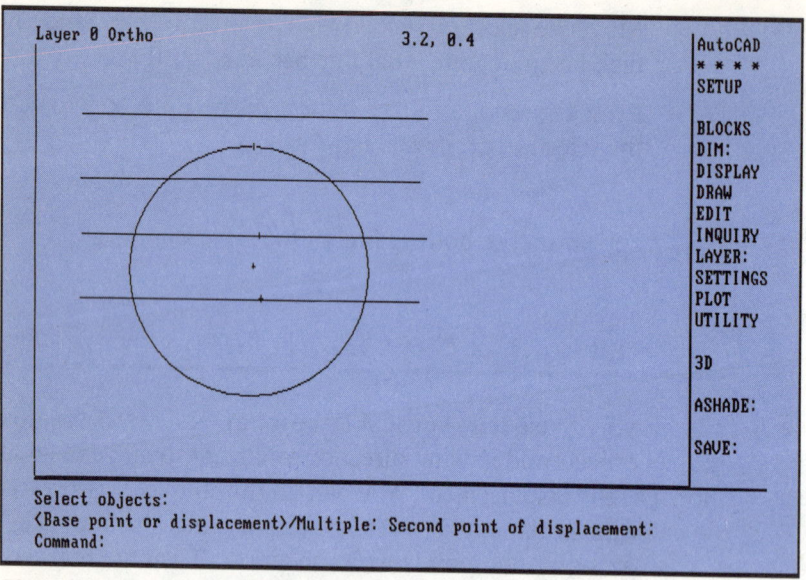

Figure 4.3: The two lines are copied and the displacement established

1. Give the command

    rotate

    and press Enter.

2. In response to the prompt

    Select objects:

    move the selection box over the upper new line and press the pick button. That line becomes spotty.

3. Move the selection box over the other new line and press the pick button. This line also becomes spotty.

4. Press the second mouse button or the Enter key to complete the selection step.

5. AutoCAD requests

    Base point

    which is the position around which rotation is to take place. Move the cursor to the top edge of the circle and press the pick button.

6. When AutoCAD requests

   <Rotation angle>/Reference:

   type the value **90** and press Enter. Notice that the two new lines are now turned 90 degrees from their previous position.

How to Make Precise Connections with the Osnap Options

In Chapter 2 you turned on Snap mode so that AutoCAD could precisely position objects. Then the cursor snapped to the nearest grid point. In a similar way, AutoCAD can position or snap the cursor to a particular part of an object, for example, to the end of a line or to the center of a circle. With this technique, AutoCAD can locate the position much more precisely than you can. This method of connection is called an *object snap* or *Osnap* for short.

Throughout this book, we will type the Osnap options from the keyboard rather than select them from the screen menu because it is faster. However, sometimes you may want to look at a list of the Osnap options to help you choose the one you want.

Displaying the Osnap Menu

Let us display the Osnap menu.

1. To see the menu of Osnap commands, move the cursor to the far right side of the screen.

2. Move up to the second line from the top, the one with four asterisks.

3. Press the pick button to change to the Osnap menu (Figure 4.4). You will use the options Center, Endpoint, Intersec, Midpoint, Quadrant, and Tangent for the drawings of this book. If you want to select an option from the Osnap menu, move the cursor to the menu item and press the pick button.

4. To change back to the Main menu, move the cursor up one line to the top row, to the words *AutoCAD,* and press the pick button.

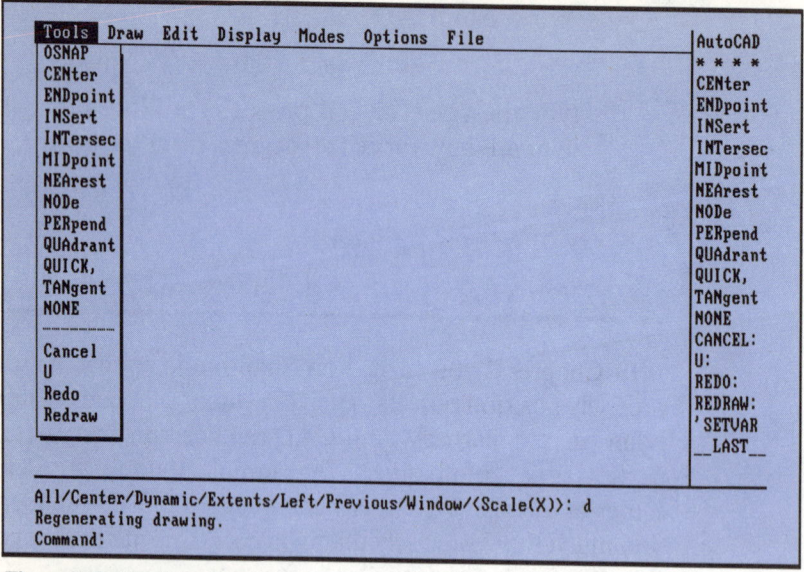

```
Tools Draw  Edit  Display  Modes  Options  File      AutoCAD
OSNAP                                                 * * * *
CENter                                                CENter
ENDpoint                                              ENDpoint
INSert                                                INSert
INTersec                                              INTersec
MIDpoint                                              MIDpoint
NEArest                                               NEArest
NODe                                                  NODe
PERpend                                               PERpend
QUAdrant                                              QUAdrant
QUICK,                                                QUICK,
TANgent                                               TANgent
NONE                                                  NONE
                                                      CANCEL:
Cancel                                                U:
U                                                     REDO:
Redo                                                  REDRAW:
Redraw                                                ' SETVAR
                                                      __LAST__

All/Center/Dynamic/Extents/Left/Previous/Window/<Scale(X)>: d
Regenerating drawing.
Command:
```

Figure 4.4: The Osnap menu

Displaying the Osnap Menu with Release 9

If you have AutoCAD release 9 or later, there is another way to display the Osnap menu.

1. Move the cursor to the top line of the screen.

2. Move the cursor to the far left corner of the top line. When the word *Tools* changes appearance, press the pick button. The Osnap menu is pulled down (displayed) on the drawing screen (Figure 4.4). If you want to select an option from this menu, move the cursor to corresponding item and press the pick button.

3. To remove this menu from the screen, shift the cursor to the drawing area and press the pick button.

Displaying the Osnap Menu with a Three-Button Mouse

If you have a three-button mouse, you can press the third button to display the Osnap menu.

How to Move Objects in a Drawing

In this section we will move the two new lines down across the circle.

1. Give the command

    move

    and press Enter.

2. Select the two new lines again by typing

    p

    for Previous and pressing Enter. As you learned in the last chapter, this selects the items you selected for the previous command (in this case, the Rotate command).

3. When both new lines are spotty, press the second mouse button or the Enter key to complete the selection process. We are going to move the two lines back down over the center of the circle. Therefore, we will reverse the pair of displacement points that we used previously. We will pick the top edge of the circle first and then the center of the circle. Previously, you selected the center and top edge of the circle by hand. However, this time you will use the Osnap commands to move the two lines.

4. In response to the line:

    Base point or displacement:

    type the Osnap command

    quad

    and press Enter. Quad is an Osnap command that precisely locates the closest quadrant of the circle; that is, it selects the top, right, bottom, or left edge, whichever is closer to the cursor.

5. Move the selection box to the top edge of the circle and press the pick button.

6. For the second point, type the Osnap command

    cen

for Center and press Enter. This command precisely locates the center of a circle.

7. With the selection box still at the top edge of the circle, press the pick button. The two vertical lines move downward. They now stick out both above and below the circle (Figure 4.5).

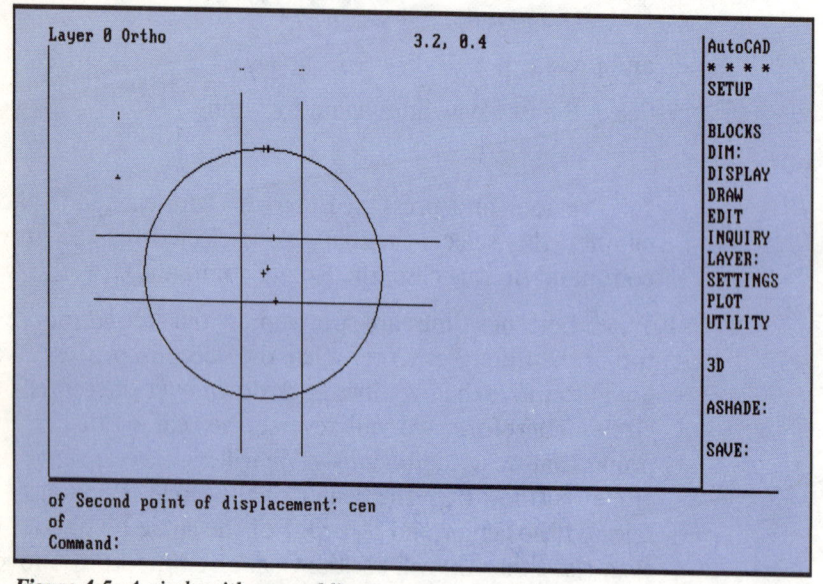

Figure 4.5: A circle with crossed lines

Before continuing, save a copy of your current work to disk. Give the command

save

and press the Enter key. Press the Enter key a second time to accept the default file name second.dwg. Now your work is safe if the electricity goes off.

Let's remove parts of the lines and the circle with the Trim command.

How to Use the Trim Command

You previously learned to use the Erase command to remove items from the drawing screen. However, the Erase command can only be used to remove complete objects such as a line or a circle. You cannot use the Erase command to remove part of a line or circle. Instead, use the Trim command.

The Trim command can be used to reduce the length of a line or a circular arc. Its use is more complicated than the Erase command because you must trim one line against a second line, called the *trim boundary*. With the Erase command, you selected the items to be erased in one step, but with the Trim command you must select items in two phases. First, you must select the boundary or lines to trim against. Then you must select the lines that are to be trimmed against the boundary. Press F8 to turn off Ortho mode.

*T*rimming Lines

Let us begin by trimming the parts of the lines that stick out of the circle. Your drawing screen should look like that in Figure 4.5.

1. Check to see that the word *Command:* shows on the bottom line of the screen. Give the ^C command if not. (You learned previously that ^C completes the current command so you can begin another.)

2. Type

    trim

    and press Enter. AutoCAD responds with the two prompts

    Select cutting edge(s)...
    Select objects:

    The cursor changes to a selection box. At this point, you must select not the object to be trimmed, but the *boundary* you want to trim against.

3. Move the selection box to the edge of the circle, well away from the lines, and press the pick button. The entire circle becomes spotty, marking it as the trim boundary. AutoCAD responds with

    1 selected, 1 found

as it does when you are selecting items for the Erase command. Then AutoCAD repeats the request

Select objects:

so you can include another boundary.

4. Since this is the only boundary we need, press the second mouse button or the Enter key to complete the boundary-selection phase. AutoCAD responds with

Select object to trim:

Now you can select the part of each line you want to trim back to the spotted boundary.

5. Move the selection box over the upper end of the left vertical line (Figure 4.6). The selection box does not have to be exactly at the end; just be sure you are outside the circle. Press the pick button. Notice that this line is neatly trimmed back to the circle. As usual, there is a mark on the screen, showing the position of the selection box when you trimmed the first line. The circle is still

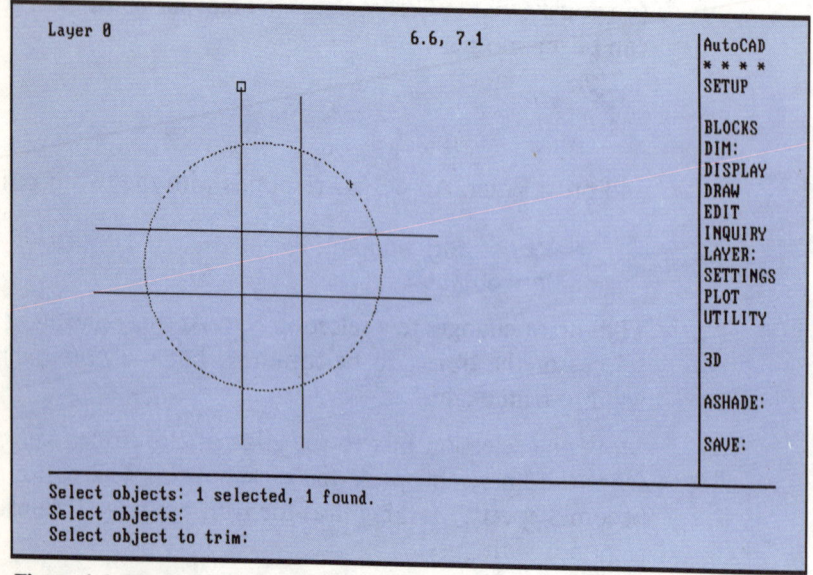

Figure 4.6: Marking a line to be trimmed back to the circle

spotty, marking it as a trim boundary. AutoCAD again issues the line

Select object to trim:

6. Move the selection box to each of the remaining seven parts that stick out of the circle, pressing the pick button to trim that part back to the circle. The screen should look like Figure 4.7. The circle is spotty because the Trim command is still active.

7. After trimming all eight pieces, try to trim the parts of the lines that are within the circle. Move the selection box to the right vertical line inside the circle and press the pick button. Nothing happens. Move the selection box to the other lines and press the pick button. Again, nothing happens. The Trim command can only erase an object on one side of the trim boundary. It cannot erase an object on both sides. Later in this chapter we will see a way to trim these interior lines.

8. Now press the second mouse button or the Enter key to complete the Trim command. The spotty circle returns to normal

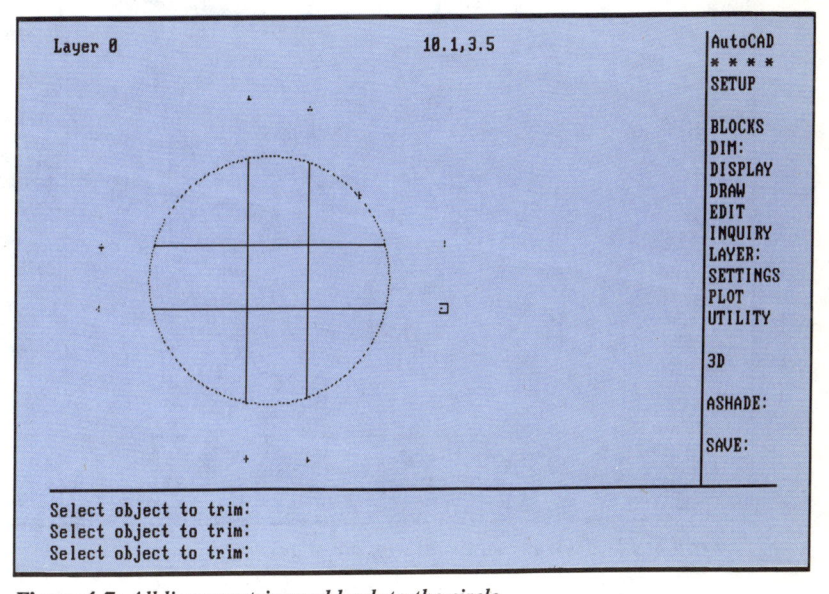

Figure 4.7: All lines are trimmed back to the circle

and the word *Command:* appears on the bottom line of the screen.

9. Press F7 twice to remove the spots marking the cursor position during trimming.

Trimming a Circle

In the previous section, you trimmed parts of the lines back to the circle, which resulted in shorter lines. Now you will trim parts of the circle against the lines by removing selected parts. Thus, the circle is converted to several independent arcs.

1. Press the second mouse button or the Enter key to restart the Trim command. The cursor changes to a selection box.

2. Move the selection box over each of the four lines to make them spotty (Figure 4.8). (Alternately, you can use a Crossing window to select all four lines at once.) The four lines are now the trim boundaries.

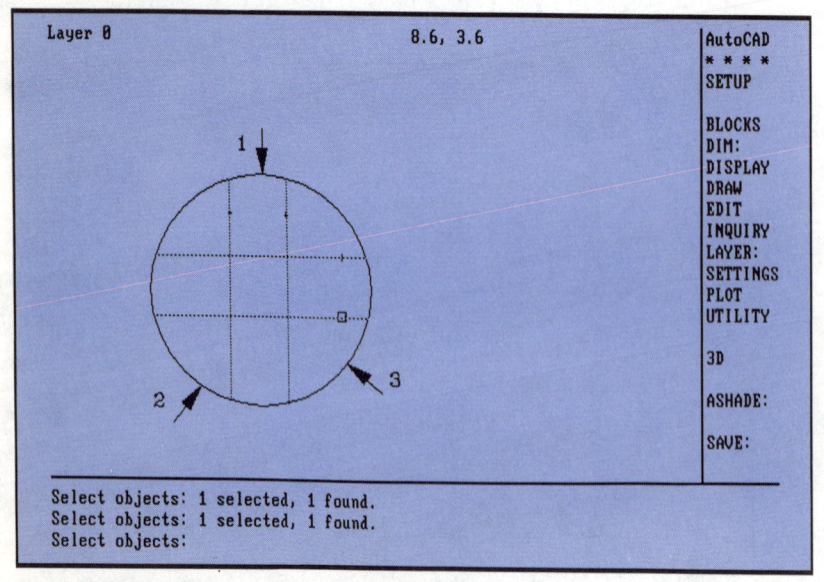

Figure 4.8: The lines are marked as trim boundaries

Changing an Existing Drawing **73**

3. Press the second mouse button or the Enter key to complete the selection of the trim boundary.

4. Move the selection box to the top edge of the circle, to the region marked 1 in Figure 4.8. Press the pick button. The top edge of the circle, between the two vertical lines, is erased (Figure 4.9). The Trim command is still active and the lines are still selected as the trim boundary.

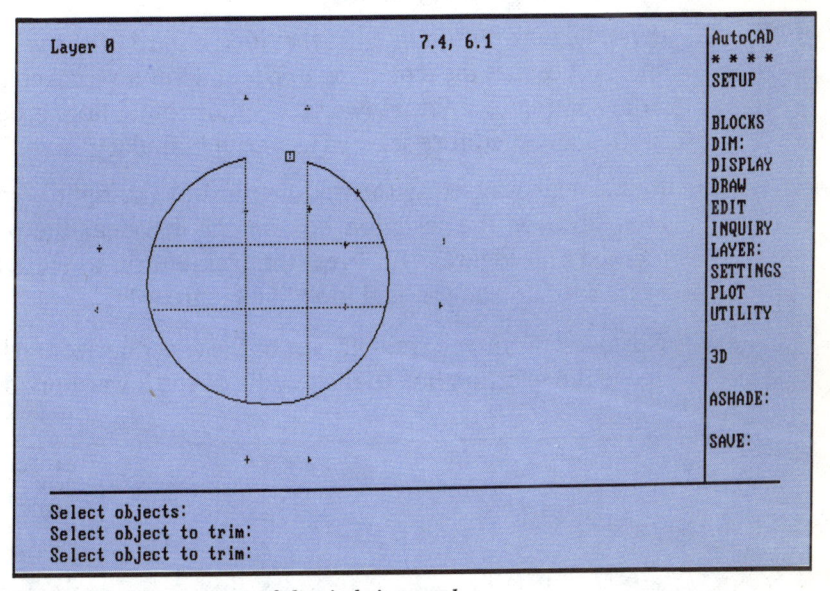

Figure 4.9: The top part of the circle is erased

5. Move the selection box to the lower-left edge of the circle, to the region marked 2 in Figure 4.8.

6. Press the pick button to erase this segment.

7. Similarly, move the selection box to the lower-right edge of the circle, to the region marked 3 in Figure 4.7. Press the pick button to erase this segment. Your drawing should now look like Figure 4.10.

*T*rimming the Trim Boundary

In the previous section you trimmed parts of the circle against the four lines that are designated as the trim boundary. It is also possible to trim parts of the boundary against other parts of the trim boundary. Let us see how by continuing the Trim command of the previous section. Your drawing screen should look like Figure 4.10.

1. The two vertical lines are divided into three parts by the horizontal lines. We are going to erase the middle third of the two vertical lines by continuing with the Trim command. Move the selection box to the middle of the left vertical line, to the place marked 4 in Figure 4.10.

2. Press the pick button to erase the middle third of the vertical line. Notice that the remaining upper and lower pieces change from spotted to solid. However, the horizontal lines are still spotted and therefore selected as a trim boundary.

3. In a similar way, erase the middle third of the right vertical line. Position the selection box on the line near the place marked 5 in Figure 4.10. Press the pick button to erase this part. Your drawing should look like Figure 4.11.

4. Next we will erase the middle part of the lower horizontal line. Move the selection box to the middle of the lower horizontal

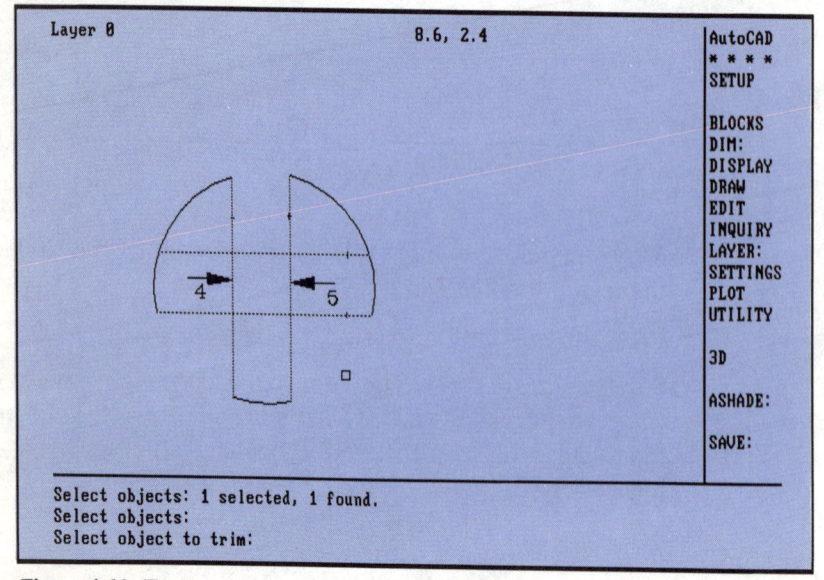

Figure 4.10: Two more parts of the circle are erased

line, to the place marked 6 in Figure 4.11. The vertical lines, which you originally designated as trim boundaries, are no longer spotted. Nevertheless, they are still acting as trim boundaries. Press the pick button to erase the middle third of the lower line. As with the vertical lines, the remaining left and right parts change from spotted to normal appearance.

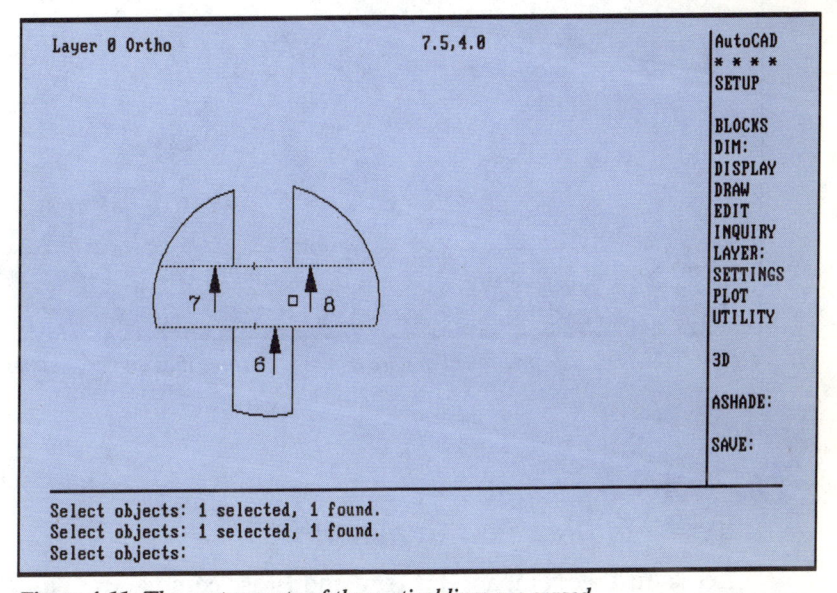

Figure 4.11: The center parts of the vertical lines are erased

5. In the same way, remove the left third of the upper horizontal line. Move the selection box to the region marked 7 in Figure 4.12 and press the pick button.

6. Now move the selection box to the right third of the upper line, near the region marked 8 in Figure 4.11. Press the pick button to erase the right third of this line.

7. Press the right mouse button or the Enter key to complete the Trim command. Your drawing screen should look like Figure 4.12.

8. Press F7 twice to remove the markers from the screen.

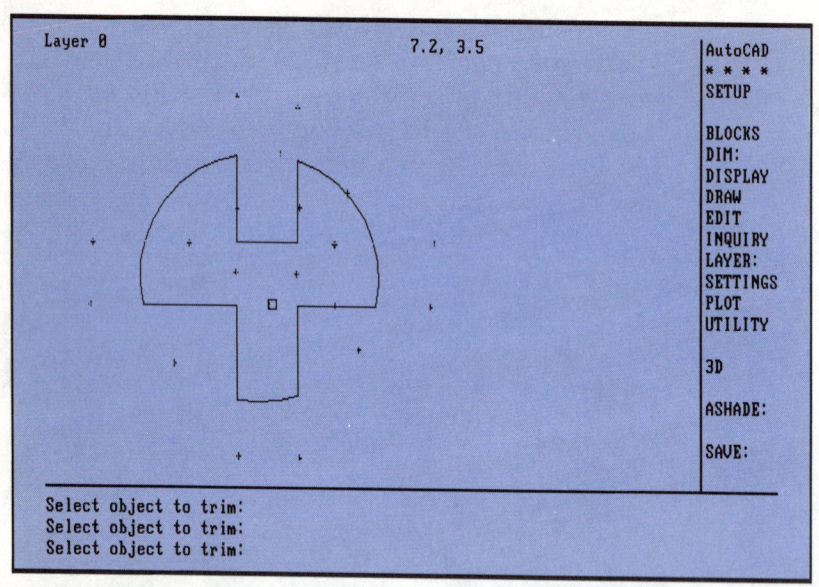

Figure 4.12: The circle and four lines are trimmed to three arcs and seven lines

The Trim Command Compared to the Erase Command

Let us further compare the Trim and Erase commands. The Trim command erases a part of an object up to a trim boundary while the Erase command removes a complete object. To illustrate this, let's erase the bottom arc.

1. Restart the Trim command by pressing the right mouse button or the Enter key.

2. Move the selection box to the lower part of the left vertical line. Press the pick button. This line becomes spotty.

3. Move the selection box to the lower part of the right vertical line. Press the pick button. This line also becomes spotty.

4. Press the right mouse button or the Enter key to complete boundary-line selection. The bottom arc now touches the trim boundaries at each end.

5. Move the selection box over the arc at the bottom of the drawing. Press the pick button. The arc does not disappear. The problem is that you are trying to trim an entire object, the bottom arc. In the previous examples, the line or curve you wanted to trim penetrated the trim boundary. After trimming one side, there was something left over because you erased only a part of an object. If you want to erase this lower arc, however, you must use the Erase command because you want to delete the entire piece.

6. Give the command

    ^C

    to cancel the Trim command.

7. Give the command

    erase

    and press Enter.

8. Place the selection box over the lower arc and press the pick button. Now, the arc becomes spotty. Notice that the other two arcs of the circle do not become spotty, because they are now separate entities.

9. Press the second mouse button or the Enter key to complete the selection process. The lower arc disappears.

10. Type

    u

    and press Enter to restore the lower arc.

11. Leave the drawing editor and save the latest version of your drawing by giving the command

    end

    and pressing Enter. This saves your work with the file name second.dwg.

5

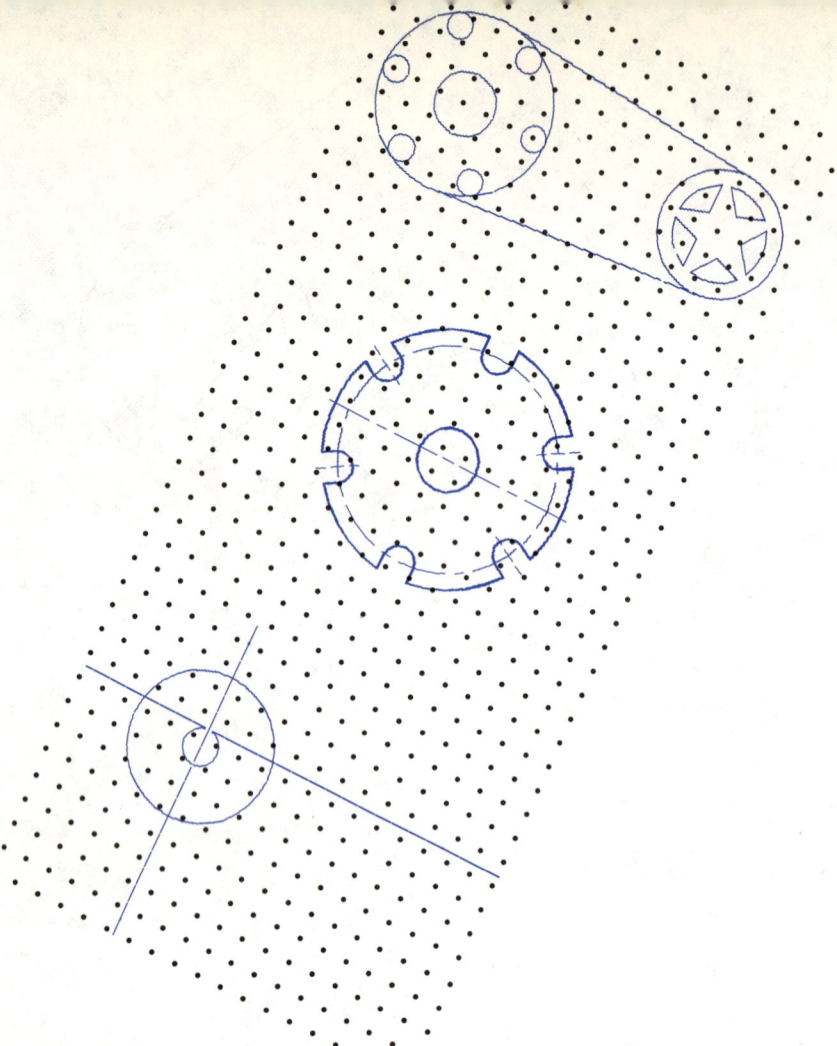

Making More Elaborate Changes

Featuring:
- Setting drawing size
- Stretching objects
- Dynamic zoom
- Mirror images

Making More Elaborate Changes 81

In this chapter we will continue working with AutoCAD commands. Using two circles and two lines, you will draw an object resembling a drive belt on pulleys. You will make it longer with the Stretch command, and magnify it with the Zoom command. Then you will remove parts of the circles with the Trim and Break commands. Finally, you will use some basic AutoCAD commands that you've already learned, plus the Array command to add detail and complexity to your drawing. New commands used in this chapter are

- Tan to make a line tangent to another object
- Stretch to move connected objects
- Regen to redraw the screen
- Break to erase part of an object
- Array to draw several copies of an object at once
- Arc to draw a part of a circle
- Mirror to make a mirror image
- Extend to lengthen a line

How to Set Up the Drawing Area

You will begin by setting up the drawing area. First you'll name your drawing and set the display, grid, and snap spacing. Then you'll set the drawing size and draw a border around the drawing area.

1. At the AutoCAD Main menu type

    1

    and press Enter to create a new drawing.

2. Type

    pulley

    and press Enter to name the new drawing.

3. Type the command

   units

   and press Enter to set the display.

4. Press Enter again to accept the current value of the prompt.
5. Type

   1

   and press Enter to set the display to one digit.

6. Press ^C to complete the Units command.
7. Press F1 to switch back to the drawing screen.
8. Type

   snap

   and press Enter to set the snap spacing.

9. Type

   0.5

   and press Enter.

10. Type

    grid

    and press Enter.

11. Type

    s

    and press Enter to set the grid spacing to the snap spacing.

Let us set the drawing size next, as you learned to do in Chapter 2.

1. Type the command

   limits

   and press Enter. AutoCAD responds with

   ON/OFF<Lower left corner><0.0,0.0>:

   showing the current coordinates for the lower-left corner.

2. Press the Enter key to accept the default value. AutoCAD then shows the current coordinates for the upper-right corner (12,9), and waits for you to enter new values.

3. Type

    22, 17

   and press Enter to change the upper-right corner to the new value. The drawing screen returns.

Now that you have enlarged the drawing limits, let us draw a border around it.

1. Type

    line

   and press Enter.

2. Type

    0.5, 0.5

   and press Enter to start the line.

3. Type

    21.5, 0.5

   and press Enter to draw the bottom edge.

4. Type

    @16<90

   and press Enter to draw the right border. (This line is off the screen.)

5. Type

    @21<180

   and press Enter to draw the top border.

6. Type

    close

   and press Enter to complete the border.

How to Draw Two Connected Circles

In this section you will begin by drawing two circles. Then you will draw lines tangent to the two circles. The finished drawing will look like two pulleys connected by a drive belt (Figure 5.1).

1. Type the command

   circle

   and press Enter.

2. Press F6 to turn on the coordinate readout.
3. The cursor will be in the lower-left corner. Move the cursor upward and to the right until the coordinate readout is

   5.0, 4.0

   (Alternatively, you can type **5,4** from the keyboard.) Press the pick button to fix the circle center. Since Snap mode is on, AutoCAD will precisely locate the center for you.

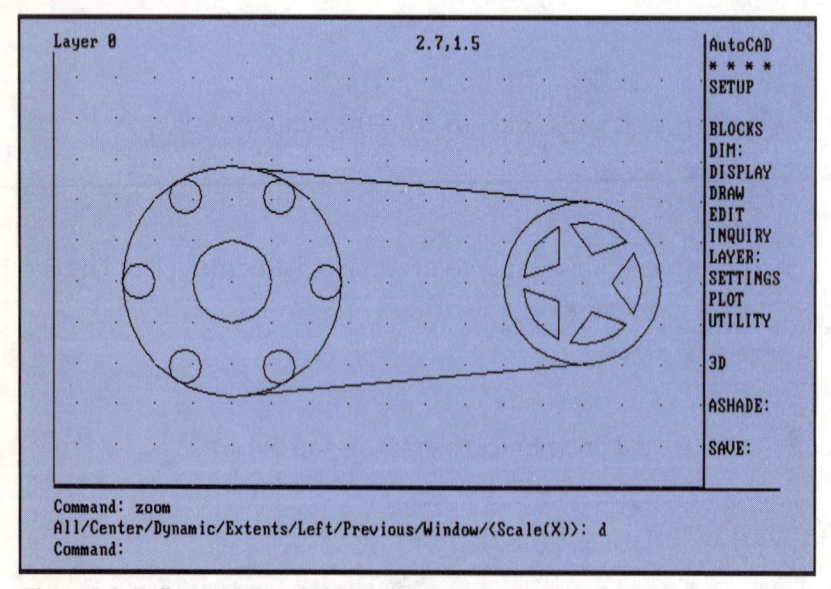

Figure 5.1: Pulleys and drive belt

Making More Elaborate Changes 85

4. Move the cursor upward and to the right, at a 45-degree angle. Snap onto the second diagonal grid point. The coordinate readout shows

    1.4<45

5. Press the pick button to establish the circle size.

6. Press the second mouse button or the Enter key to restart the Circle command and draw the second circle.

7. Move the cursor upward and to the right until the coordinate is

    8.0, 7.0

    Press the pick button to fix the center of the second circle.

8. Move the cursor to the right two grid points. The coordinate readout shows

    1.0<0

    Press the pick button. Good. Your screen should look like Figure 5.2.

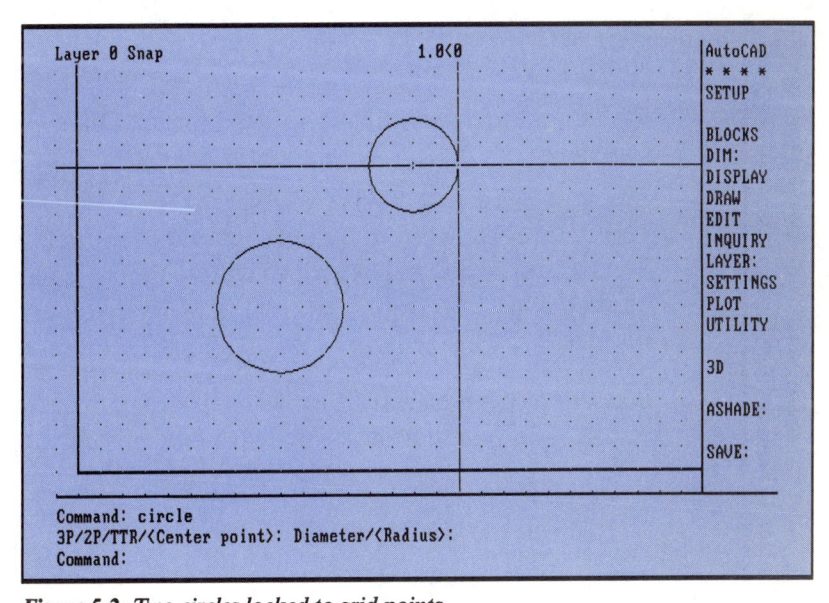

Figure 5.2: Two circles locked to grid points

9. Press F9 to turn off Snap mode so we can draw lines that do not connect to grid points.

How to Draw Tangent Lines with the Tan Command

Now you will draw two lines tangent to the two circles. The Osnap Tan command will help with this task. Tan forces a line to be tangent to the circle (or arc) you select. You previously used the Center and Quad Osnap commands.

1. Give the command

    line

    and press Enter.

2. In response to the statement:

    From point:

    type

    tan

    for Tangent and press Enter. As it did for the Cen and Quad commands, the cursor changes to a selection box with crossed lines.

3. Move the selection box to the top edge of the left circle, where the line will begin, as shown in Figure 5.3. The coordinate position is

    4.2, 5.1

    Press the pick button and the cursor returns to normal. There is no change in your drawing as yet, but AutoCAD responds with

    To point:

4. To complete the line, type

    tan

    and press Enter. The cursor again changes to include a selection box.

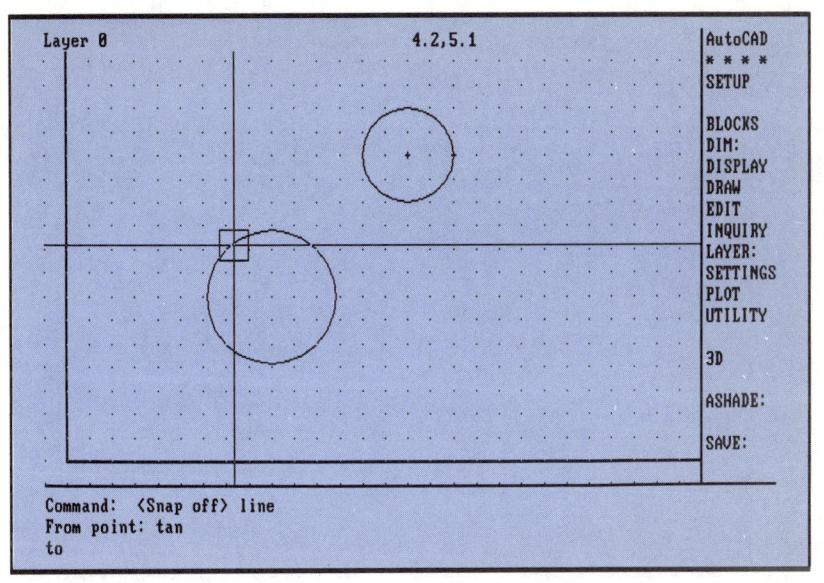

Figure 5.3: The selection box marks the position for the first tangent line

5. Move the selection box to the top edge of the right circle—the end point of the line—as shown in Figure 5.4. This is location

    7.4, 7.8

    Press the pick button. Now a line appears that is tangent to both circles. (Figure 5.5).

6. Press the second mouse button or the Enter key to complete the Line command.

Now let's draw a second line along the bottom of the circles. The procedure is the same as above.

7. Press the second mouse button or the Enter key to start the Line command again.

8. In response to the statement

    From point:

    type

    tan

    and press Enter.

88 *The ABC's of AutoCAD*

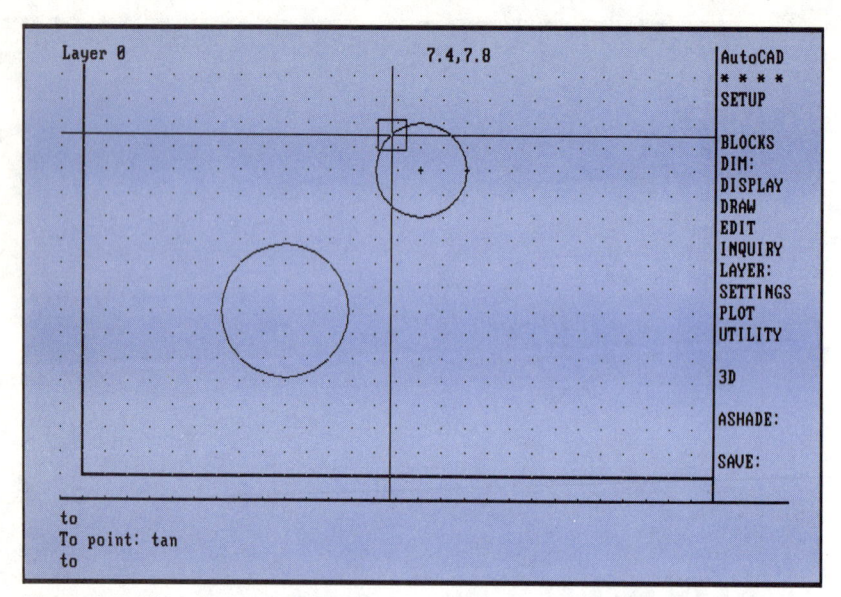

CH. 5

Figure 5.4: The selection box marking the location for the second tangent line

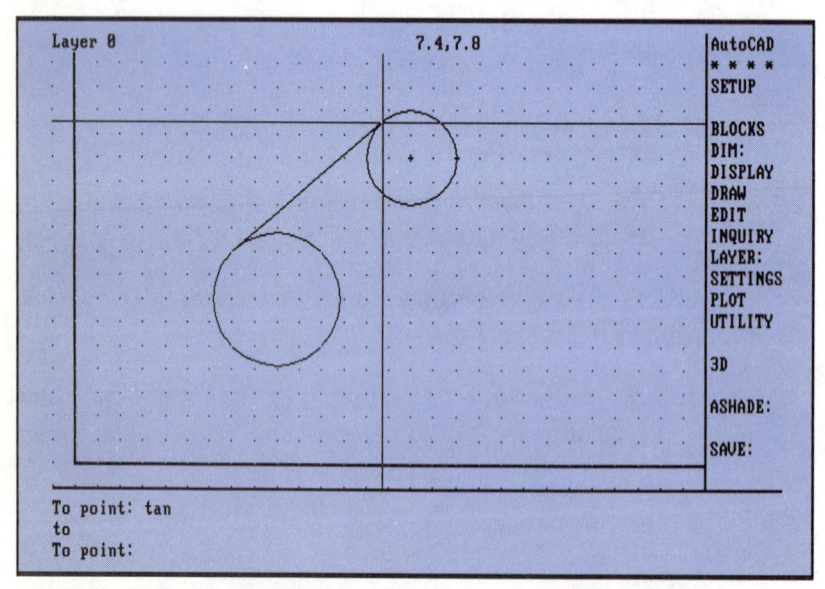

Figure 5.5: The upper tangent line is drawn

Making More Elaborate Changes 89

9. Move the selection box to the bottom edge of the right circle near location

   8.6, 6.2

   Press the pick button and the cursor returns to normal.

10. Type

    tan

    and press Enter.

11. Move the selection box to the bottom edge of the left circle near location

    5.7, 2.8

    Press the pick button. Now a line that is tangent to both circles appears across the bottom (Figure 5.6).

12. Press the second mouse button or the Enter key to complete the Line command.

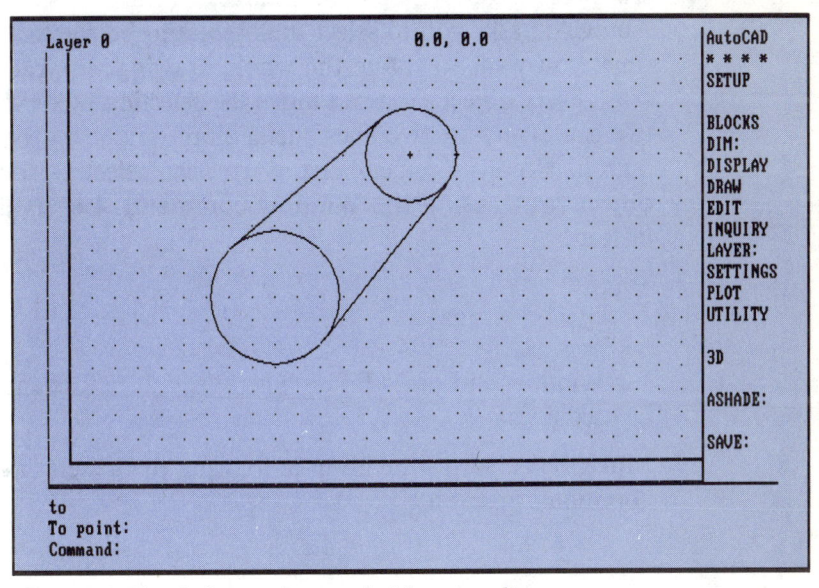

Figure 5.6: The circles are connected with tangent lines

Good. You've completed the basic drawing. Keep the drawing on the screen. In the next sections you'll move objects in the drawing.

How to Rotate the Drawing

The object you just drew is inclined upward at a 45-degree angle. Suppose after drawing it you realize that you want it in a horizontal position. You can easily do this with the Rotate command. In the previous chapter you used the Rotate command to turn two lines by 90 degrees. However, the Rotate command is quite general. You can turn selected parts or the entire drawing. Furthermore, you can rotate by any desired angle. Follow these steps, using the drawing you just completed.

1. Give the command

   rotate

   and press Enter. The cursor changes to the selection box. AutoCAD asks you to select the objects to be rotated. This time, you want to rotate the whole drawing, so you must select every object. You can move the selection box over the two circles and the two lines one at a time and press the pick button. However, remember that you can select a group or object faster using the Window command. Let us use it instead.

2. Type

   w

   for Window and press Enter. The selection box changes to crossed lines.

3. Move the cursor to the lower-left corner of the left circle to coordinate position

   3.4, 2.4

   and press the pick button.

Making More Elaborate Changes 91

4. Move the cursor to the upper-right corner of the right circle near location

    9.2, 8.3

    Notice that a window grows as the cursor is moved.

5. When the selection window covers all parts of your object, press the pick button. The parts become spotty to show that they are selected.

6. Press the second mouse button. The expression

    Base point:

    appears on the bottom line. AutoCAD needs to know what point to rotate the object around.

7. This time, we will rotate the object about the center of the left circle. Give the command

    cen

    for Center and press Enter. As you learned in the previous chapter, this is an object snap or Osnap command that locks onto the center of a circle when you select the rim of that circle.

8. Move the selection box to the rim of the left circle, well away from the tangent lines, and press the pick button. Now as you move the cursor, an image of your object, centered on the left circle, moves on the screen.

9. In the previous chapter we rotated in the positive or counter-clockwise direction. Type the number

    −45

    to rotate the object 45 degrees in a minus (clockwise) direction this time (Figure 5.7). Alternatively, you could have moved the cursor until the object rotated into the desired position and then pressed the pick button. But then it would not be as precisely located.

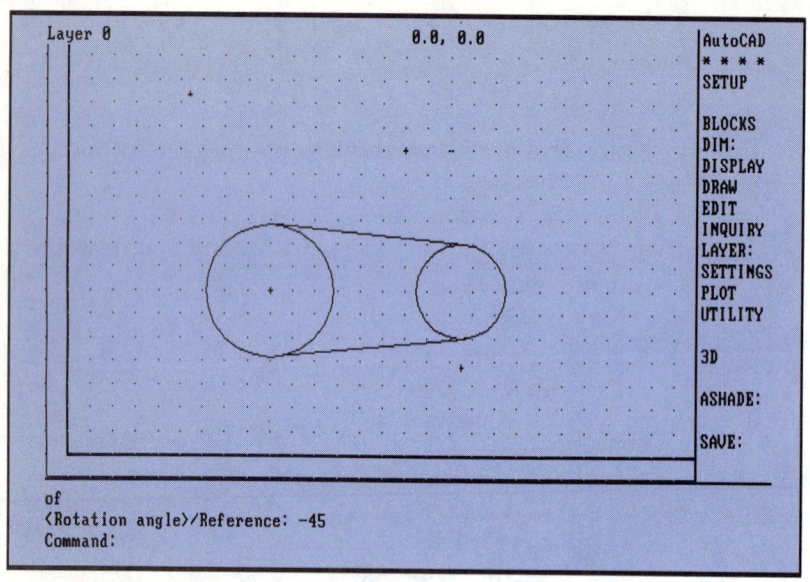

Figure 5.7: The object is rotated 45 degrees

How to Move an Object with the Stretch Command

In the previous chapter, you used the Move command to move objects. However, with the Move command, if the moved items are connected to other items, the connections will be broken.

The Stretch command is similar to the Move command, but it enables you to move items that are connected to other items and preserve the connections. For example, if you move the right circle and the tangent lines of your drawing with the Move command, the lines will no longer connect to the left circle. However, if we use the Stretch command, the connecting lines will automatically change length and remain tangent to both circles.

Let's try the Stretch command. In this section you are going to move the right circle a little farther to the right, away from the left circle.

1. Check that Snap mode is off.

2. Type the command

    stretch

    and press Enter. The cursor changes to the familiar selection box. AutoCAD asks you to select the objects to stretch. You want to select the right circle and the two tangent lines connecting the circles. Of course, you can point to each of the three objects separately. However, let us use a Crossing window instead, as you did in the previous chapter.

3. Type

    c

    for Crossing window and press Enter. The cursor changes back to crossed lines.

4. Move the cursor to the lower-right side of the right circle to location

    11.1, 2.4

    and press the pick button. The cursor changes to a window.

5. Move the window left and upward until it includes the right circle and parts of the two lines. You can see that it would be impossible to use a Regular window for this process. Be careful that the window does not touch the left circle. Press the pick button. The right circle and the two lines become spotty to show that they have been selected.

6. Press the right mouse button or the Enter key to complete the selection process. Now you're ready to move the selected items.

7. AutoCAD responds with the prompt

    Base point:

    as with the Move command. Type the Osnap command

    cen

    for Center of a circle and press Enter. The cursor shows a selection box around the crossed lines.

8. Move the selection box to the right edge of the right circle, well away from the straight lines. Press the pick button.

9. Move the cursor to the right. Notice that the right circle moves too. Furthermore, the two tangent lines "stretch" and remain connected to the circles.
10. Turn on Snap mode by pressing F9. The right circle will snap to the next grid point.
11. Press the left mouse button or the Enter key to lock the right circle and complete the Stretch command.
12. Press F9 to turn off Snap mode.

You can use the Stretch command to move parts of your drawing either closer together or farther apart. Continue to the next exercise where you'll enlarge a part of the drawing.

How to Enlarge an Object with the Zoom Command

In this section you will enlarge the left circle with the Zoom command. This command enables you to work with objects in a more convenient scale. AutoCAD draws circles with straight lines. When you enlarge a circle, the lines cause the circle to have flat sides. To make the circle look rounder on the screen, you can use the Regen, or Regenerate, command. Then AutoCAD will redraw the circle using more sides so it will look round once more. However, this does not change the final drawing.

Follow these steps to enlarge and regenerate the right circle of your drawing.

1. Give the command

    zoom

    and press the space bar.
2. Now select the circle. Type

    w

    for Window and press Enter.

3. Move the cursor to the upper-left side of the left circle, to location

   2.9, 5.6

   and press the pick button.

4. Move the cursor to the lower-right side of the same circle to enclose it in a window.

5. When the coordinate readout is

   7.2, 2.4

   press the pick button. The image within the window enlarges to fill the screen (Figure 5.8).

6. To make the enlarged circle look rounder, give the command

   regen

   and press Enter. The circle will now appear as it does in Figure 5.9.

Before continuing, save a copy of your current work to disk.

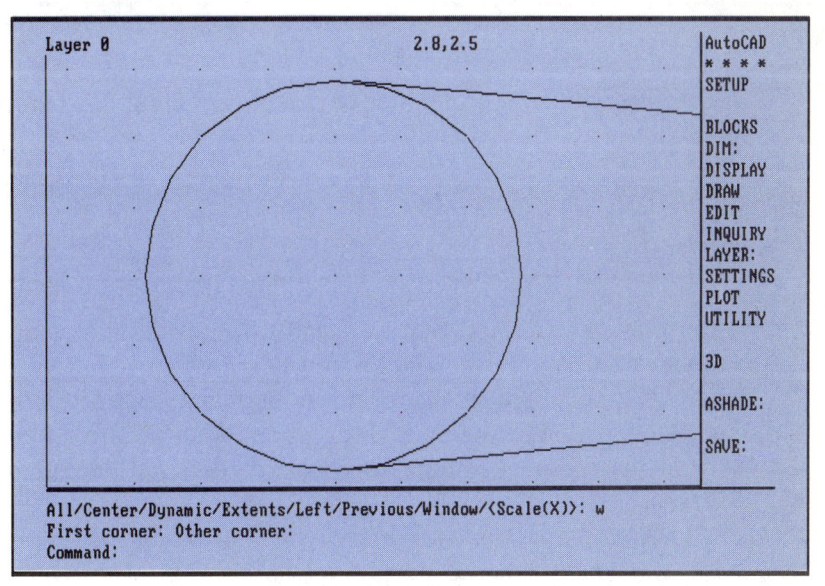

Figure 5.8: An enlarged view of the left circle showing flat sides

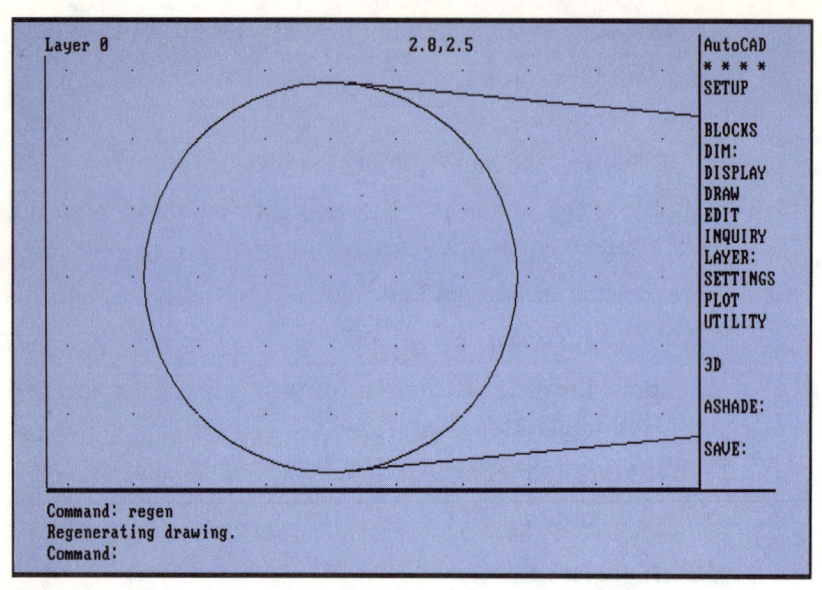

Figure 5.9: Enlarged view of the circle after regeneration

7. Give the command

    save

    and press the Enter key.

8. Press Enter a second time to accept the default file name.

How the Use the Mark Option to Undo Your Work

You may have noticed that we usually abbreviate the secondary commands such as W for Window and Cen for Center. On the other hand, we do not abbreviate the primary commands such as Circle and Line. An apparent exception is U for Undo. We have already used U to undo the previous command. However, the Undo command is different.

When you give the Undo command, you must also give a second part to the command. If the second part is a number, AutoCAD will undo that many previous commands. For example, if you want to undo the last five commands you have given, type

undo

and press Enter. Then in response to the prompt

Auto/Back/Control/End/Group/Mark/<Number>:

type 5 and press Enter. AutoCAD will undo the last five commands. Thus the U command does the same thing as Undo followed by the number 1, except it is shorter.

Other useful features of Undo are the Mark and Back options. If you give the Undo command, followed by a large number such as 9999, your work will be undone all the way back to the beginning. However, it is also possible to undo your work back to a special place. You mark this place with the Undo command and the Mark option. (Mark can be abbreviated to M but Undo cannot be abbreviated.) Later, you can undo your work to this point by giving the Undo command with the Back option. (Back can also be abbreviated to B.)

Thus, at any point you can give the Undo command, then choose the Mark option. You can then try out a new set of commands. If the result is not what you wanted, give the Undo command again with the Back option. The drawing is returned to the state at which it was when you gave the Undo-Mark command. To see how the Mark option works, we'll use it as we make some temporary changes to the drawing. In the following section, you'll learn how to use the Break command to erase parts of the circle. Then you'll undo your changes.

How to Use the Break Command

We are going to experiment on our enlarged circle with the Break command. We will not keep the results, but will return to the present form.

1. Give the command

    undo

    and press Enter. Be careful to spell out the full name. Do not use the abbreviation U.

2. Type the option

    m

    for Mark and press Enter.

As you have seen, the Erase command erases a complete object and the Trim command erases a part of an object. To use the Trim command you must first select the trim boundary and then select the object to be trimmed against the boundary.

The Break command is primarily used to break an object into two separate objects. While it can also remove a part of an object, you will generally want to use the Trim command for this task.

When you use the Break command you only have to select one object, the object to be broken. There is no trim boundary as there is with the Trim command. The Break command has two forms—the two point and the three point. With the first method, you can remove a part of an object by selecting two points, then the part between the points is erased. This is a simple process with a line or an arc. However, it is more complicated for a circle. When you break a circle, the part between the first and second points, in a *counterclockwise* direction, is erased.

You must be careful when you want to break an object at the intersection of two lines. You cannot simply select the intersection point, or AutoCAD will not know which line to break. In this case you use the three-point method. First you select the object to be broken. Then you type F to signal that the first point to break will follow and then press Enter. Then you select the two points to be broken.

*E*rasing Part of a Circle

Let us use the Break command to erase the right side of the circle.

1. Type the command

    break

    and press Enter. The cursor changes to a selection box.

2. Move the cursor to the right edge of the circle to location

    6.4, 4.3

Making More Elaborate Changes 99

Press the pick button. The circle becomes spotty and the cursor changes back to crossed lines.

3. Move the cursor *downward* about an inch along the edge of the circle to location

   6.4, 3.7

   Press the pick button a second time. Notice that most of the circle is erased (Figure 5.10). AutoCAD erased all of the circle between your two selected points, but in a *counterclockwise* direction. If you want to erase the part that remains and keep the part that was erased, you must select the two points in the opposite order. The Break command always deletes part of a circle in a counterclockwise direction. Therefore, you must pick the two points with this in mind.

4. Give the command

   U

   and press Enter to undo the last step so you can erase in the other direction. The screen should look like Figure 5.9.

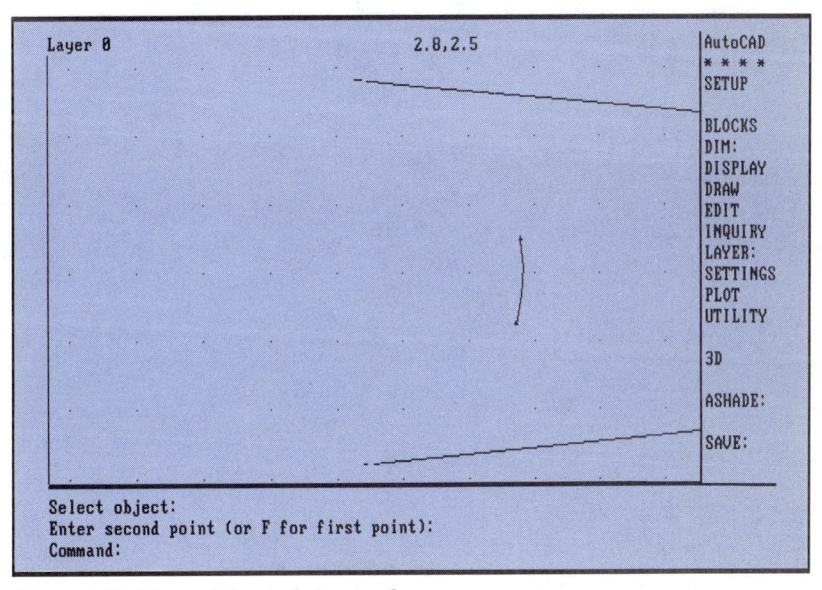

Figure 5.10: Most of the circle is erased

Now that the U command has restored the circle, let us try to erase a small part of the right side.

1. Give the command

   break

   and press Enter. (Don't try to repeat the previous command by pressing the right mouse button. That command was U not Break.)

2. As before, move the cursor to the right edge of the circle near location

   6.4, 3.7

   Press the pick button.

3. Move the cursor *upward,* in a counterclockwise direction, about an inch along the edge of the circle near location

   6.4, 4.3

   Press the pick button. This time only a small part of the right edge of the circle is erased (Figure 5.11).

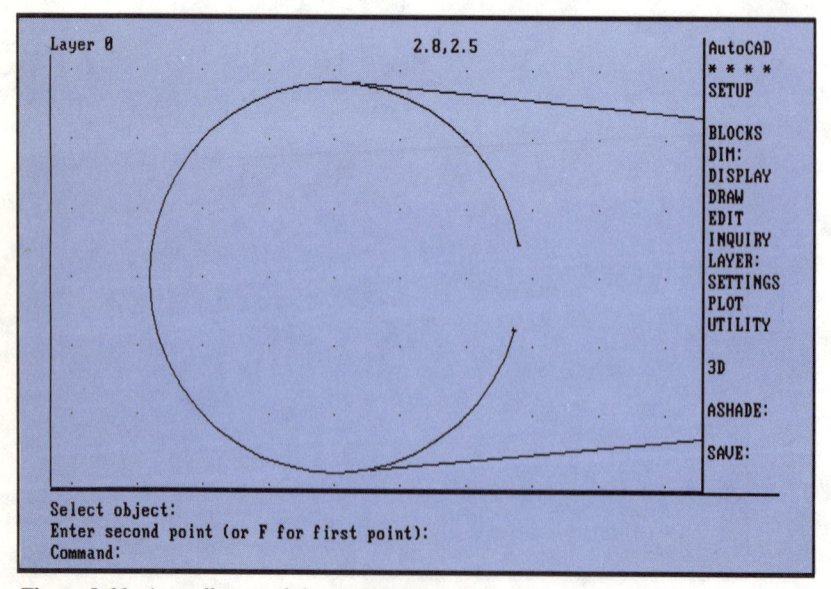

Figure 5.11: A small part of the circle is erased

Let us continue removing parts of the broken circle.

The Trim Command Compared to the Break Command

From the previous examples you can see that special care must be taken when you remove part of a circle with the Break command. You must select the two points, marking the part to be removed, in a counterclockwise direction. Of course, you can recover with the U command if you make a mistake. Let's try erasing a fragment with the Trim command now.

Erasing the Upper Fragment with the Trim Command

In this section you will erase the upper piece of the broken circle using the Trim command. Your screen should look like Figure 5.11.

1. Give the command

    trim

    and press Enter.

2. Move the selection box over the upper tangent line and press the pick button. That line becomes spotty.

3. Press the right mouse button or Enter to complete the selection process. You have set the trim boundary.

4. Move the selection box to the upper right edge of the circle, between the opening in the circle and the upper line.

5. Press the pick button and the upper part is trimmed back to the upper tangent line.

6. Press Enter to complete the Trim command.

Erasing the Lower Fragment with the Break Command

Let us erase the lower fragment back to the tangent point by using the Break command.

1. Type the command

    break

    and Press Enter.

2. Type the Osnap command

    end

    for Endpoint and press Enter. This Osnap option locks onto the endpoint of a line or arc. The cursor changes to a double selection box.

3. Move the selection box to the end of the lower arc. Press the pick button and the arc becomes spotty.

4. Type the Osnap command

    int

    for Intersection. This Osnap option locks onto the intersection of two objects.

5. Move the selection box to the lower tangent point and press the pick button. The lower fragment disappears.

6. Press the right mouse button or the Enter key to complete the Break command.

7. Restore the complete circle by giving the command

    undo

    and pressing Enter. (Be careful not to abbreviate this command.)

8. Give the option

    b

    for Back and press Enter. The screen will be restored back to the stage where you gave the Undo-Mark command (Figure 5.9).

Notice that in the previous section you erased the lower arc in a clockwise direction. When you erase a part of a line or arc, you can go in either direction. It is only when a complete circle is to be broken that you must mark the two points in a counterclockwise direction.

There is a further complication in this example. If you had selected the lower tangent point first, AutoCAD would not know which of the two objects, the arc or the tangent line, you wanted to break. Therefore, you must not choose the first point to be broken where there is more than one line. But you might sometimes want to erase an object between places where several lines cross. Let us see how to do this with the Break command.

Erasing the Right Part of a Circle with the Break Command

In this section you will erase the right part of the circle yet another time. You will erase the entire piece with one command. Since you want to erase between both intersection points, you must use the three-point rather than the two-point method. With this method, the first point selects the object to be broken. Then the other two points mark the portion to be erased. Since we are erasing a circle, we must be careful to mark the second and third points in a counterclockwise direction.

1. Type the command

    break

    and press Enter.

2. Move the selection box to the right edge of the circle and press the pick button. The entire circle becomes spotty.

3. Press

    f

    for First and press the Enter key.

4. Give the Osnap command

    int

    for Intersection and press Enter.

5. Put the selection box over the *lower* tangent point and press the pick button.

6. Give the Osnap command

    int

    again and press Enter.

7. Put the selection box over the *upper* tangent point and press the pick button. The right part is erased.

8. Give the command

    u

    and press Enter to restore the circle. The screen should look like Figure 5.9.

How to Draw Concentric Circles

Drawing concentric circles is easy—you simply use the Circle command and Snap mode to place a circle within another circle. Let's try it. We'll draw a smaller concentric circle to represent a shaft for this pulley drawing.

1. Give the command

    circle

    and press Enter. You will use the center of the existing circle for the center of the new circle.

2. Turn on Snap mode by pressing F9 so you can snap to the circle center.

3. Move the cursor to the center of the circle. When the coordinate readout shows

    5.0, 4.0

    press the pick button.

4. Move the cursor to the right until the circle snaps to the next grid point. The coordinate reads

    0.5<0

5. Press the pick button to fix the circle size.

6. Press F9 to turn off Snap mode.

How to Draw Tangent Circles

In this section you will draw a third circle. This will be a small circle drawn inside and tangent to the large circle. You previously drew circles by marking the center and then one edge. This time we will draw a circle by designating two points on opposite sides of the circle.

1. Type the command

    circle

Making More Elaborate Changes **105**

and press Enter. (You can also just press Enter to repeat the previous command.)

2. Select the two-point option by typing

    2p

    and pressing Enter.

3. Type the Osnap command

    quad

    for Quadrant and press Enter. A selection box is added to the cursor.

4. Move the selection box to the left edge of the circle and press the pick button. This locks the left edge of the new circle to the left edge of the larger circle.

5. Press F9 to turn on Snap mode.

6. Define the right edge of the circle by moving the cursor to the right until it snaps onto the next grid point. Press the pick button to establish the circle size. Your drawing should look like Figure 5.12.

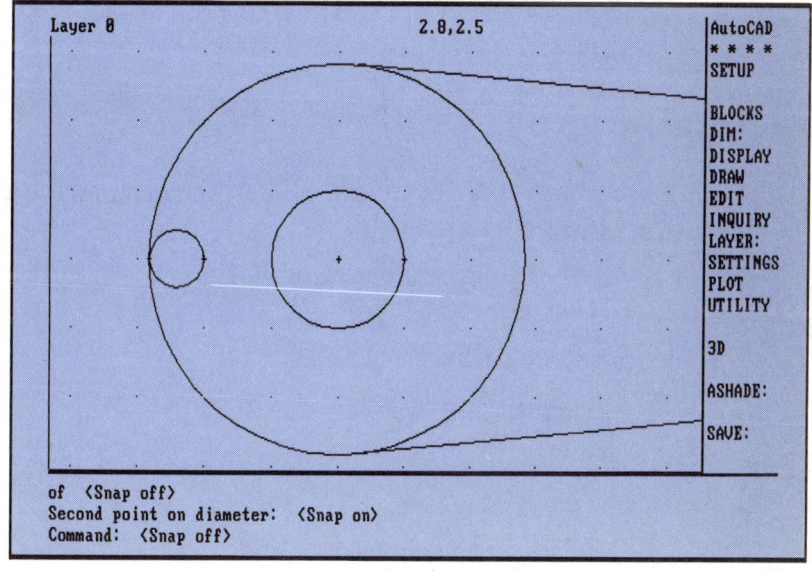

Figure 5.12: Two circles drawn in the larger circle

7. Press F9 to turn off Snap mode.

How to Make Multiple Copies with the Array Command

In the previous chapters you used the Copy command to duplicate a pattern. This command is suitable for making one copy. However, if you want to make several regularly spaced copies of an object, the Array command is more suitable. To gain experience with this powerful command, you will use it to make multiple copies of a circular pattern and decorate a circle with a five-pointed star.

Duplicating a Pattern

We are going to make a pattern of six circles around the enlarged left circle.

1. Type the command

    array

    and press Enter. AutoCAD then asks you to select the objects you want to replicate.

2. Give the command

    L

    for Last item drawn and press Enter. The small circle becomes spotty as it is selected.

3. Press the right mouse button or the Enter key to complete the selection process.

4. When you see the prompt:

    Rectangular or Polar array (R/P):

    Type

    p

    for Polar and press Enter.

5. AutoCAD then wants to know where you want the center of the polar array. We want to select the center of the large circle. Therefore, type the Osnap command

   cen

   for Center and press Enter so that AutoCAD can precisely find the center.

6. Move the cursor to the rim of the larger circle, well away from the small circle and the tangent lines, and press the pick button.

7. Next, AutoCAD needs to know the number of items, including the original, in the new array. Type the value

   6

   and press Enter. This will replicate the original circle until there are six copies altogether.

8. Finally, in response to the prompt

   Angle to fill (+ = CCW, − = CW) <360>:

   press Enter to accept the default value. This will draw the copies equally spaced around the circle. The prompt, however, allows you to select less than a full circle by specifying the angle and the direction.

9. Press Enter again to select rotation during copy. There will now be six small circles equally spaced around the larger circle (Figure 5.13).

Good. You have seen how Array can duplicate an item. Now go to the next section and see how Array can be used to decorate your drawing to add interesting detail.

How to Draw an Arc

In the remainder of this chapter you will decorate the right circle with a five-pointed star. You will start with a line and an arc, form a wedge, then use Array to make the star. First we will want an enlarged view of the right circle. Let's get it with the Dynamic Zoom command.

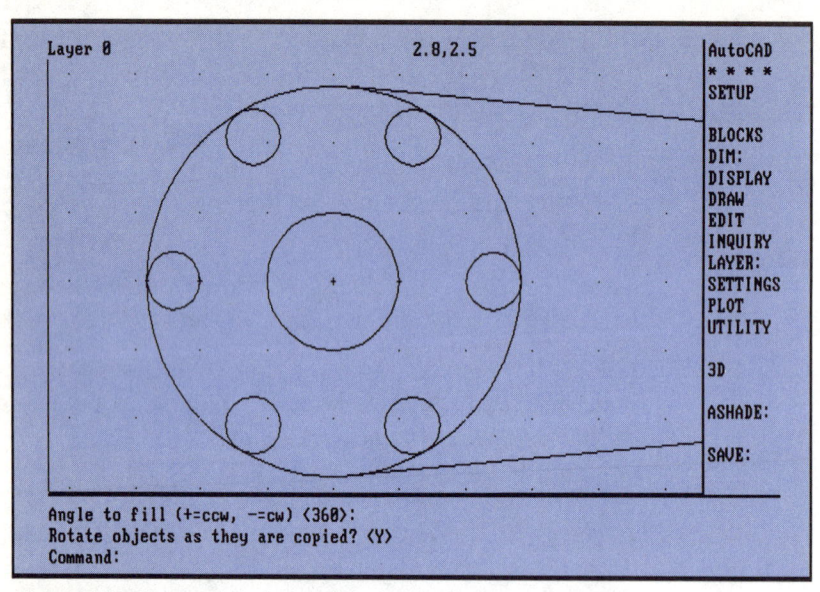

Figure 5.13: Six small circles produced with the Array command

1. Type the command

    zoom

    and press the space bar.

2. Type

    d

    for Dynamic Zoom and press Enter.

The screen changes to show the entire drawing area that you previously defined (Figure 5.14). The two connected circles are shown along with two windows, one dotted and one solid. The dotted window marks the limits of the previous view, the left circle. The other window, with an X in the middle, moves with your mouse. It will define the next view.

3. Move the selection window so the X is centered on the right circle as shown in Figure 5.14. The coordinate readout shows

    9.5, 4.0

4. Press Enter to select the next view (Figure 5.15).

Making More Elaborate Changes **109**

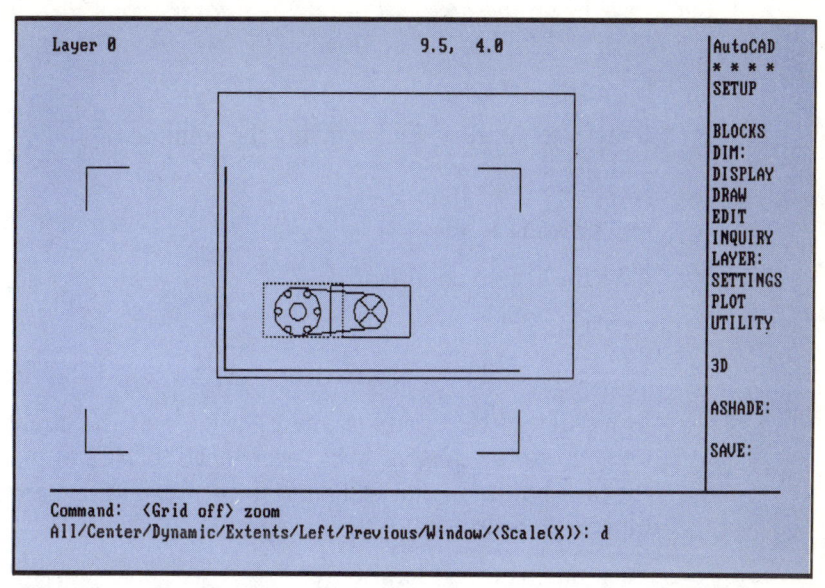

Figure 5.14: Dynamic Zoom command shows the entire drawing area

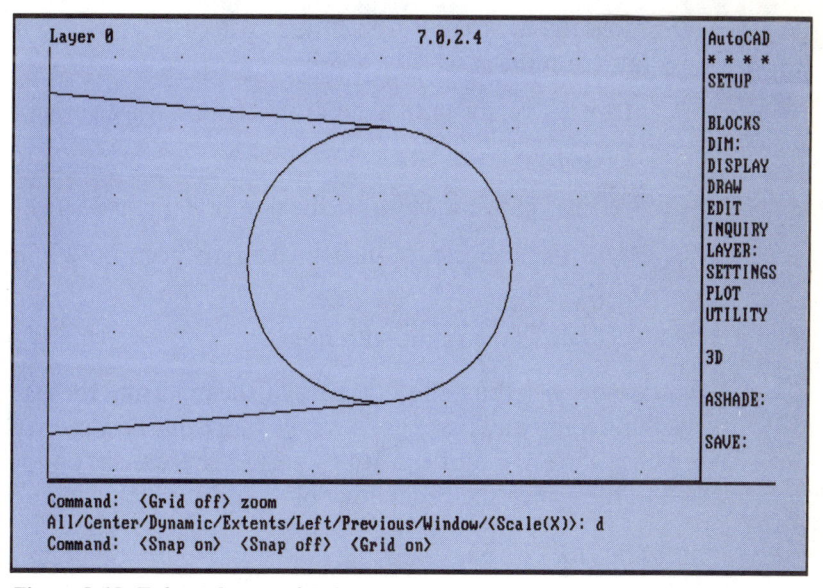

Figure 5.15: Enlarged view of right circle

Before we begin the arc, let's draw a *temporary construction line*. You'll use this line as an aid in drawing the arc. We will remove this line later.

1. Draw a temporary line by giving the command

    line

    and pressing Enter.

2. Give the Osnap command

    cen

    for Center and press Enter.

3. Move the selection box to the right edge of the circle, well away from the tangent lines (near location 10.5, 4.0). Press the pick button to start a line at the center of the circle. The other end is fastened to the the cursor.

4. Turn on Ortho mode with F8.

5. Move the cursor so its horizontal line goes through the circle center.

6. Move the cursor upward a little so you can distinguish the new line from the cursor.

7. Move the cursor until the coordinate position shows

    0.7<0

    Press the pick button to fix the new line (Figure 5.16).

8. Press the second mouse button to complete the Line command.

9. Turn off Ortho mode with F8.

Good. Now let's draw the first part of the arc using the Arc command. This command has a great many variations because you need to establish three parts of the arc by choosing from six options. We will select the center, the beginning point, and the included angle.

1. Give the command

    arc

    and press Enter.

Making More Elaborate Changes 111

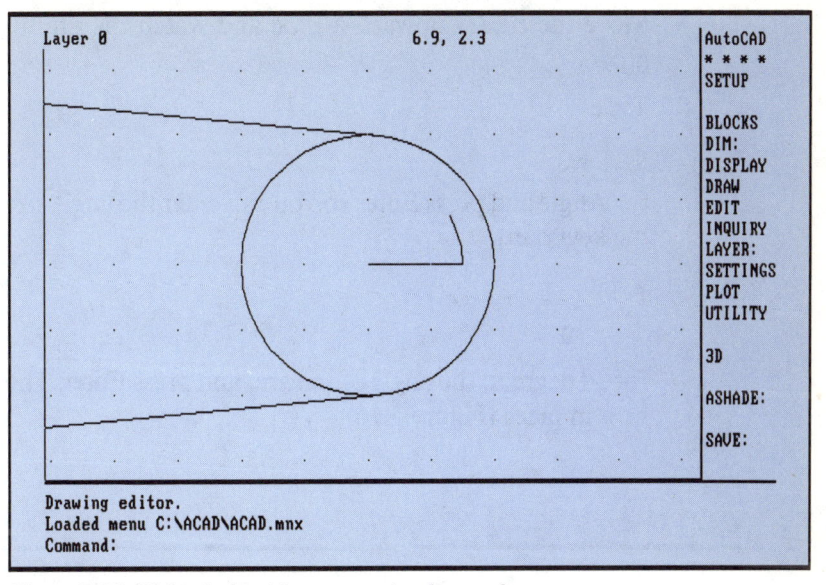

Figure 5.16: Right circle with construction line and arc

2. Type

    c

    and press Enter to designate the center of the arc first.

3. Give the Osnap command

    cen

    and press Enter to lock onto the center of the circle.

4. Move the selection box to the right edge of the circle and press the pick button. This makes the center of the arc coincide with the center of the circle.

5. Give the Osnap command

    end

    and press Enter so you can lock onto the right end of your construction line.

6. Move the selection box to the right end of the construction line and press the pick button.

7. Be sure Ortho mode is off.

8. Move the cursor upward a little and watch the arc begin to grow.
9. Type

    a

    for Angle and press Enter so you can enter the angle size from the keyboard.
10. Type

    30

    for 30 degrees, the angle of the arc, and press Enter. The arc is now in place (Figure 5.16).

How to Draw a Wedge

Working from the arc, you will now add to it to draw a wedge.

1. Give the command

    line

    and press Enter.

2. Give the Osnap command

    end

    and press Enter.

3. Move the cursor to the upper end of the arc (near 10.0, 4.4) and press the pick button. One end of the new line is fixed to the upper part of the arc.

4. Give the Osnap command

    mid

    and press Enter to lock onto the middle of a line.

5. Move the cursor near the middle of the construction line at location

    0.4<237

    (Figure 5.17) and press the pick button.

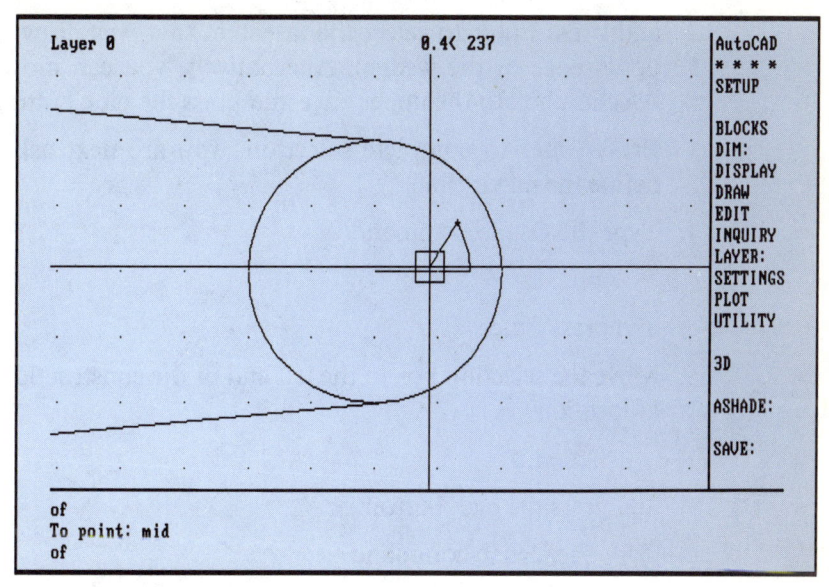

Figure 5.17: Upper wedge line is added

6. Press the right mouse button or the Enter key to complete the Line command. You now have the upper edge of the wedge.

Replicating an Object with the Mirror Command

We are going to draw the lower edge of the wedge with the Mirror command. This command makes a copy that is a mirror image. That is, it reverses the direction of objects with respect to a mirror line. To specify the reflection line, you designate two points. We will use the construction line as the mirror line.

1. Type the command

    mirror

    and press Enter. AutoCAD asks you to select the object to be mirrored.

2. Type

    L

and press Enter to select the last item that was drawn (the upper edge of the wedge). Alternatively, you can move the selection box to the upper edge and press the pick button.

3. Press Enter to complete selection. You are next asked to define the mirror line.

4. Type the Osnap command

   end

   and press Enter.

5. Move the selection box to the left end of the construction line at location

   9.5, 4.0

   and press the pick button.

6. Type the Osnap command

   end

   again.

7. Move the selection box near the right end of the construction line and press the pick button.

8. AutoCAD wants to know whether to delete the original line that is being mirrored. However, since we want the default answer (No), just press the right mouse button or the Enter key. The upper radial line is now mirrored below the construction line.

Doubling the Arc Length with the Extend Command

In this section you will double the arc length with the Extend command. The Extend command can extend lines and arcs to an extension boundary that you specify. This command is like the Break command because you first select a boundary, then you select the item to extend.

1. Give the command

   extend

   and press Enter.

Making More Elaborate Changes 115

2. Type

   L

   and press Enter to select the last item drawn, the lower wedge edge. This will be the boundary for the extension.

3. Press the right mouse button or the Enter key to complete the boundary-selection step. Now you must select the item to be extended.

4. Move the selection box to the arc as shown in Figure 5.18. Press the pick button. The arc is extended until it reaches the lower wedge edge.

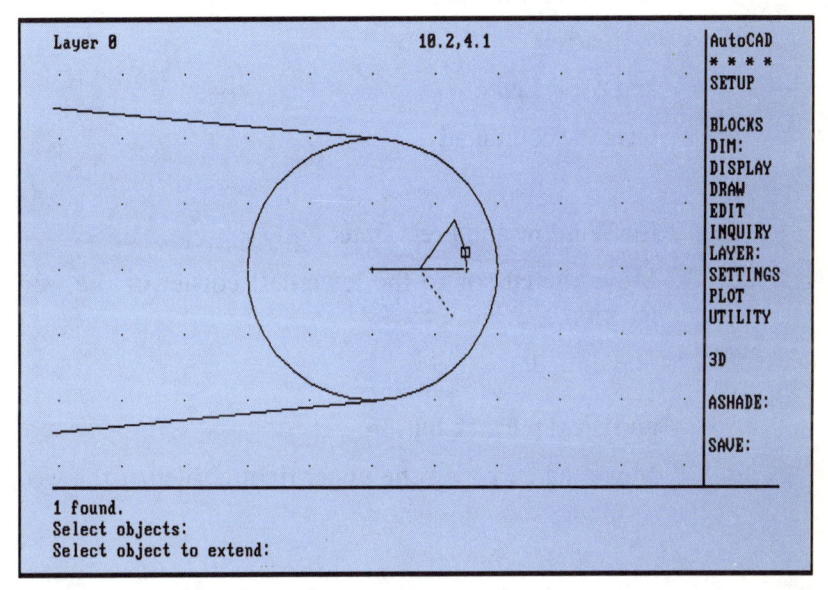

Figure 5.18: Marking the arc for extension

5. Press Enter to complete the Extend command.

Erasing the Construction Line

1. To erase the construction line, type

   erase

   and press Enter.

2. Move the selection box to location

    9.6, 4.0

    and press the pick button.

3. Press Enter to erase the construction line.

Replicating the Wedge with the Array Command

Now you will use the Array command to replicate the wedge around the circle, so there will be five wedges.

1. Give the command

    array

    and press Enter.

2. Give the command

    w

    for Window and press Enter.

3. Move the cursor to the lower-left corner of the wedge to location

    9.8, 3.6

    and press the pick button.

4. Move the cursor to the upper-right corner of the wedge to location

    10.3, 4.4

5. When the window encloses the wedge, press the pick button (Figure 5.19).

6. Press Enter to complete the selection step.

7. Type

    p

    for Polar and press Enter.

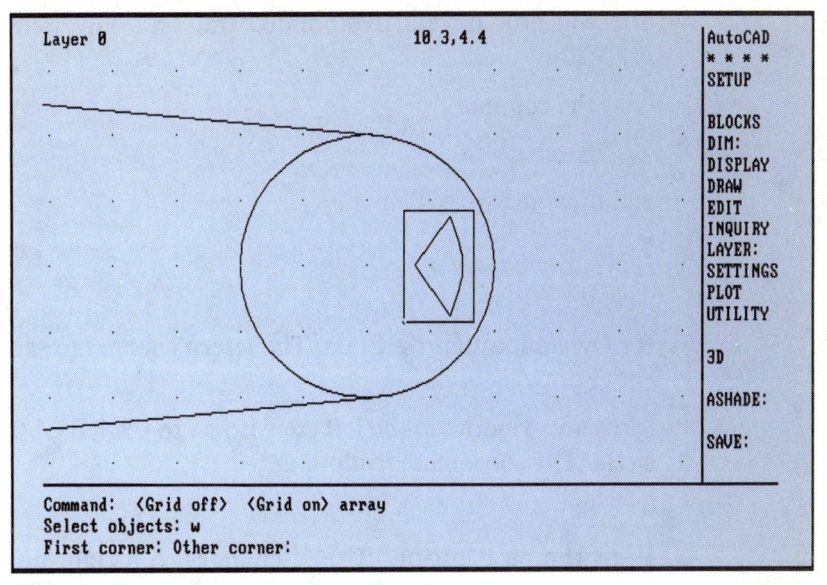

Figure 5.19: Selecting the arc for replication

8. To the prompt

    Center point of array:

    type the Osnap command

    cen

    for Center and press Enter.

9. Move the selection box to the edge of the large circle and press the pick button.

10. To the prompt

    Number of items:

    type the value

    5

    and press Enter to make a total of five copies of the wedge.

11. As before, press Enter twice to the questions

    Angle to fill (+ = CCW, − = CW)<360>:

    and

    Rotate objects as they are copied?:

You will now have a five-pointed star on your circle (Figure 5.20).

12. Give the command

    zoom

    and press the space bar.

13. Type

    d

    for Dynamic and press Enter. The screen changes to show the entire drawing area.

14. Move the window so the left edge is just to the left of the left circle. The coordinate readout is

    5.0, 4.0

    Press the pick button. The X changes to a right-pointing arrow. Move the cursor to the right to enlarge the window.

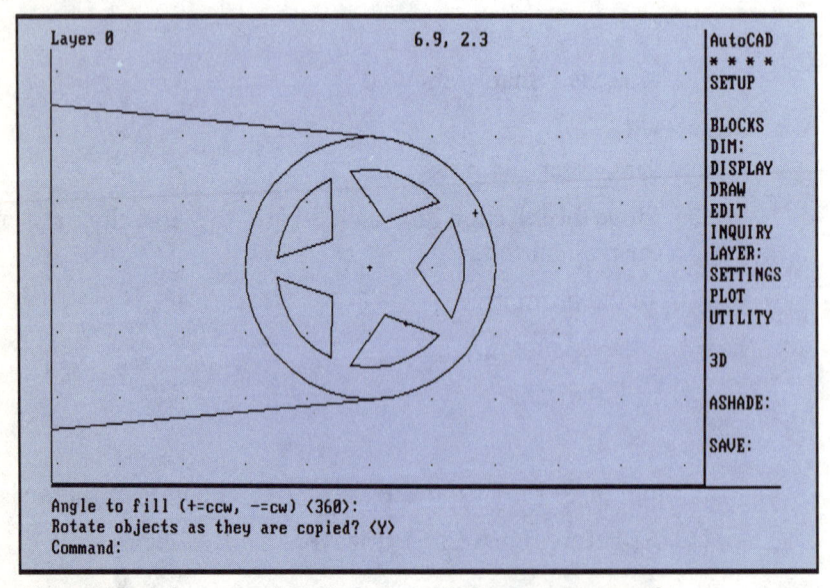

Figure 5.20: A five-pointed star is drawn with the Array command

When the window encloses the two circles, press Enter. The screen is filled with your drawing.

15. Give the command

    end

    and press Enter to complete the drawing and return to the AutoCAD Main menu.

6

Creating a Three-View Mechanical Drawing

Featuring:
- Drawing wide lines
- Drawing squares
- Separating a square with Explode
- Drawing ellipses
- Drawing hidden lines

Creating a Three-View Mechanical Drawing 123

In the previous chapters you learned how to draw lines and circles. You saw how to use AutoCAD's grid-snap and object-snap features to precisely position objects in your drawing on the screen. Then you learned how to select portions of your drawing and to make changes to them. In this chapter you will apply your knowledge to creating a three-view drawing of the bracket shown in Figure 6.1. The three views show the front, top, and right side of an object. The top view is aligned above the front view and the right view is placed on the right side of the front view.

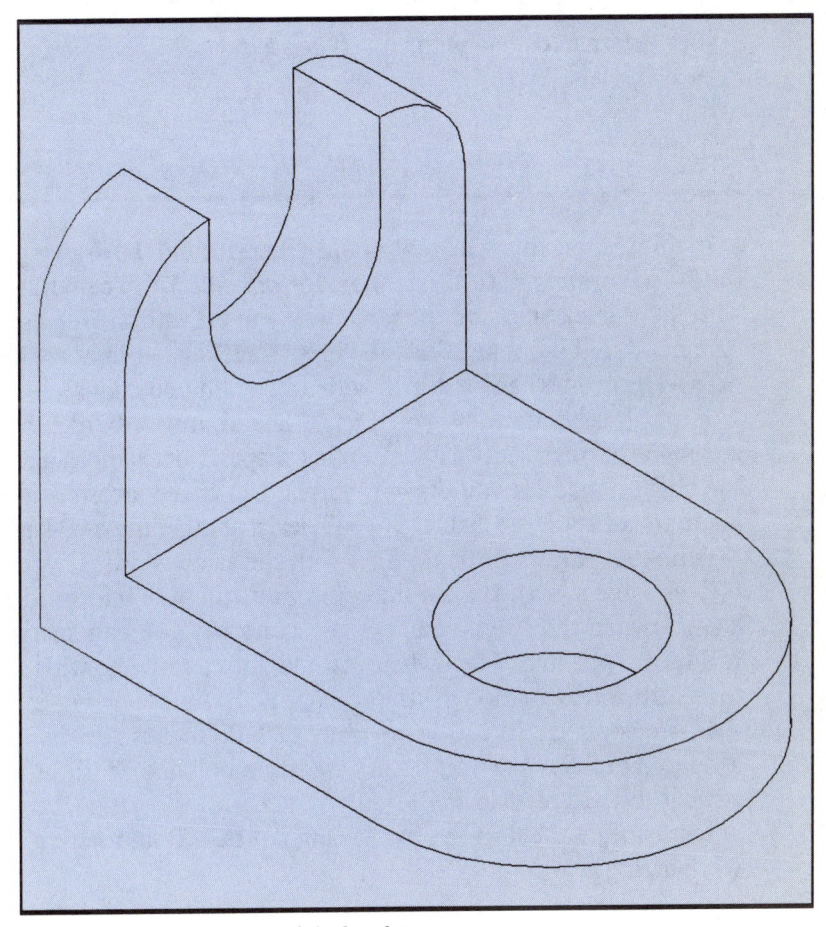

Figure 6.1: Isometric view of the bracket

The bracket will be drawn with continuous lines for the boundaries and dashed lines for the hidden parts. In addition, the drawing will be enclosed in a heavy line to mark the border.

New AutoCAD commands in this chapter are

- P-line (or polyline) to draw wide lines
- Polygon to draw a square
- Explode to separate a square
- Ellipse to draw a circle
- Ltscale to change the line type scale

How to Draw Borders with the P-line Command

In this section you will draw a border line around the drawing using the P-line command. (P-line is short for *polyline*.) You can draw lines with the P-line command the same way you do with the regular Line command, but it has an added feature. While regular lines are always narrow, polylines can be drawn with any width you choose.

In our bracket drawing, you'll use P-line to draw a border, but this command also can be used to draw other shapes. For example, a polyline can change width as you draw it, so you can create arrows and other interesting shapes. In Chapter 9, you'll learn another use of P-line.

AutoCAD draws ordinary lines with the same width. If you magnify an object with the Zoom command, the line width does not change when the length changes. By contrast, you can specify the width of a polyline. Then when you magnify a polyline with Zoom, the width will grow along with the length.

It is customary to use line widths of 0.03 inches for the border around a drawing. (If you do not specify a polyline width, it will be zero, just like a regular line.)

Let us begin the drawing by starting AutoCAD and setting up the work area.

1. Start AutoCAD.
2. From the Main menu, press 1 and then Enter to start a new drawing.

3. Type the file name

   bracket=

   and press Enter. (The = sign resets the default values.)

4. Type the command

   units

   and press Enter to change the way numbers are displayed.

5. Accept the default display of decimal numbers (2) by pressing Enter.

6. To the next question

   Number of digits to right of decimal point

   Type

   1

   and press Enter. Now AutoCAD will display numbers with only one digit past the decimal point rather than the default four, making the numbers easier to read.

7. Press ^C to skip over the remaining items that set the display of fractions and angles.

8. Press the F1 key to return to the graphics screen.

9. Type the command

   snap

   and press Enter so you can set the snap spacing.

10. Type the value

    0.5

    and press Enter to set the spacing.

11. Type the command

    grid

    and press Enter to set the grid spacing.

12. Type

    s

    and press Enter to set the grid spacing to the snap spacing.

13. Move the cursor to see that it snaps from one grid point to the next.

Good. Now you're ready to draw. We'll start with the border. You are going to draw a line around the edge of the screen following the line of grid points one-half inch inside the limits. You can create the lines by giving the coordinate values from the keyboard as you have done previously with the Line command. However, let's use the mouse this time instead.

1. Type the command

    pline

    and press Enter.

2. Press F8 to turn on Ortho mode. The word *Ortho* shows on the top line of the screen.

3. Turn on the coordinate display by pressing F6.

4. Move the cursor to the lower-left corner of the screen. The coordinate display will read 0,0. Notice that there is a row of grid points along the bottom edge of the drawing area.

5. Move one grid point up and one to the right from the lower-left corner. The cursor should snap to the point you select. When the coordinate position

    0.5, 0.5

    shows on the coordinate display, press the pick button to set the beginning of the polyline.

6. Before we draw the first line segment, we will set the line width. Type

    w

    for Width, and press Enter.

7. Give the value

    0.03

    and press Enter to set the beginning width.

8. Press Enter a second time to set the ending width to the same value as the beginning width. (The default shows 0.0 because we only display one digit past the decimal point.)

9. Move the cursor to the right and stop at the next-to-last grid point. The coordinate position is shown as

    11.0 <0

    This is a relative polar reference from the previous point. That is, the line has a length of 11 and is oriented at an angle of zero degrees (to the right).

10. Press the pick button to fix the first line segment. The polyline should be noticeably wider than the regular lines you drew previously.

11. Move the cursor straight up to the next-to-last grid point. The coordinate position should read

    8.0 <90

    to show a line 8 inches long at an angle of 90 degrees.

12. Press the pick button to fix the second line segment.

13. Move the cursor horizontally across to the left side of the screen. Stop at the next-to-last grid point on the left. The coordinate position here is

    11.0 <180

    or 11 inches to the left of the previous point. Press the pick button to fix the third segment.

14. Type

    c

    for Close and press Enter to complete the border line and finish the polyline command. Notice that AutoCAD automatically drew the final line segment. The word *Command:* on the bottom line shows that AutoCAD is ready for another command.

Your border should look like the one around the drawing in Figure 6.3.

How to Make a Border Template

Since you will want to place a border around many of your drawings, let's save the border you just drew as a separate disk file. Then you can use the border for your other drawings.

1. Give the command

    save

    and press Enter.
2. Type the file name

    border

    and press Enter. (If there is already a file with this name, you will be given a warning. Then you will be asked if you want to erase the original file. You can type Y to overwrite the original file with the new one.) You will use this border when you begin a new drawing in chapter 8.

How to Draw Rectangles

In this section, you will begin the three orthographic views—front, right, and top—of the bracket. These three views are shown in Figure 6.2.

You will first draw the rectangular portions of all three of these views using the regular Line command. In later sections you will draw the parts requiring arcs and circles. The Grid, Snap, and Ortho features will help you draw these parts precisely.

An isometric view of the bracket is shown in Figure 6.1. In contrast to orthographic views, which have two axes at right angles, isometric views show all three axes. Compare the three orthographic views in Figure 6.2 to the isometric view of the same object shown in Figure 6.1. Refer to these views to help you visualize the front, top, and right views as you draw them. (You will draw this isometric view of the bracket in Chapter 11.)

Drawing a Rectangle

Let us begin with the L-shaped front view. To make this part of the bracket, you will draw six line segments.

1. Press F8 if the word *Ortho* does not show on the top line.
2. Check that the word *Snap* is shown on the top line of the screen. Press F9 if it is not.

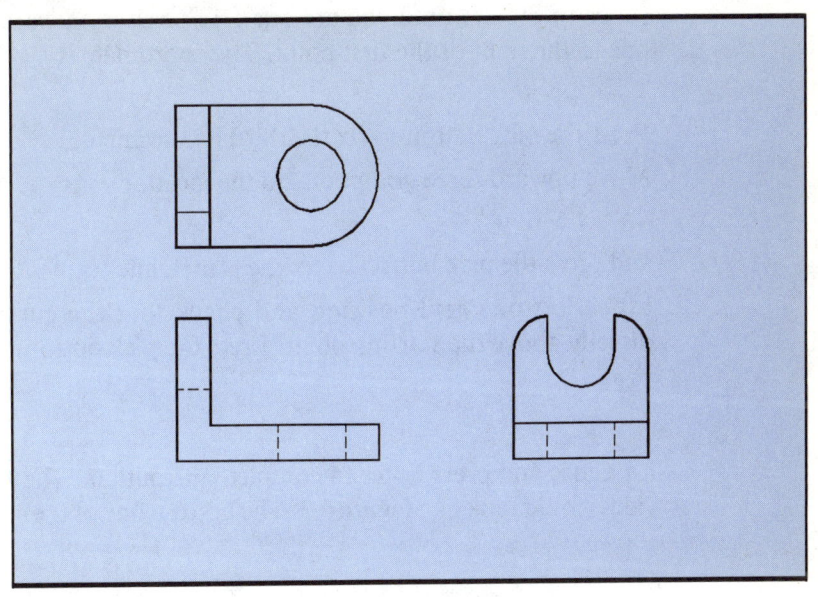

Figure 6.2: Front, right, and top views of the bracket

3. Type the command

   line

   and press Enter.

4. Move the cursor right four grid points and up three grid points from the lower-left corner of the polyline border. Check that the coordinate readout shows

   2.5, 2.0

   If the coordinate display shows something else, move the cursor until the coordinates show this position.

5. Press the pick button to start a line.

6. Move the cursor to the right six grid points, until the coordinate readout is

   3.0 <0

   Press the pick button to fix the first line of the front view.

7. Move the cursor straight up one grid point and press the pick button to fix the second line segment.

8. Move to the left until you are one grid position upward and one to the right of the first point. The coordinate is

   2.5 <180

   Press the pick button to fix the third line segment.
9. Move upward three grid points to the location

   1.5 <90

   and press the pick button to fix the fourth line segment.
10. Move left one grid position and check that the cursor is directly above the starting point. Press the pick button.
11. Type

    c

    for Close and press Enter to complete the outline. The front view should look like Figure 6.3. The bottom line of the screen shows

    Command:

    to indicate that the Line command is complete.

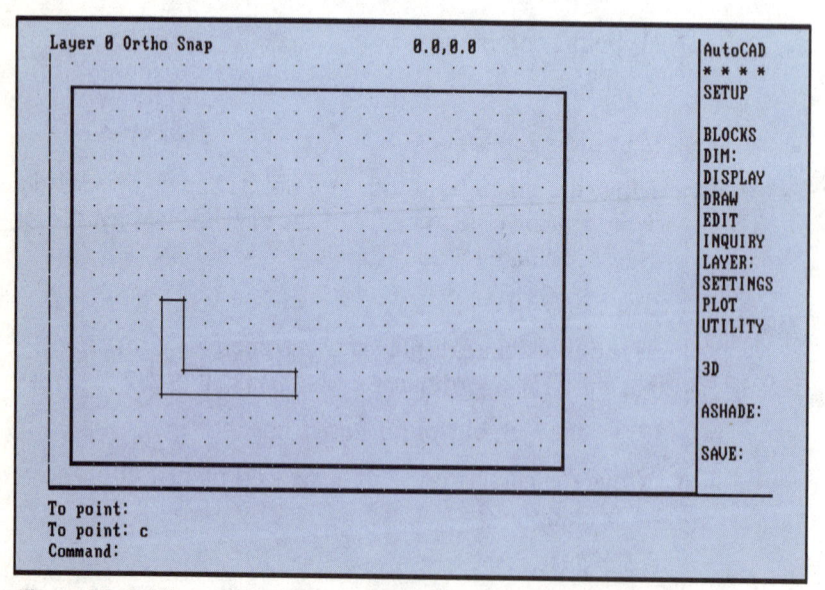

Figure 6.3: Outline of the bracket front view

Drawing a Square with a Polygon Command

Let us start the right and top views next. Since the outlines of these views are squares, we can greatly simplify the work by drawing squares. We use the AutoCAD Polygon command for this. We'll draw the right view first.

1. Type the command

    polygon

    and press Enter.

2. AutoCAD asks how many sides. Answer

    4

    and press Enter to create a square.

3. In response to the AutoCAD prompt

    Edge/<Center of polygon>:

    type

    e

    for Edge and press Enter.

4. Move the cursor downward to the lower edge of the front view. Then move over to the right side of the screen. Stop at the coordinate position

    7.5, 2.0

    The horizontal line of the cursor aligns with the bottom part of the front view.

5. Press the pick button to fix the first corner of the square.

6. Move the cursor four grid points to the right to the location

    9.5, 2.0

    Watch the square grow larger as you move the cursor. Press the pick button to fix the square with sides of two inches (Figure 6.4).

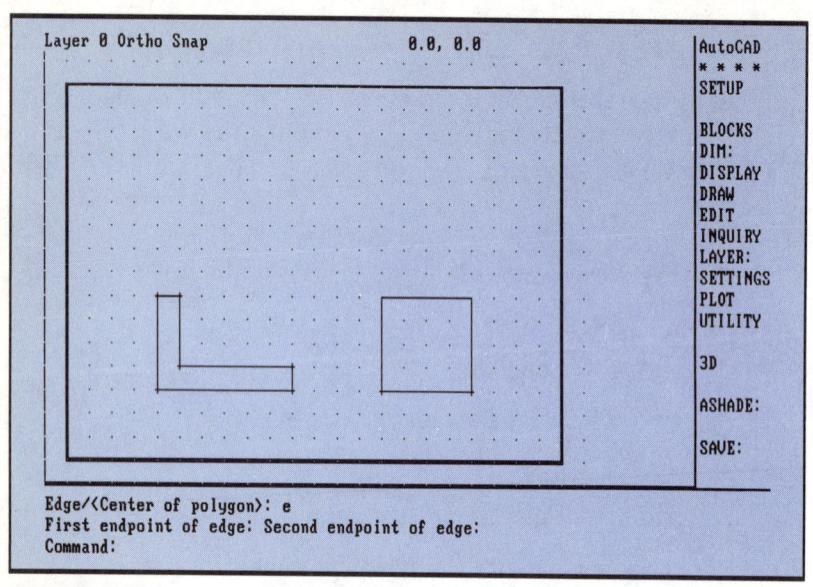

Figure 6.4: The square part of the right view

Good. Now let's use the same procedure to draw the straight parts of the top view. The square will be the same size as the one in the right view, but you will draw it in the upper-left corner of the screen.

1. Press the right mouse button or the Enter key to restart the Polygon command.

2. AutoCAD again asks how many sides. Answer

    4

    and press Enter to create another square.

3. In response to the AutoCAD statement

    Edge/<Center of polygon>:

    type

    e

    again for Edge and press Enter.

4. Move the cursor to the left side of the front view. Then move upward until you reach the position

    2.5, 5.0

At this point the vertical line of the cursor aligns with the left edge of the front view.

5. Press the pick button to start another square.
6. Move the cursor four grid points to the right to the location

    4.5, 5.0

Watch a second square grow as you move the cursor. Press the pick button to fix a second square with sides of two inches (Figure 6.5).

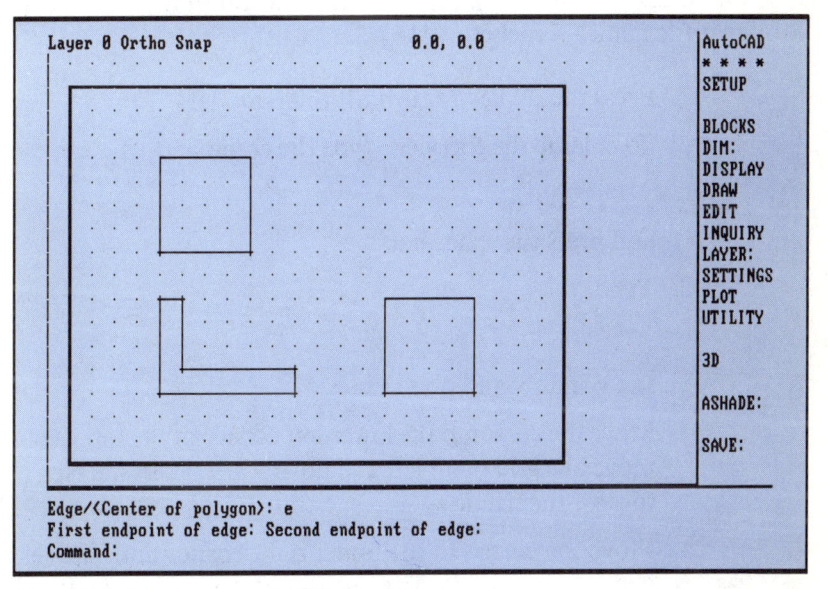

Figure 6.5: The square part of the top view

How to Use the Explode Command

You have just created squares for the right and top views. In this section, you will remove parts of each square so you can draw a circle and arcs. Unfortunately, you cannot simply erase a part without erasing the whole square, since we drew each box as one object, not as four separate lines. You first have to separate the square into its constituent parts. The AutoCAD Explode command is used for this purpose. The command name is misleading—the components do not move apart, that is, "explode" in the usual sense. After you give the Explode command, there is no apparent change. Rather, Explode references each part of the object as separate entities. Let's see how it works. First you will explode the square in the top view, then you'll erase one edge and add three more lines. You'll repeat a similar procedure for the right view.

First, save a copy of your current work. Give the command

> **save**

and press the Enter key. Press Enter a second time to accept the current file name—bracket.

1. Press the F9 key to turn off Snap mode.
2. To enlarge the top view, type the command

   > **zoom**

   and press the space bar.
3. Type

   > **w**

   for Window and press Enter.
4. Move the cursor to the lower-left corner of the top view. Then move one grid point left and downward. Press the pick button to start the window.
5. Move the cursor to the upper-right corner until the selection window surrounds the top view.
6. Press the pick button to enlarge the top view.
7. Type the command

   > **explode**

   and press Enter. The cursor changes to a selection box.
8. Move the selection box to any edge of the square and press the pick button. No change is apparent, but you have just exploded the square. Since it now consists of four separate lines, you can erase one edge without erasing the other edges.

9. Type the command

    erase

    again and press Enter.

10. Move the selection box over the right edge of the square, and press the pick button. The right edge becomes spotted but the other three edges do not change.

11. Press the right mouse button or the Enter key to erase the right edge of the square.

Now that the top view has been exploded and the right edge erased, you will add one vertical and two horizontal lines.

1. Check the top line of the screen for the word *Snap*. Press the F9 key to turn on Snap mode if necessary.

2. Check that Ortho mode is on. Press the F8 key if necessary.

3. Type the command

    line

    and press Enter.

4. First draw the vertical line. Move the cursor to the lower-left corner of the top view, then move one grid point to the right. The coordinate location is

    3.0, 5.0

5. Press the pick button to begin the new line.

6. Move straight upward to the top line of this view and press the pick button.

7. Press the right mouse button or the Enter key to complete the Line command.

8. Draw the upper horizontal line next. Restart the Line command by pressing the right mouse button or the Enter key.

9. Move down one grid point to the coordinate position

    3.0, 6.5

    and press the pick button to start another line.

10. Move one grid point to the left edge and press the pick button to fix the line.

11. Press the right mouse button or the Enter key to complete the Line command.

12. Draw the lower horizontal line next. Restart the Line command by pressing the right mouse button or the Enter key.

13. Move down the left edge two grid points to coordinate position

    2.5, 5.5

    Press the pick button to start the third line.

14. Move right one grid point and press the pick button again to fix the line.

15. Press the right mouse button or the Enter key to complete the Line command. Compare your top view with the one shown in Figure 6.6.

16. Return to the original drawing size by typing the command

    zoom

    and pressing the space bar. AutoCAD responds with the prompt

    All/Center/Dynamic/Extents/Left

17. Type

    a

    for All and press Enter to see all the drawing.

See how easily your bracket is taking shape? Soon you'll add the circular parts to this view, but first let's complete the straight parts of the right view. To do this you'll draw three more straight lines on the right view. First, though, you'll need to explode this square.

1. Move the cursor to the right view.

2. Give the command

    explode

    and press Enter. The cursor changes to a selection box.

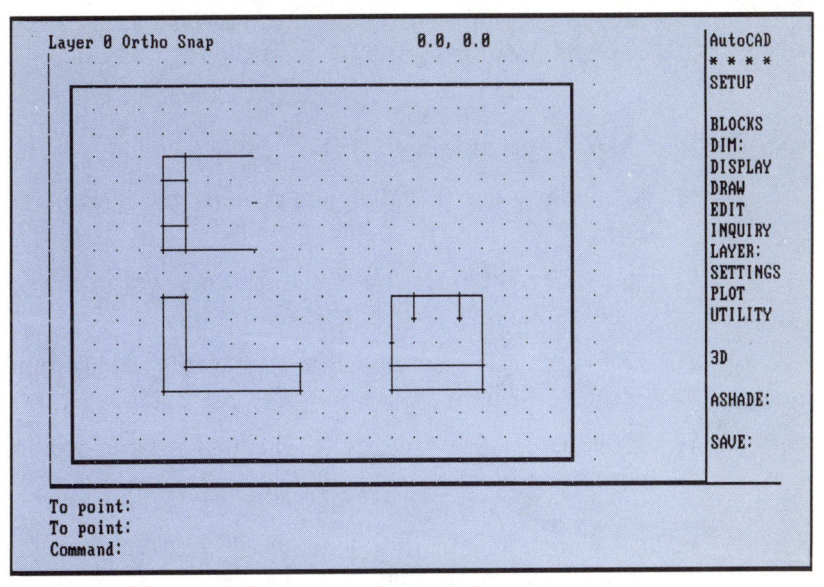

Figure 6.6: The rectangular parts of the bracket

3. Move the selection box to any edge of the square and press the pick button. As before, no change is apparent, but you have just exploded the square in the right view.

4. Type the command

    line

    and press Enter.

5. Move the cursor to the lower-left corner of the right view, then move one grid point upward. The coordinate location is

    7.5, 2.5

6. Press the pick button to begin a new line.

7. Move four grid points to the right edge and press the pick button.

8. Press the right mouse button or the Enter key to complete the Line command.

9. Draw the left short line next. Restart the Line command by pressing the right mouse button or the Enter key.

10. Move to the upper-left corner of the right view. Then move one grid position right to the coordinate position

    8.0, 4.0

    Press the pick button.

11. Move down one grid point and press the pick button to fix the line.

12. Press the right mouse button or the Enter key to complete the Line command.

13. Draw the right short line next. Restart the Line command by pressing the right mouse button or the Enter key.

14. Move across the top edge to the next-to-last grid position. The coordinate location is

    9,0, 4.0

    Press the pick button to start the line.

15. Move down one grid point and press the pick button to fix the line.

16. Press the right mouse button or the Enter key to complete the Line command. Compare your right view with Figure 6.6.

How to Modify a Drawing with Circles and Arcs

In this section you will add a circle and arcs to the top and right views. You will also remove some lines. As you use AutoCAD, you frequently will use procedures like this to change basic, simple shapes into more complex objects. In this section, you will learn a new command to draw a circle—Ellipse. We will use Ellipse here because in the next chapter we will widen the lines of this view by converting them to polylines. Since a circle cannot be converted to a polyline and an ellipse is a polyline (and can also be a circle), we will draw our circle with the Ellipse command.

An ellipse can be an oval or a circle. As an oval, one direction or axis is longer than the other. If both axes are the same, the ellipse is a circle. You draw an ellipse with AutoCAD by giving three points. The first two define the long axis. The third point is on the short axis. To draw a circle, make the second and third points the same.

Let's begin by drawing a circle on the top view.

1. Give the command

    ellipse

    and press Enter.

2. Move the cursor to the lower-right corner of the top view to the coordinate position

    4.5, 5.0

3. Move the cursor upward one grid point to coordinate position

    4.5, 5.5

    and press the pick button to establish the first point of the ellipse.

4. Move the cursor up two grid points to the coordinate position

    1.0 <90

    Press the pick button to establish the second point of the ellipse. An outline of the ellipse is now visible.

5. Because the two axes are equal, the ellipse is in the shape of a circle, which is the shape we want. Therefore, press the pick button to complete the circle-shaped ellipse.

We will draw ellipses with oval shapes in Chapter 11. (Notice the ovals in Figure 6.1.)

Continue your modification of the top view by drawing an arc that is concentric with the circle. This will add a curved edge to one side of the view. Use the Arc command, as you learned in the previous chapter.

1. Type the command

    arc

    and press Enter to start a circular arc.

2. Type the command

    c

    and press Enter to establish the center of the arc.

3. Move the cursor to the center of the circle and check that the cursor is at coordinate position

   4.5, 6.0

   Press the pick button. Now the arc will be concentric with the circle. Of course, you could have used the Center Osnap option instead of the regular Snap mode.

Next you will establish two positions on the arc. It is important to remember that AutoCAD always draws arcs in a counterclockwise direction. Therefore, start at the lower right corner of the top view.

4. Move the cursor to coordinate position

   4.5, 5.0

   and press the pick button. This is the beginning of the arc.

5. Move the cursor upward and to the right to see an arc grow from the selected point. The arc is concentric with the circle.

6. Move the cursor straight upward through the center of the circle to the top edge of the top view. Stop at coordinate position

   1.0 <90

   and press the pick button to complete the arc.

Compare your top view with the one shown in Figure 6.7.

Good. You can see how your drawing is becoming more detailed. Now go to the right view and add an arc to the two short lines. We will draw this second arc in a slightly different manner. Last time we first chose the center, then the first point, and lastly the second point of the arc. This time we will change the order to first point, center, and last point.

1. Press the right mouse button or the Enter key to restart the Arc command.

2. Move the cursor to the right view. Stop at the lower end of the left short line. The coordinate position is

   8.0, 3.5

Creating a Three-View Mechanical Drawing **141**

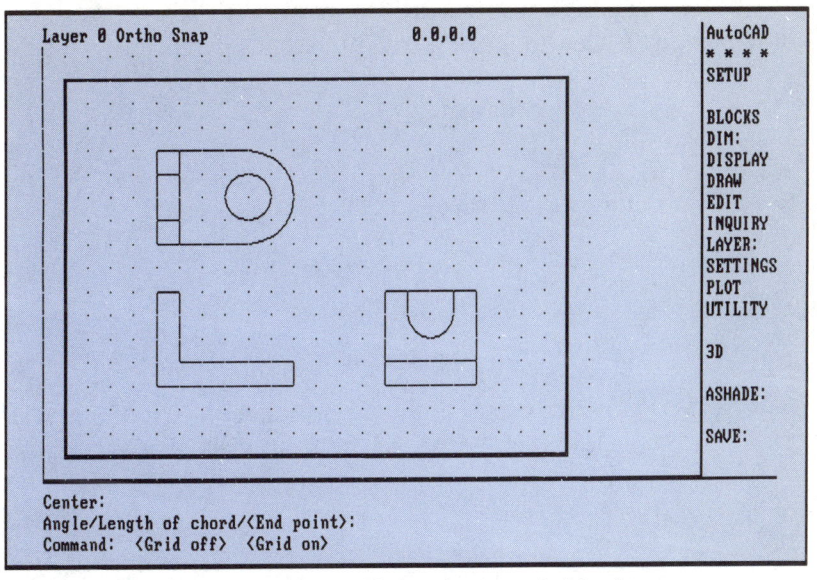

Figure 6.7: A circle and an arc are added to the top and right views

3. Press the pick button to establish the starting position of the arc. (This is the default option for the first step.)

4. Type

    c

    and press Enter to choose the arc center, overriding the default choice of the arc end point for the second step.

5. Move one grid position to the right, halfway between the two short lines. This is the center of the arc.

6. Press the pick button to fix the arc center.

7. Move one grid position right to the lower end of the other short line. Press the pick button for the third step to complete the arc.

8. Check that your right view looks like the one shown in Figure 6.7.

Now add the last two arcs to the corners in the right view. But first, enlarge the view to make it easier to see the detail.

1. Give the command

    zoom

    and press the space bar.

2. Type in

    w

    for Window and press Enter.

3. Move the cursor one grid position to the left of and one below the lower-left corner of the front view. The coordinate position is

    7.0, 1.5

    Press the pick button.

4. Move the cursor one grid position to the right of and one above the upper-right corner of the front view. The coordinate position is

    10.0, 4.5

    Press the pick button. The front view fills the screen.

5. Type the command

    arc

    and press Enter to draw an arc in the upper-left corner.

6. Type

    c

    and press Enter to choose the center location.

7. Move the cursor to the upper-left corner. Then move one grid point down and one to the right. This is the position where you started the previous arc. The coordinate position is

    8.0, 3.5

8. Press the pick button to fix the arc center.

9. Move upward one grid point to the top edge. Press the pick button to start the arc.
10. Move one grid point left and one downward. Press the pick button to complete the arc.
11. Press the right mouse button or the Enter key to restart the Arc command.
12. Give the command

    c

    and press Enter to choose the center.
13. Move three grid points to the right to grid position

    9.0, 3.5

    Press the pick button to fix the center.
14. Move one grid position to the right and press the pick button to start the arc.
15. Move one grid position upward and one to the left. Press the pick button to complete the arc. Compare your screen to Figure 6.8.

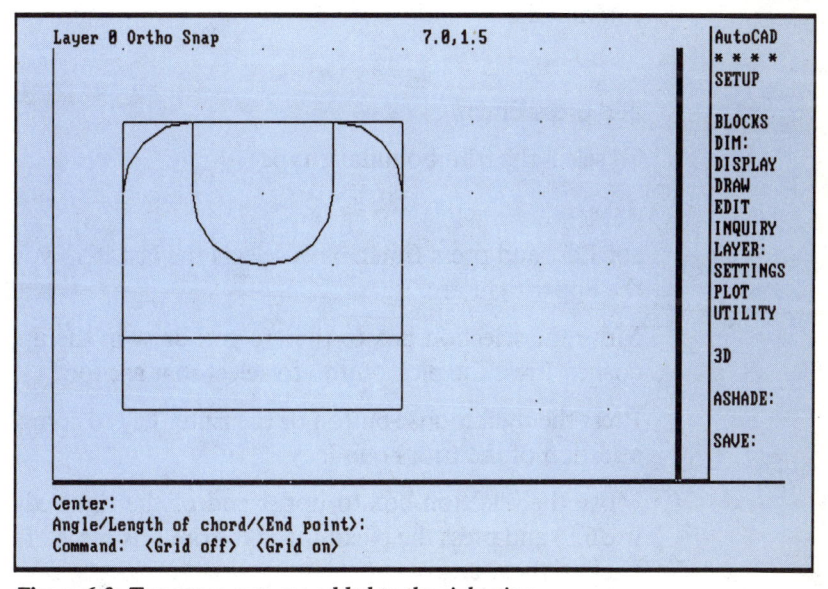

Figure 6.8: Two more arcs are added to the right view

16. Press F9 to turn Snap mode off.

Your right-view drawing is nearly completed. You have one more task, though—the line across the opening and the parts at the corners must be removed. First you will erase the top line, then trim the left and right edges.

1. Give the command

    erase

    and press Enter.

2. Move the selection box to the middle of the top line, well away from any other lines.

3. Press the pick button. The top line becomes spotted to show that it is selected.

4. Press the right mouse button or the Enter key to erase the top line. This fixes two problems at once—the opening in the middle and the parts at the corners.

5. We used the Erase command to remove the entire top line. Now we want to remove just the top end of the left and right lines. We can use the Trim command for this step. Give the command

    trim

    and press Enter.

6. To select the trim boundary, type

    L

    for Last and press Enter. This selects the last item you drew, the upper-right arc.

7. Move the selection box to the arc you drew in the upper-left corner. Press the pick button to select that arc too.

8. Press the right mouse button or the Enter key to complete the selection of the trim boundary.

9. Move the selection box to upper end of the right edge (Figure 6.9) and press the pick button to trim this piece of the line back to the arc.

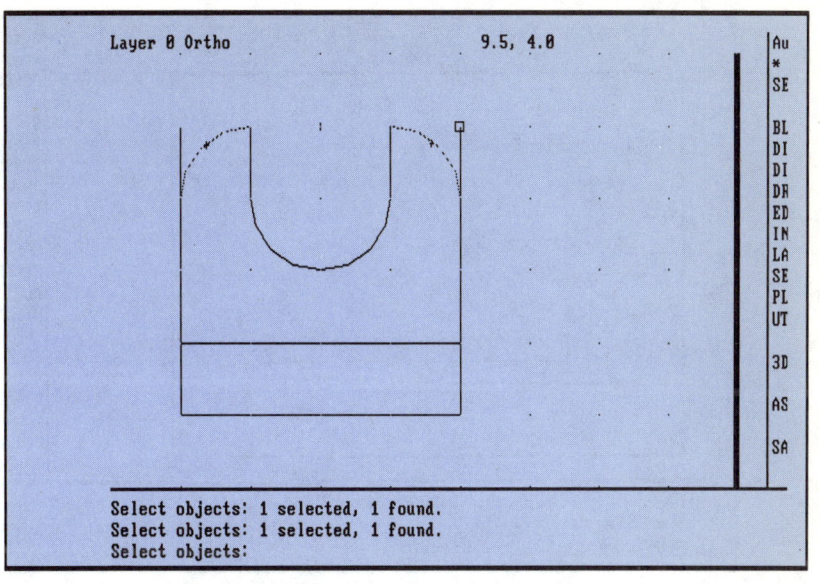

Figure 6.9: The left and right edges are trimmed to the arcs

10. In a similar way, mark the upper-left line to trim it back to its arc.

11. Press the right mouse button or the Enter key to complete the Trim command.

12. Return to the full view by typing the command

    zoom

    and pressing the space bar.

13. Type

    a

    for All and press Enter. Your screen should look like Figure 6.10.

How to Use AutoCAD's Standard Line Types

Engineering drawings use lines of different thickness and style to designate different ideas. For example, wide, continuous lines mark

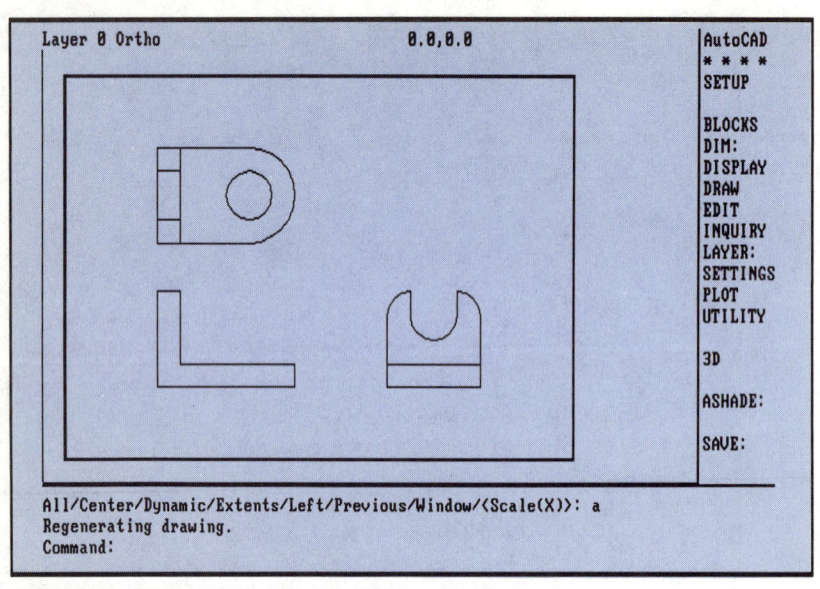

Figure 6.10: Three views of the bracket

the edges of an object, and thin lines with alternating dashes and dots mark the center lines of circles and arcs. Thick lines with an alternation of a dash and two dots mark a section plane. AutoCAD can readily produce all of these line types and set the line width. Figure 6.11 shows the standard line types available with AutoCAD. In this chapter we will use the hidden line type.

How to Draw Hidden Lines

The lines we have drawn so far represent visible edges, that is, edges that we could see if we looked at the object we are drawing. We also have to include lines for edges that are not visible because they are on the back side or in the middle. These are called *hidden lines*. Of course, hidden lines are not actually hidden. Rather they represent hidden edges.

Hidden lines are shown on shop drawings with dashed rather than solid lines. In this section you will draw five hidden lines on your figure. These represent the circular openings cut into the bracket. The

Creating a Three-View Mechanical Drawing **147**

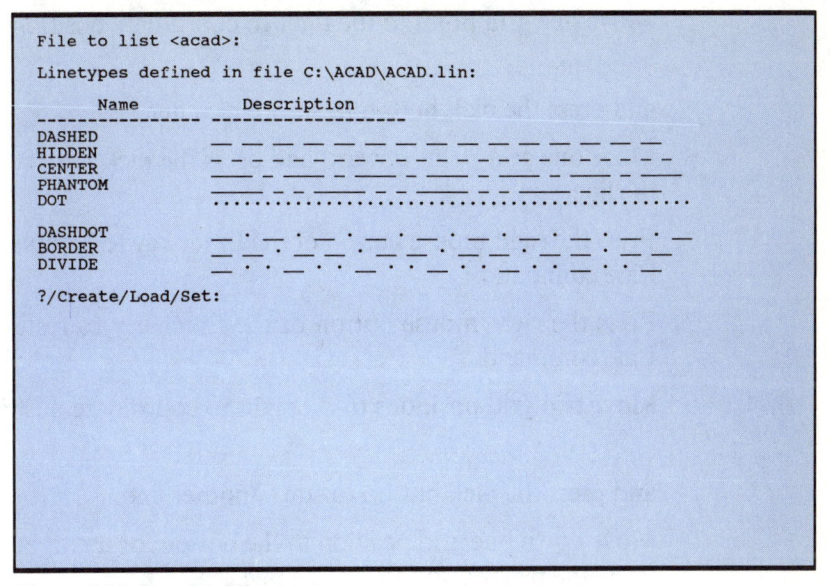

```
File to list <acad>:

Linetypes defined in file C:\ACAD\ACAD.lin:

     Name          Description
     ----          -----------
  DASHED           _ _ _ _ _ _ _ _ _ _ _ _ _ _ _ _
  HIDDEN           _ _ _ _ _ _ _ _ _ _ _ _ _ _ _ _ _ _
  CENTER           ____ _ ____ _ ____ _ ____ _ ____ _
  PHANTOM          ____ _ _ ____ _ _ ____ _ _ ____
  DOT              ................................................

  DASHDOT          __ . __ . __ . __ . __ . __ . __ . __ .
  BORDER           __ __ . __ __ . __ __ . __ __ . __ __ .
  DIVIDE           __ . . __ . . __ . . __ . . __ . . __

?/Create/Load/Set:
```

Figure 6.11: Standard line types

hidden line-type is built into AutoCAD. There are two different methods for drawing hidden lines with AutoCAD. With one method, you change the line type setting from continuous (which is the type of line you've used so far) to hidden, draw the lines, then change the line type back to continuous. With the second method, you draw the line first, then change the line type to hidden afterward. We will draw the hidden lines with the second method because it is easier.

In this exercise you'll add lines to the right and front views. Then in the next section you'll change these lines to hidden lines. First draw two lines in the right view.

1. Give the command

    line

    and press Enter.

2. Move the cursor to the lower-left corner of the right view.

3. Press F9 to turn on Snap mode if necessary.

4. Press F7 to turn on the grid if necessary.

5. Move one grid point to the right to coordinate position

   8.0, 2.0

   and press the pick button to start a new line.

6. Move one grid point upward and press the pick button to fix the line.

7. Press the right mouse button or the Enter key to complete the Line command.

8. Press the right mouse button or the Enter key to restart the Line command.

9. Move two grid positions to the right to coordinate position

   9.0, 2.5

   and press the pick button to start another line.

10. Move down one grid position to the bottom of the right view. Press the pick button to fix this line.

11. Press the right mouse button or the Enter key to complete the Line command.

Now you'll draw three lines on the front view.

1. Press the right mouse button or the Enter key to restart the Line command.

2. Move the cursor left to the lower-right corner of the front view.

3. Move one grid point to the left. The coordinate location is

   5.0, 2.0

   The vertical line of the cursor should align with the right edge of the circle in the top view.

4. Press the pick button to start the first line.

5. Move one grid position upward and press the pick button to fix the line.

6. Press the right mouse button or the Enter key to complete the Line command.

7. Press the right mouse button or the Enter key to restart the Line command.

8. Move left two grid positions to the coordinate position

    4.0, 2.5

    The vertical line of the cursor should align with the left edge of the circle in the top view. Press the pick button to start the second line.

9. Move down one grid position to the bottom of the front view. Press the pick button to fix this line.

10. Press the right mouse button or the Enter key to complete the Line command.

11. Press the right mouse button or the Enter key to restart the Line command.

12. Move to the lower-left corner of the front view.

13. Move upward two grid points to coordinate position

    2.5, 3.0

    The horizontal line of the cursor should align with the bottom of the circular opening of the right view. Press the pick button to start the third line.

14. Move right one grid position. Press the pick button to fix this line.

15. Press the right mouse button or the Enter key to complete the Line command.

16. Press F9 to turn Snap mode off.

Changing the Line Type to Hidden

You have just added five lines that mark hidden parts of the drawing. Because these lines represent hidden edges, they should be the hidden line type. However, you drew them with the continuous line type because it was easier. Therefore, you must now change the line type to hidden. One way to do this is to use the Change command. But first, enlarge the view.

1. Give the command

    zoom

    and press the space bar.

2. Type

    w

    for Window and press Enter.

3. Move the cursor to the lower-left corner of the front view to location 2.2, 1.7 and press the pick button to start the window.

4. Move the cursor to the upper-right corner of the right view to location 9.7, 4.2 and press the pick button to enlarge the front and right views together.

5. Give the command

    change

    and press Enter.

6. When AutoCAD asks you to select the lines to be changed, move the selection box over each of the five lines and press the pick button. As usual, each line becomes spotty as you select it.

7. Press the right mouse button or the Enter key to complete the selection.

8. To the AutoCAD prompt

    Properties/<Change point>:

    type **p** and press Enter.

9. AutoCAD then displays the prompt:

    Change what property (Color/Elev/LAyer/LType/Thickness)?

10. Type

    lt

    for Line Type and press Enter to select a change of line type.

AutoCAD responds with the prompt:

New linetype <BYLAYER>:

11. Type

    hidden

    and press Enter. AutoCAD repeats the prompt:

    **Change what property
    (Color/Elev/LAyer/LType/Thickness)?**

12. Simply press the right mouse button or the Enter key to complete the Change command. The lines are now broken, indicating that they are hidden.

13. Give the command

    zoom

    and press the space bar.

14. Type

    p

    for the Previous view and press Enter. Now you can see all three views again.

Changing the Scale of the Line Type

The five lines you changed in the previous section are drawn with a broken line, but there is only one opening in each line because the length is so short. You can make hidden lines show more openings by changing the scale of the line type. Let's do that now.

1. Give the command

    ltscale

    for Line Type Scale and press Enter. You can see that the default line-type scale is 1.0.

2. First, just to see what happens, change to a larger scale by giving the value

    1.5

    and pressing Enter.

3. All five hidden lines immediately change. However, now they appear to be continuous. The problem is that you have selected a scale that is too large.
4. Press Enter to restart the Ltscale command.
5. Type

   0.6

   and press Enter to change the scale to a smaller value. With this smaller scale, two openings are shown on each line (Figure 6.12).

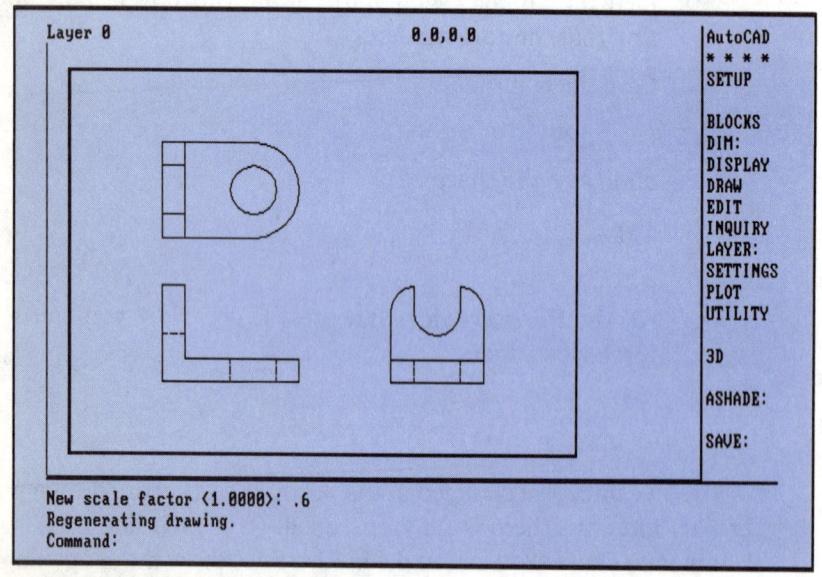

Figure 6.12: Hidden lines are added

6. Save the latest version by typing the command

   save

   and pressing Enter.
7. Press Enter a second time to accept the current file name of bracket.

7

Printing the Drawing

Featuring:

Getting a printout
with a printer

Widening the object
lines

Printing the final
copy

Now that you have completed the three views of the bracket, you're ready to print it. First you will create a small copy of the drawing using a dot-matrix printer. You will then widen the object lines around the bracket by conversion to polylines. Finally, you will create a second, full-scale version of the bracket using the dot-matrix printer. While this second version is not as good as can be obtained with a plotter, it would be satisfactory for submission to a machine shop.

New AutoCAD commands in this chapter are

- Prplot to print your drawing
- P-edit to widen polylines

How to Print a Drawing

If there is a plotter attached to your computer, you can obtain a finished drawing by giving the Plot command. However, you can also obtain a good version of your work if you have a dot-matrix or laser printer. Even if you do have a plotter, you may want to use the printer for copies of intermediate stages because it is much faster. Therefore, in this section you will make a copy of your work on a printer. (Except for the initial command, the sequence of steps is similar for either method.)

If you have neither a plotter nor a printer, you can select the option of plotting to a floppy disk. Then you can take the disk to another computer that has a plotter or a printer and make a copy there. Auto-CAD is not needed on the other computer.

Because you can either plot the entire drawing or only a part of it, you must tell AutoCAD what part of your drawing you want to plot. There are five possibilities—Display, Extents, Limits, View, or Window. The first choice, Display, and the last, Window, will generally be most useful. If you choose Display, which is the default, you get exactly what is shown on the video screen. Thus, if you have zoomed onto one part of your work, only that zoomed part will be plotted.

The second choice, Extents, shows everything you have drawn. This is a good choice if you have not made any mistakes. Unfortunately, this method includes regions where you have erased items.

Thus, if you accidentally draw items outside of your boundary and then erase them, that region will still be shown on the plot. The third choice, Limits, includes the defined limits of your drawing. The View option gives a view you have previously selected and named. With the last method, you place a selection window around the parts you want to plot. You'll make two sizes of your drawing—one small and one large. Before you make the larger copy, you'll widen the object lines. Let's start with the first printout.

1. Give the command

    prplot

    for Printer Plot and press Enter. AutoCAD asks

    What to plot - Display, Extents, Limits, View, or Window<D>

2. Press the Enter key to accept the default option of Display. The screen changes to text mode. Information such as the size of the plot and rotation of the figure are given (Figure 7.1). Then you are asked if you want to change anything.

```
Plot will NOT be written to a selected file
Sizes are in Inches
Plot origin is at (0.00,0.00)
Plotting area is 7.90 wide by 6.00 high (USER size)
Plot is NOT rotated 90 degrees
Hidden lines will NOT be removed
Plot will be scaled to fit available area
Do you want to change anything? <N> y

Write the plot to a file? <N>
Size units (Inches or Millimeters) <I>:
Plot origin in Inches <0.00,0.00>:
Standard values for plotting size
Size    Width    Height
MAX     7.99     11.00
USER    7.90     6.00

Enter the Size or Width,Height (in Inches) <USER>:
Rotate 2D plots 90 degrees clockwise? <N>
Remove hidden lines? <N>
Specify scale by entering:
Plotted Inches=Drawing Units or Fit or ? <F>:
Effective plotting area:  7.90 wide by 4.92 high
Position paper in printer.
```

Figure 7.1: The plotting screen

3. Type

   y

   and Press Enter.

4. To the next prompt:

   Write the plot to a file? <N>

   Press the Enter key to make a printer plot on your printer. (You have to use the Enter key at this stage; you cannot use the mouse buttons.)

   At this point you could also type Y and press Enter to make a disk file that can be run on another computer. Take the disk to the other computer and at the DOS prompt give the command

   copy fname.dwg prn

   where *fname* is the file name you assign.

5. Press Enter to select inches instead of millimeters.
6. Press Enter again to select 0, 0 as the plot origin.
7. Type

   7.9,6

   and press Enter to select the width and height. Width is always the horizontal direction along the printer platen. Height is always the vertical direction, the way the paper rolls.

8. At the next prompt

   Rotate 2D plots 90 degrees clockwise <N>

   press Enter so the plot will not be rotated.

9. Press Enter two times to accept the next two options. The effective plotting area will then be given.

10. Finally, you are instructed to position the paper in the printer and press the Enter key. When you do, the printer plot begins. If your printer is buffered, you can immediately return to work on your drawing while the printer is drawing your figure. Your printout should look like Figure 7.2.

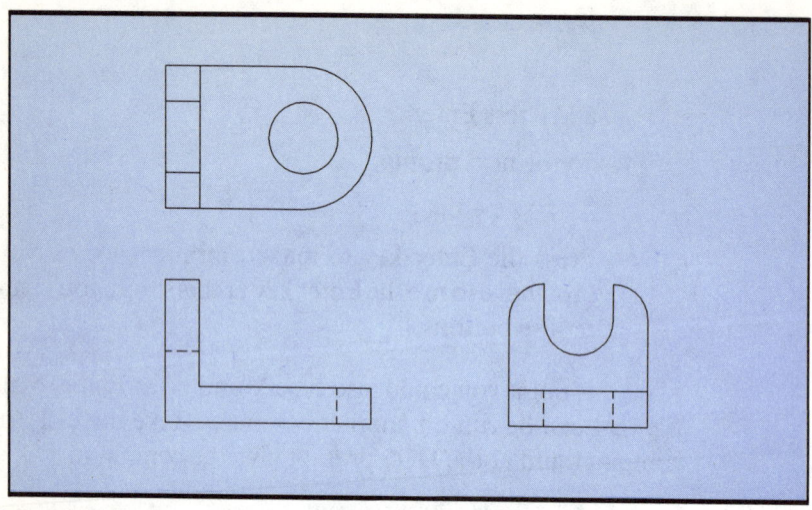

Figure 7.2: Printout of bracket views with normal object lines

Good. You've just printed a hard copy of your first drawing. Notice that it has wider lines for the border, but thin lines for the other parts. However, it is customary to draw the object lines—those that surround the object—with wide lines (about 0.02 inches wide). In the next section you'll widen these lines. But first, save the current version of your drawing under a different name, just in case something goes wrong.

1. Give the command

    save

    and press Enter.

2. Then give the filename

    bracketn

    for the version of the bracket that has narrow object lines.

3. As a second check, give the command

    undo

    and press Enter.

4. Follow this with the option

    m

for Mark and press Enter. Then you can easily return to this point if you have trouble with the next section.

How to Widen Lines with the P-Edit Command

In the following section you will widen the object lines in all three views by converting them to polylines. To do this, you will use the P-edit (for polyline edit) command. The P-edit command can widen only polylines or lines that can be converted into polylines. Circles cannot be widened.

Changing Lines to Polylines

Let us widen the object lines of the front view first. We used polylines to draw the wide border around the edge. Now we will change the object lines of the front view to polylines.

1. Type the command

    pedit

    and press Enter to start the polyline editor.

2. AutoCAD responds with the prompt

    Select polyline:

    Move the selection box to the lower line of the front view and press the pick button. The lower line becomes spotty.

3. Next, you are informed that the object you have selected is not a polyline. (Of course, you know that. You want to convert a regular line to a polyline.) Next, you are asked if you want to convert this line to a polyline. Press the second mouse button or the Enter key to accept the default value of Y for Yes. The line you marked is converted to a polyline.

4. Type

    w

    for Width and press Enter to set the polyline width.

5. Give the value 0.02 and press Enter. Notice that the bottom line becomes wider.

6. Type

    j

    for Join and press Enter to convert the other straight lines around the object into polylines.

7. Type

    w

    for Window and press Enter to choose a regular selection window.

8. Enclose the entire front view in a selection window. Move the cursor to the lower-right corner of the front view. Press the pick button.

9. Move the cursor to the upper-left corner or the front view. When the window covers the entire front view, press the pick button. The entire front view becomes spotty (Figure 7.3).

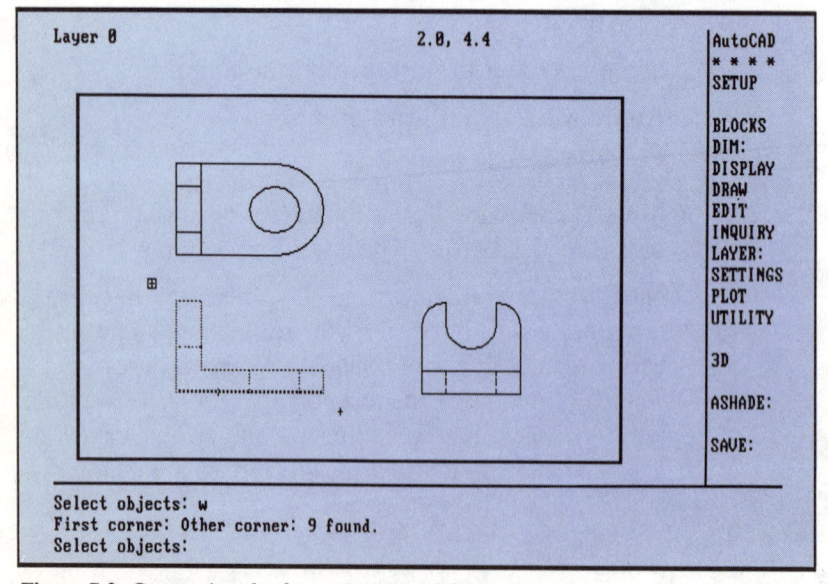

Figure 7.3: Converting the front view to polylines

10. Press the second mouse button or the Enter key to complete the selection. All the object lines around the front view become wide, matching the width you gave for the bottom line. Notice that the three interior hidden lines do not change.

11. Press the second mouse button or the Enter key to complete the P-edit command.

Converting Right-View Object Lines

Now continue on to convert the object lines of the right view to polylines. You will use the same procedure as before.

1. Press the second mouse button or the Enter key to restart the P-edit command.

2. Move the selection box to the bottom line of the right view. Press the pick button to select this line.

3. Again, you are informed that the object you have selected is not a polyline. Press the second mouse button or the Enter key to accept the default value of Y to convert this line to a polyline.

4. Type

    w

    and press Enter to set the polyline width.

5. As before, give the value 0.02 and press Enter. Notice that the bottom line of the right view becomes wider.

6. Type

    j

    for Join and press Enter to make the other lines around this view become polylines.

7. Type

    w

    for Window and press Enter.

8. Enclose the right view in a selection window. Move the cursor to the lower-right corner of the front view and press the pick button.

9. Move the cursor to the upper-left corner of the right view. When the window covers the entire front view, press the pick button. The front view becomes spotty.

10. Press the second mouse button or the Enter key to complete the selection. All the object lines around the perimeter of the right view become wide, matching the width you gave for the bottom line. Notice that neither the two interior hidden lines nor the horizontal object line near the bottom changes.

11. Press the second mouse button or the Enter key to complete the P-edit command.

Now you will convert the interior object line to a polyline. This line must be separately changed since a closed polyline cannot be joined to another line.

1. Press the second mouse button or the Enter key to restart the P-edit command.

2. Move the selection box to the horizontal line just above the bottom line of the right view. Press the pick button to select this line.

3. You are informed that the object you have selected is not a polyline. Press the second mouse button to accept the default value of Y to convert this line to a polyline.

4. Type

    w

    and press Enter to set the polyline width.

5. Give the value 0.02 and press Enter. Notice that this line becomes wider.

6. Press the second mouse button or the Enter key to complete the P-edit command.

Converting Object Lines in the Top View

Let us change the top view next. This view is more complicated because we have to convert the three interior lines separately from the perimeter lines.

1. If Snap mode is on, turn it off with the F9 key.
2. Enlarge the top view by typing the command

    zoom

    and pressing the space bar.
3. Type

    w

    for Window and press Enter.
4. Put a window around the top view in the usual way. Move the cursor to the lower-left corner and press the pick button.
5. Move to the upper-right corner and press the pick button again.
6. Type

    pedit

    and press Enter to start the polyline editor.
7. Move the selection box to the bottom line of the top view. Press the pick button to select this line.
8. Press the second mouse button or the Enter key to convert this line to a polyline.
9. Type

    w

    and press Enter to set the polyline width.
10. Give the value 0.02 and press Enter. Notice that the bottom line becomes wider.
11. Type

    j

    for Join and press Enter to make the other lines around this view become polylines.
12. Type

    w

    for Window and press Enter to make a selection window.

13. Enclose the top view in a selection window. Move the cursor to the lower-left corner of the front view and press the pick button.

14. Move the cursor to the upper-right corner of the top view. When the window covers the entire front view, press the pick button. The entire top view becomes spotty.

15. Press the second mouse button or the Enter key to complete the selection. All the object lines around the perimeter of the top view become wide, matching the width you gave for the bottom line. Notice that the three interior lines and the circle do not change. They must be separately converted.

16. Press the second mouse button or the Enter key to complete the first part of the P-edit command.

Now you will change the interior straight lines to a polyline. You must run the polyline editor again to convert these lines.

1. Press the second mouse button or the Enter key to restart the P-edit command.

2. Move the selection box to the vertical line near the left edge. Press the pick button to select this line.

3. Press the second mouse button or the Enter key to convert this line to a polyline.

4. Type

    w

    and press Enter to set the polyline width.

5. Give the value 0.02 and press Enter. Notice that this line becomes wider.

6. Press Enter to complete the P-edit command.

7. Repeat steps 1-6 twice to convert the two horizontal lines to wide polylines.

Printing the Drawing   **165**

Widening the Ellipse Line Width

Now we will increase the line width of the circle-shaped ellipse. This is a simpler process than we used for the lines and arcs since the ellipse is already defined as a polyline.

1. Give the command

    pedit

    and press Enter to start the polyline editor.

2. Move the selection cursor to the edge of the ellipse and press the pick button.

3. Type

    w

    and press Enter to set the polyline width.

4. Give the value 0.02 and press Enter. Notice that the ellipse becomes wider.

5. Press the second mouse button or the Enter key to complete the P-edit command.

6. Give the command

    zoom

    and press the space bar.

7. Type

    a

    for All and press Enter to see all your drawing.

8. Press the F7 key to turn off the grid.

You now have widened the object lines and arcs of the three views of the bracket. You may notice that some of the polylines appear to be wider than others even though you gave the same width for all polylines. The problem is that the line width has a value between two and three scan lines on the video screen. Therefore, sometimes these lines are drawn with two scan lines and sometimes with three. A similar problem may occur with a dot-matrix printer, although not with a regular plotter or laser printer.

How to Make a Larger Printer Plot

Let us now make a second larger printer plot of our drawing to see how the wider object lines appear. This drawing will just fill a standard 8.5 by 11-inch sheet.

1. Give the command

    prplot

    and press Enter.

2. Press the Enter key to accept the default option of D, to plot what is shown on the display.

3. When you are asked if you want to change anything, type

    y

    and press Enter to override the default options.

4. Press Enter to the next three questions to accept the default values.

5. Two plot sizes are offered this time. The one called MAX is 8 inches by 11 inches. The other is called USER and is the size you selected last time. This time, type

    max

    and press Enter to select the larger size. Notice that the width is the smaller dimension now. Since the larger dimension is given second, you must rotate the plot so the longer dimension is vertical.

6. For the next question, answer

    y

    and press Enter so the plot will be rotated.

7. Press Enter two times to accept the next two options. The effective plotting area will then be given.

8. Finally, press the Enter key to start the plot. The result will look like Figure 7.4 .

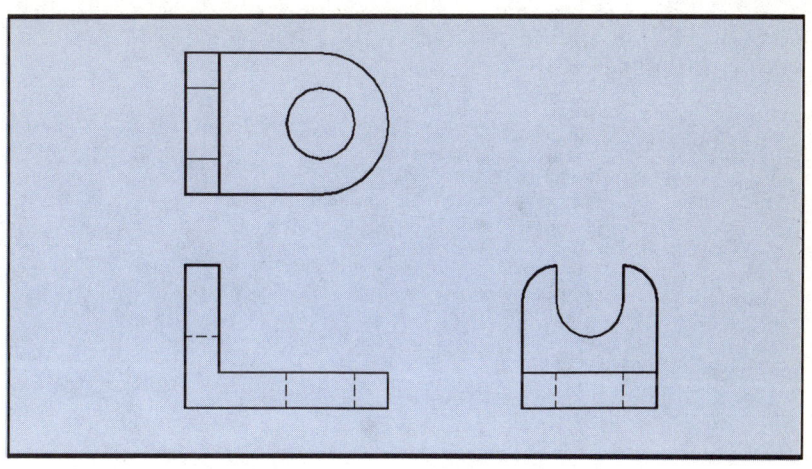

Figure 7.4: Laser printer version of bracket with wide object lines

8

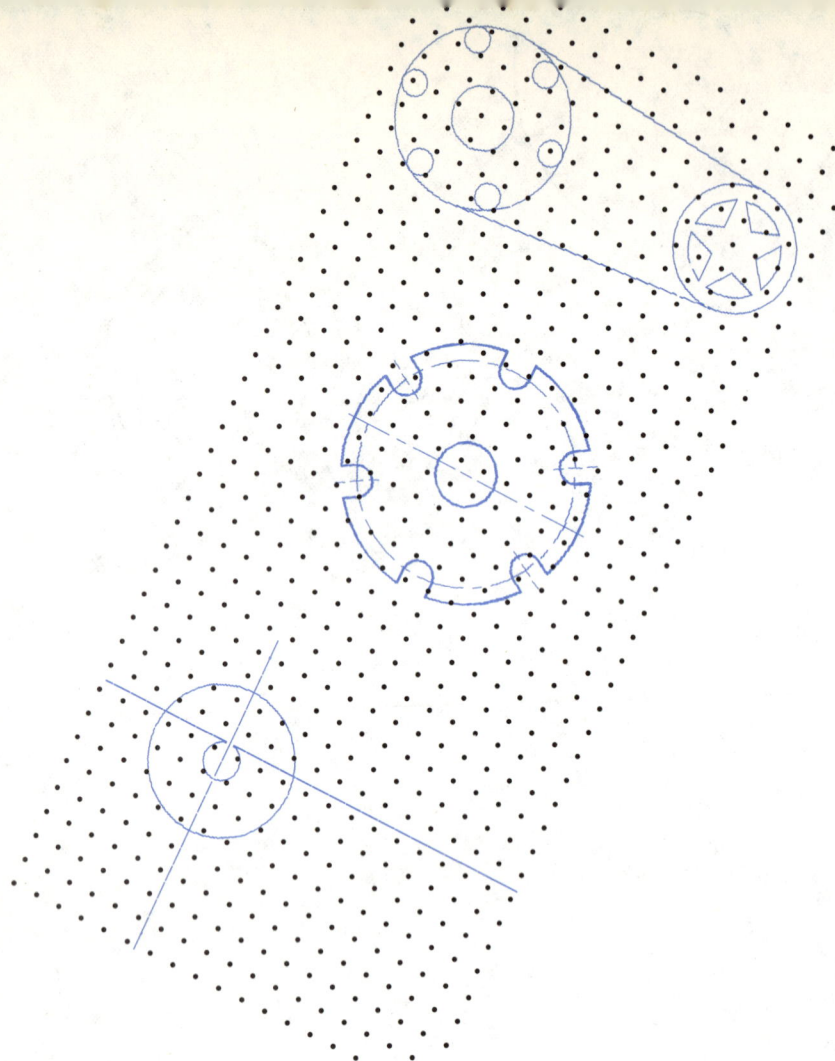

Some Shortcuts and Enhancements

Featuring:
    Inserting another drawing
    Drawing a sectional view
    Extending lines
    Breaking a line
    Using hatching

In the previous two chapters you drew three views of a bracket. In this chapter you will draw the top and front views of a circular flange. Only two views are needed for this object because of circular symmetry. This drawing will demonstrate another feature of mechanical drawing—the sectional view. Both the figure border and the object lines will be drawn wider than normal using polylines.

The views in the previous chapters show features that are visible on the outside of an object. Wide object lines are used to represent these visible lines. With this method, internal features that are not visible on the surface are drawn with thin, dashed hidden lines.

An alternative method for showing internal details is the *sectional view*. With this technique, we draw a view that is obtained by slicing through the object with a *cutting plane*. The part on one side of the cutting plane is removed to expose the cut surface. With this method, hidden lines are not needed. The sectioned area, representing the material cut by the plane, is surrounded by regular visible-type lines and cross hatched with thin parallel lines. Because different styles of hatch pattern show different types of material, AutoCAD is provided with a wide selection of hatch patterns.

The cutting plane in the view adjacent to the section view is marked with a *cutting-plane line*. This is a wide line formed with long dashes alternated with two short dashes. The cutting-plane line is created with the AutoCAD phantom line type. Arrow heads are placed at the ends of the cutting-plane line to show the direction of the cut-away view.

Commands introduced in this chapter are

- Hatch to fill an area with a hatching pattern

How to Insert a Standard Border

In Chapter 6 you drew a wide border line using the P-line command. Then you saved the border as a separate disk file so you could use it for other drawings. If you did not save this border, please return to that chapter and do this before continuing. You'll insert this border into your flange drawing.

Before beginning the drawing, we perform the usual housekeeping chores.

1. Start AutoCAD.
2. Select item 1 from the Main menu and press Enter to start a new drawing.
3. Type the file name

    flange =

    and press Enter.
4. Type the command

    insert

    and press Enter to retrieve the border you previously drew and saved.
5. For the file name, type

    border

    and press Enter.
6. To put the origin at the standard location, type

    0, 0

    and press Enter.
7. Answer the remaining three questions by pressing the Enter key three times. The wide border now appears on the screen.
8. As before, type the command

    units

    and press Enter.
9. Press Enter to accept the default display of decimal numbers (item 2).
10. Type

    1

    and press Enter to set the display to one digit past the decimal point.
11. Press ^C to skip over the remaining questions.

12. Press the F1 key to change back to the drawing screen.
13. Give the command

    snap

    and press Enter.
14. To set the snap spacing, type

    0.5

    and press Enter.
15. Type the command

    grid

    and press Enter.
16. Then set the grid spacing to the snap spacing by typing

    s

    and pressing Enter.

How to Draw the Top View

In this section you will draw the top view of the flange shown in Figure 8.1. First, you draw three circles—one large, one medium, and one small. The large and medium circles are concentric while the smaller one is tangent to the rim of the larger one. Parts of the large and small circles are removed to create a bolt slot. Then the slot is replicated around the rim of the larger circle with the Array command.

Drawing the Three Circles

We will begin by drawing the largest of the three circles.

1. Press the F6 key to turn on the coordinate display.
2. Give the command

    circle

    and press Enter.

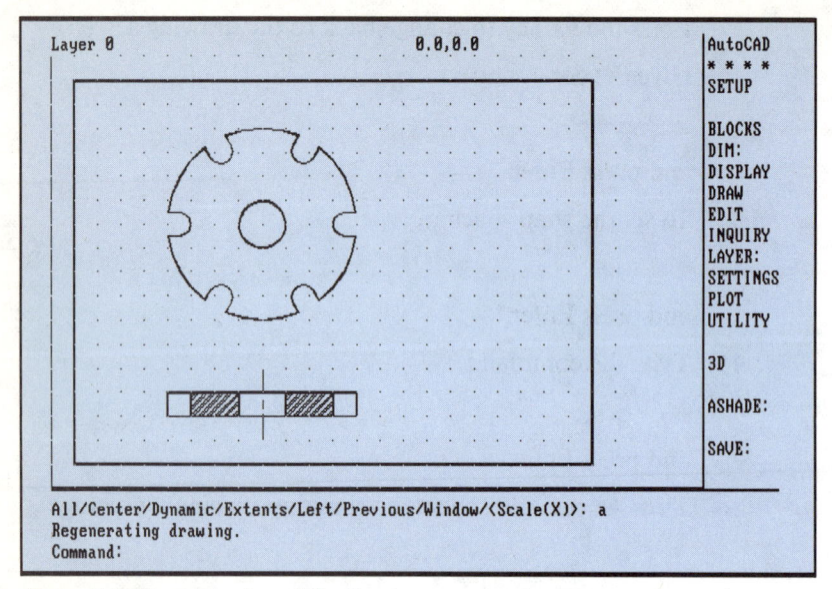

Figure 8.1: Complete view of the flange

3. Move the cursor to the coordinate position

    4.5, 5.5

    and press the pick button to establish the circle center. Alternatively, type the coordinates and press Enter.

4. Move the cursor right four grid points to the coordinate location

    2.0 <0

    and press the pick button to complete the larger circle.

In Chapter 6 you converted lines, arcs, and ellipses to wide polylines. However, you cannot easily convert a circle to a polyline. Therefore, in this section, you will draw the medium-size circle using the Ellipse command, which is already a polyline.

1. Give the command

    ellipse

    and press Enter.

2. Move to the center of the large circle, then move down one grid point to coordinate location

    4.5, 5.0

Press the pick button to start an ellipse.

3. Move straight upward two grid points to the coordinate location

    1.0 <90

    and press the pick button again. The outline of a circle should be apparent.

4. Press the pick button a third time to fix the circular ellipse (Figure 8.2).

Next you'll draw the small circle. You are going to make six circular notches around the rim of the flange. First you will draw one circle, then you will copy it with the Array command. But first enlarge the view.

1. Give the command

    zoom

    and press the space bar.

2. Type

    w

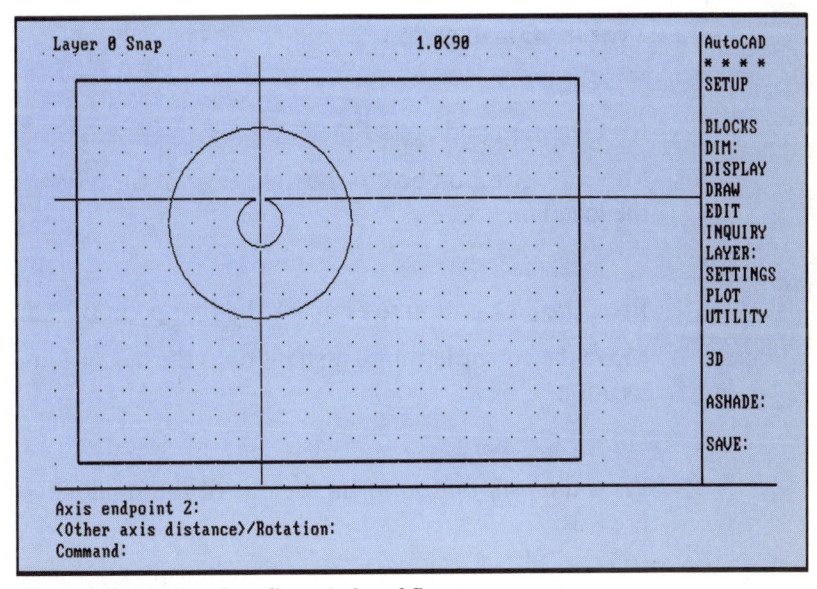

Figure 8.2: Large and medium circles of flange

for Window and press Enter.

3. Move the cursor to the lower-left side of the large circle to the location

    2.0, 3.0

    and press the pick button.

4. Move the cursor to the upper-right side of the large circle to the location

    7.0, 8.0

    and press the pick button to enlarge the view.

5. Type the command

    circle

    and press Enter.

6. Type the option

    2p

    and press Enter. With this method you specify the circle size by giving two points on the diameter rather than the usual center and radius.

7. Type the Osnap option

    quad

    for Quadrant and press Enter.

8. Move the selection box to the right edge of the large circle to the location

    6.5, 5.5

    Press the pick button to establish the first point of the circle.

9. Move the cursor left until it snaps onto the next grid point at location

    6.0, 5.5

    Press the pick button to fix the size of the small circle (Figure 8.3).

Some Shortcuts and Enhancements **177**

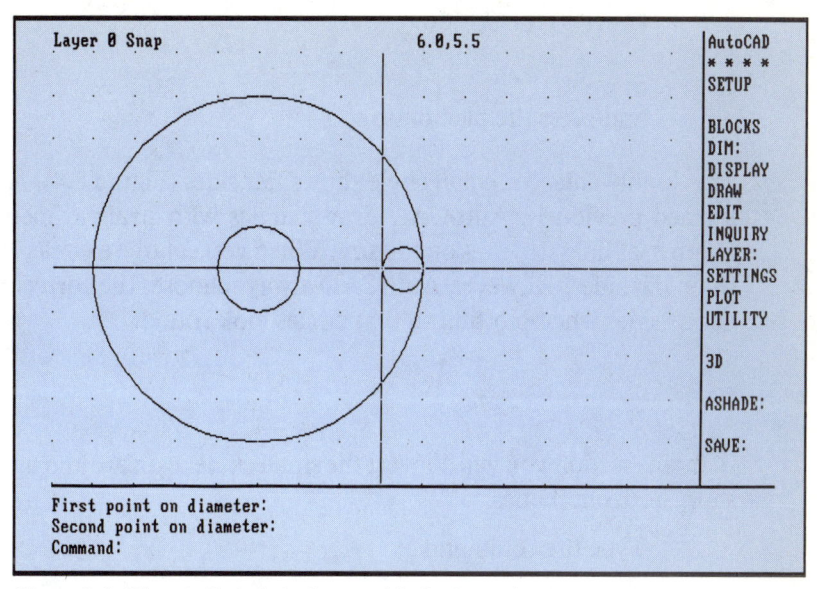

Figure 8.3: The small circle is drawn with the 2p option

Converting a Circle to an Arc

In this section you will remove part of the small circle, converting it into an arc. Then, you will remove part of the large circle. First, enlarge the view a second time.

1. Press the F9 key to turn off Snap mode.
2. Give the command

    zoom

    and press the space bar.
3. Type

    w

    for Window and press Enter.
4. Put a window around the new small circle to enlarge it. Move the cursor to

    5.8, 5.1

    and press the pick button.

5. Move to the position

    6.7, 5.9

    and press the pick button.

The doubly enlarged small circle shows flat sides (Figure 8.4). As you learned previously, AutoCAD draws circles with straight lines. The number of lines depends on the size. When you enlarge a circle, it may show flat sides. However, AutoCAD always chooses the correct number of sides when plotting so that circles look round.

Connecting Two Circles

In this section you will convert the small circle to an arc and add two short horizontal lines.

1. Type the command

    line

    and press Enter.

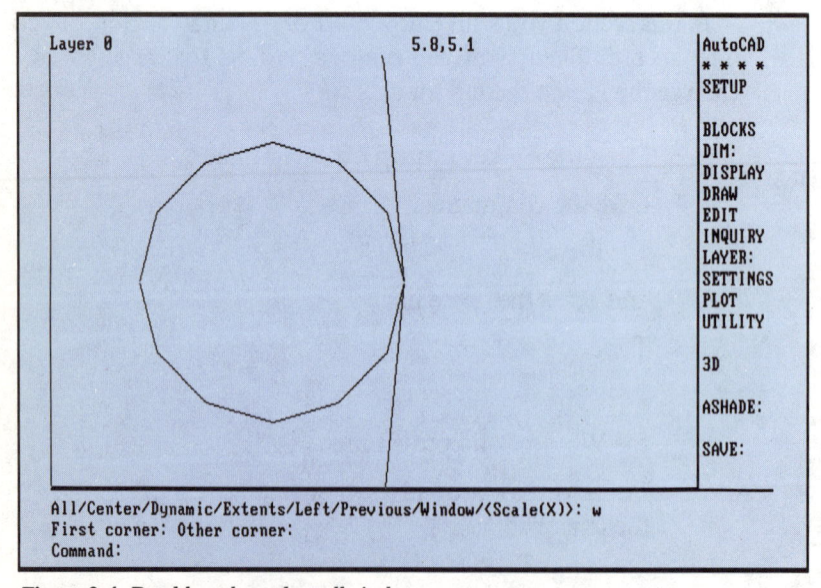

Figure 8.4: Doubly enlarged small circle

2. Type the Osnap option

   quad

   and press Enter.

3. Move the cursor to the top edge of the small circle and press the pick button. As you learned previously, you do not have to precisely locate the cursor. The Osnap command will do that for you.

4. Press the F8 key to turn on Ortho mode.

5. Move the cursor to the right, stopping short of the large circle (Figure 8.5). Press the pick button to establish the right end of this line.

6. Press the right mouse button or the Enter key to complete the Line command.

7. Press the right mouse button or the Enter key to restart the Line command.

8. Type the Osnap option

   quad

   again and press Enter.

9. Move the cursor to the bottom edge of the small circle and press the pick button.

10. Move the cursor to the right, stopping short of the large circle. Press the pick button to fix the right end of the second line.

11. Press the right mouse button or the Enter key to complete the Line command. Your screen should look like Figure 8.5.

*E*xtending Lines with the Extend Command

In this section you will have AutoCAD extend the two short lines until they meet the large circle. This will make a precise connection. By contrast, if you try to make the connection yourself, it will not be as accurate.

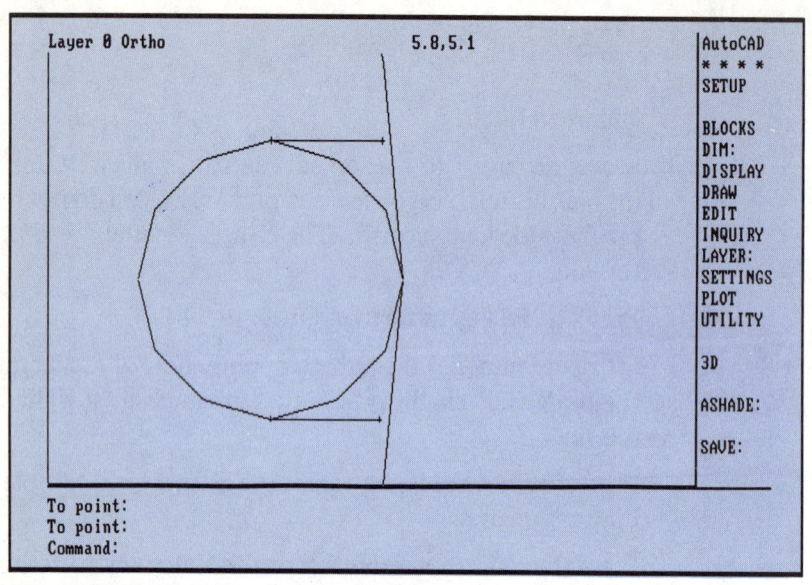

Figure 8.5: Small circle and connecting lines

1. Type the command

    extend

    and press Enter.

2. Move the selection box to the edge of the large circle, well away from the small circle. Press the pick button. The large circle becomes spotty showing that it is marked as an extension boundary.

3. Press the second mouse button or the Enter key to complete selection of the extension boundary.

4. Move the selection box to the short line at the top of the small circle. Press the pick button. The upper line extends until it connects to the large circle.

5. Move the selection box to the short line at the bottom of the small circle. Press the pick button. The lower line extends until it connects to the large circle.

6. Press the second mouse button or Enter to complete the Extend command.

Some Shortcuts and Enhancements   181

*T*rimming the Circle Opening

In this section you will trim part of the small and large circles to make a bolt slot.

1. Press the F8 key to turn off Ortho mode.

2. Type the command

    trim

   and press Enter.

3. Move the selection box to the upper line that connects the small circle to the large circle. Press the pick button to mark this line as a trim boundary.

4. Move the selection box to the lower line that connects the small circle to the large circle. Press the pick button to mark this line as a trim boundary (Figure 8.6).

5. Press the right mouse button or the Enter key to complete the selection of the trim boundary. Now you must select the lines to be trimmed.

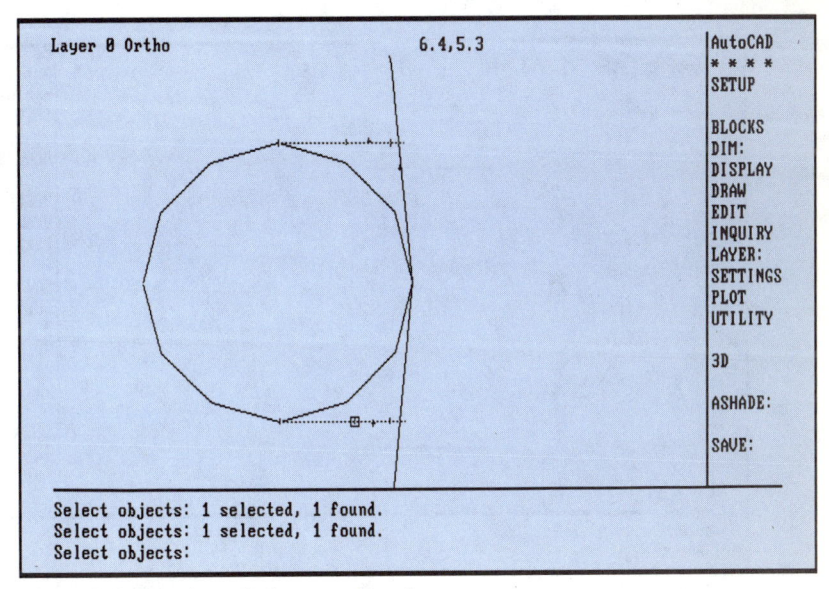

Figure 8.6: *Trim boundaries are selected*

6. Move the selection box to the right edge of the small circle, well away from the large circle. Press the pick button to remove the right half of the circle.

7. Move the selection box to the right edge of the large circle. Position it between the two short lines, and press the pick button to remove a small part of the large circle (Figure 8.7). The opening now looks like a slot for a bolt.

8. Press the second mouse button or Enter to complete the Trim command.

Replicating the Circle Opening

In the following sections you will replicate the bolt slot to create six copies. We will remove all but one sixth of the large circle. Then we will replicate this part.

Drawing a Temporary Construction Line

Drawing a temporary construction line from the center of the large

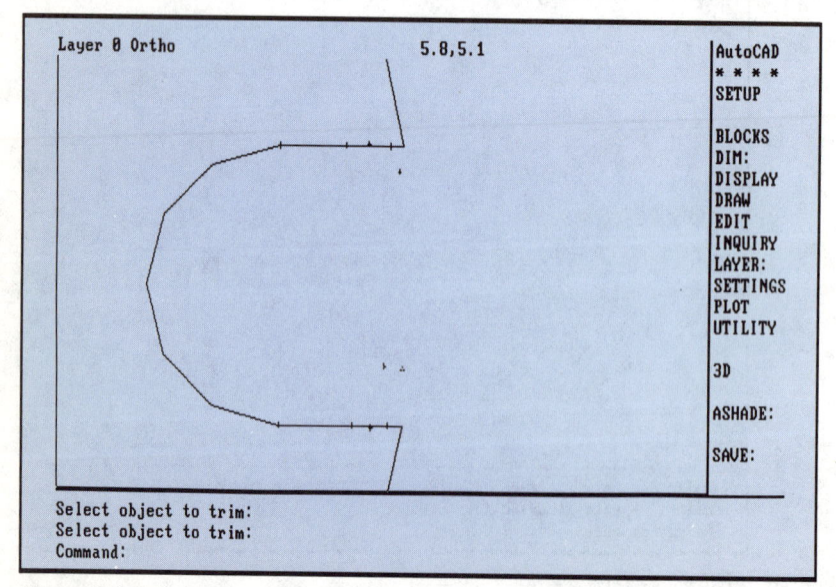

Figure 8.7: Bolt slots are opened

circle to the diameter will make our task easier.

1. Give the command

    zoom

    and press the space bar.
2. Type

    p

    for Previous and press Enter. This returns you to the previous view.
3. Type the command

    line

    and press Enter.
4. Type the Osnap command

    cen

    for Center and press Enter.
5. Move the selection box to the edge of the large circle and press the pick button to start a radial construction line from the center of the large circle.
6. Type the Osnap command

    int

    for Intersection and press Enter.
7. Move the cursor to the intersection of the large circle and the lower short line that extends from the small circle. Press the pick button to create a temporary construction line (Figure 8.8). Be sure that the right end of the line connects to the right end of the lower short line from the small circle.
8. Press the second mouse button or Enter to complete the Line command.

Now rotate the construction line 60 degrees. We need to erase most of the large circle, leaving only 60 degrees of arc. We will use the construction line to mark the 60-degree point.

184 *The ABC's of AutoCAD*

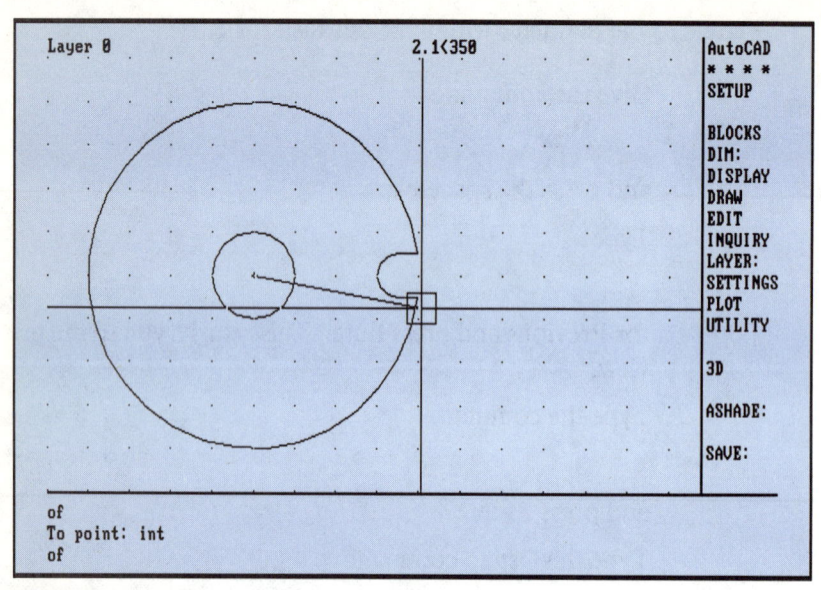

CH. 8

Figure 8.8: Adding a temporary construction line

1. Give the command

    rotate

    and press Enter.

2. Move the selection box to the new construction line and press the pick button. The line becomes spotty. (You can also type L for last item drawn.)

3. Press the second mouse button or the Enter key to complete the selection.

4. In answer to the question

    Base point:

    type the Osnap option

    cen

    for Center and press Enter.

5. Move the selection box to the edge of the large circle and press the pick button. This designates the center of the large circle as the center of the rotation.

6. Type the angle

    60

    and press Enter to rotate the construction line 60 degrees.

Trimming the Circle

Now we are ready to remove most of the large circle.

1. Give the command

    trim

    and press Enter.

2. Move the selection box first to the new construction line and press the pick button or L for Last.

3. Move the selection box to the lower short line connecting the small circle to the large circle. Press the pick button.

4. Press the second mouse button or the Enter key to complete the selection process.

5. Move the cursor to the left edge of the large circle. Press the pick button to erase most of the large circle.

6. Press the second mouse button or Enter to complete the Trim command.

Erasing the Temporary Construction Line

Now we will erase the construction line.

1. Type the command

    erase

    and press Enter.

2. Move the selection box to the middle of the construction line and press the pick button.

3. Press the second mouse button or Enter to erase the line. Your screen should look like Figure 8.9.

186 The ABC's of AutoCAD

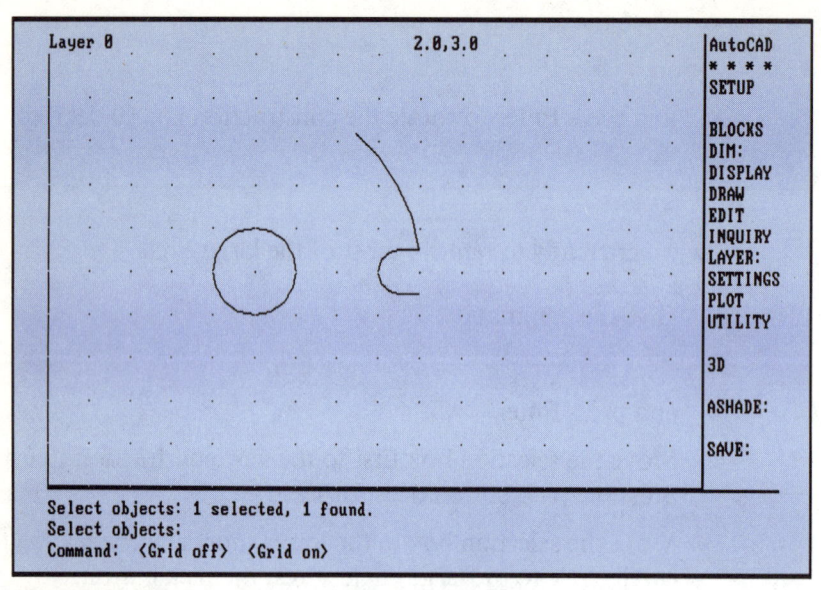

CH. 8

Figure 8.9: A 60-degree sector is ready for replication

Replicating the 60-Degree Sector

Now we are ready to replicate the bolt hole around the flange.

1. Give the command

    array

    and press Enter.

2. We will choose four items—the remaining arc of the large circle, the left half of the small circle, and the two short horizontal connecting lines—by moving the selection box to each in turn and pressing the pick button. Of course, you could also select these four items with a window.

3. Press the right mouse button or the Enter key to complete the selection process.

4. Type

    p

    for Polar array and press Enter.

5. In response to the question

    Center point of array

    type the Osnap option

    cen

    and press Enter.

6. Move to the arc of the large circle and press the pick button. This will replicate the arc around the center of the large circle.

7. For the number of items to create, answer

    6

    and press Enter.

8. Press Enter twice to accept the defaults of counterclockwise rotation and rotation during copying.

You now have a full circle with six bolt holes (Figure 8.10). Before continuing to the next section, save a copy of your current work to disk.

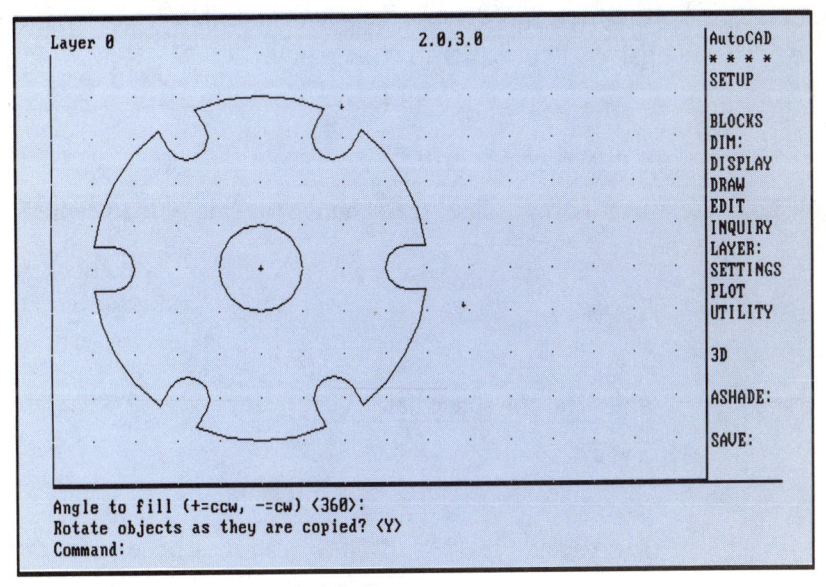

Figure 8.10: Flange with six bolt holes

1. Give the command

    save

   and press the Enter key.

2. Press Enter a second time to accept the current file name of flange.

How to Draw the Front View

Let's draw the rectangular front view next. Since this is to be a sectional view, there will be interior lines representing the small and medium circles. There will also be cross hatching for the part of the diameter that is cut by the section plane. We will draw the left and right halves of this view in two different ways to show alternate techniques.

First, you'll draw the center line, then the left half, and finally, the right half. The left side will be drawn as a rectangle with two dividing lines added. The right half will be drawn as a zig-zag line. Both methods will give us a correct view. The left side will be easier to draw but the right side will be easier to cross hatch.

Drawing the Center Line

Here you'll draw a line, then change the line type to center. You'll also change the scale.

1. Type

    zoom

   and press the space bar.

2. Type

    a

   for All and press Enter. The screen shows the entire drawing.

3. Press the F9 key to turn on Snap mode.

4. To draw the center line on the front view, type

   line

   and press Enter.

5. Move the cursor to the position

   4.5, 2.5

   The vertical line of the cursor should align with the center of the large and medium circles of the top view. Press the pick button to start a new line.

6. Move down three grid points to the position

   1.5 <270

   and press the pick button.

7. Press the second mouse button or the Enter key to complete the Line command.

8. To convert the continuous line to a center line, type

   change

   and press Enter.

9. When AutoCAD asks you to select the objects to be changed, type

   L

   for Last and press Enter. The line becomes spotty as you select it.

10. Press the right mouse button or the Enter key to complete the selection. AutoCAD then displays the prompt:

    Properties/<Change point>:

11. Type

    p

    and press Enter to select property change.

12. AutoCAD then displays the prompt:

    **Change what property
    (Color/Elev/LAyer/LType/Thickness)?**

13. Type

    lt

    for Line Type and press Enter to select a change of line type. AutoCAD responds with the prompt:

    New linetype<BYLAYER>:

14. Type

    center

    and press Enter. AutoCAD repeats the prompt:

    (Color/Elev/LAyer/LType/Thickness)?

15. Press the right mouse button or the Enter key to complete the Change command. The new line does not appear to change because the scale is wrong.

16. Type the command

    ltscale

    and press Enter.

17. To the prompt

    New scale factor <1.0000>:

    type

    0.6

    and press Enter. The new line changes to alternating long and short segments.

Drawing the Left Side of the Front View

In this section you will draw the left side of the front view starting from the center line. Three lines will define the perimeter. Then you will add two short lines across the center.

1. Give the command

    line

    and press Enter.

2. Move the cursor to the center line at coordinate position

   4.5, 2.0

   and press the pick button to start a new line.

3. Move the cursor to the left four grid points until the vertical line of the cursor nearly aligns with the left side of the top view. Press the pick button to fix the first line of this view. (Of course, the cursor will not precisely align with the large circle because we have cut away a small part of it.)

4. Move downward one grid point and press the pick button.

5. Move right four grid points and connect again with the center line. Press the pick button.

6. Press the second mouse button or Enter to complete the Line command.

Adding Detail with Interior Lines

Since this is a sectional view, we need to show detail down the center of the view.

1. Press the right mouse button or the Enter key to restart the Line command.

2. Move the cursor to the lower-left corner of the front view to location

   2.5, 1.5

   Move right one grid point to position

   3.0, 1.5

   At this point the vertical line of the cursor aligns with the right end of the left bolt slot in the top view.

3. Press the pick button to start a new line.

4. Move upward one grid point and press the pick button to complete the short line.

5. Press the right mouse button or the Enter key to complete the Line command. Look for the word *Command:* on the bottom line of the screen.

6. Press the right mouse button or the Enter key to restart the Line command.

7. Move the cursor right two grid points to coordinate position

    4.0, 2.0

    The vertical line of the cursor now aligns with the left edge of the medium circle in the top view. Press the pick button to start the next line.

8. Move down one grid point and press the pick button to fix the end of the next line.

9. Press the right mouse button or the Enter key to complete the Line command. The word *Command:* appears on the bottom line. You should now have a row of three box-shaped regions on the left side of the front view.

Drawing the Right Side of the Front View

In this section you will draw the right side of the front view starting at the center line. By using short, zig-zag lines you will be able to draw all of the right side except for two segments.

1. Give the command

    line

    and press Enter.

2. Move the cursor to the center line at coordinate position

    4.5, 2.0

    Press the pick button to start a new line.

3. Move the cursor one grid point to the right and press the pick button to fix the next line.

4. Move downward one grid point and press the pick button to draw a second connected line.

5. Move right two grid points until the vertical cursor aligns with the left end of the right bolt slot in the top view. Press the pick button to fix the third connected line.

6. Move upward one grid point and press the pick button.

7. Move one grid point to the right. Check that the vertical line of the cursor nearly aligns with the right edge of the large circle in the top view. Press the pick button.

8. Move down one grid point and press the pick button.

9. Move left one grid point and press the pick button. Your view should look like Figure 8.11.

10. Press the second mouse button or Enter to complete the line command.

Good. We will now draw two line segments to close the gaps in the front view.

1. Press the second mouse button or the Enter key to start the line command.

2. Move left two grid points to position

    5.0, 1.5

    and press Enter.

3. Move left one grid point to the center line and press the pick button to fill in one gap.

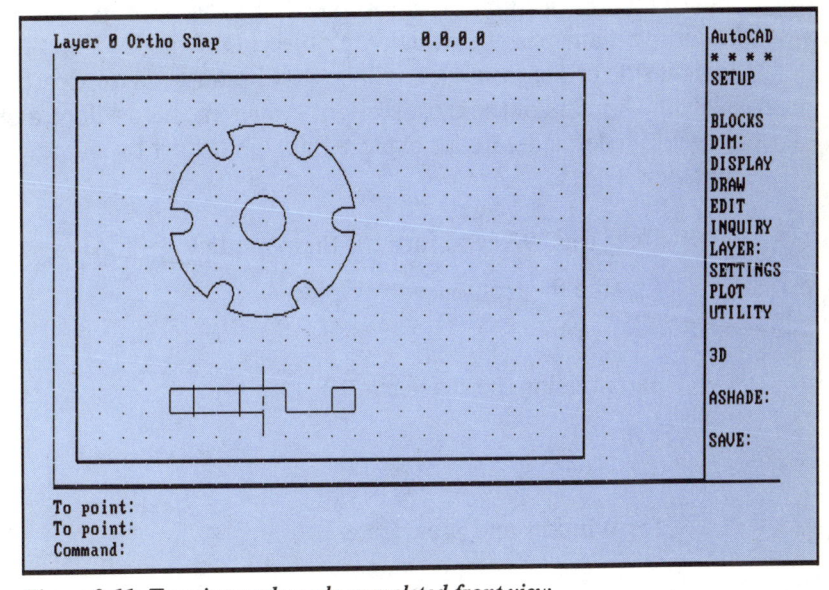

Figure 8.11: Top view and nearly completed front view

4. Press the second mouse button or Enter to complete the Line command.
5. Press the second mouse button or Enter to restart the Line command.
6. Move to location

    5.0, 2.0

    and press the pick button to start the last line segment.
7. Move two grid points right and press the pick button.
8. Press the second mouse button or Enter to complete the Line command. Look for the word *Command:* on the bottom line.

Both halves of the front view should look the same, although they are in fact different. Consequently, we will use different methods to add section lines to the two halves.

How to Add Section Lines with Hatching Patterns

Since this is a sectional view, we need to show section lines where the cutting plane passes through the object. Drawing section lines on the right side of the front view will be easy because we were careful to isolate the borders of the cross section. However, there will be a problem with the left side. Let us explore this. We'll start by enlarging the front view.

1. Press the F9 key to turn off Snap mode.
2. Enlarge the front view by typing

    zoom

    and pressing the space bar.
3. Type

    w

    for Window and press Enter.

4. Move the cursor to the location

   2.3, 1.0

   and press the pick button to start the window.

5. Move to the position

   6.7, 2.6

   and press the pick button to complete the window.

You can fill a closed area with a pattern using the Hatch command. AutoCAD provides several different hatch patterns. Some patterns are standard such as Steel and Brass, while others are decorative such as Stars and Honey (comb). If you have AutoCAD release 9 or later, you can display the patterns on the screen and then select one with the mouse. Just type **hatch** and press Enter, then type **?** and press Enter. The pattern names appear on the screen. The listing stops when the screen is filled. Press Enter to see the next screen. Let's choose a hatching pattern for the drawing now.

1. Type the command

   hatch

   and press Enter.

2. In response to the prompt

   Pattern (?or name/U,style):

   type

   steel

   and press Enter.

3. In response to the prompt

   Scale for pattern <1.000>:

   press Enter to accept the default.

4. In response to the prompt

   Angle for pattern <0>:

   press Enter to accept the default.

5. Now, the familiar prompt

   Select objects

   appears. Type

   w

   for Window and press Enter.

6. To box in the right side of the front view, move the cursor to the location

   4.8, 2.1

   and press the pick button.

7. Move to the location

   6.2, 1.3

   and press the pick button. The right-center rectangle becomes spotted to show that it is selected.

8. Press the second mouse button or the Enter key to fill in the selected area with the Steel hatch pattern.

Good. Now repeat the previous technique to add a hatch pattern to the left side.

1. Press the second mouse button or the Enter key to repeat the Hatch command. This time the beginning prompts are omitted.

2. When the prompt

   Select objects

   appears, type

   w

   for Window and press Enter.

3. Move to the location

   4.1, 1.4

   and press the pick button.

4. Move to the location

   2.8, 2.2

Some Shortcuts and Enhancements 197

to box in the left-center rectangle. Press the pick button. Notice that the top and bottom lines of the center rectangle around which you placed the window were not selected. Only the two vertical lines on either side were selected (Figure 8.12).

5. Move the selection cursor to the top line and press the pick button. Notice that the entire left half of the top line becomes selected.

6. Move the selection cursor to the bottom line and press the pick button. Notice that the entire left half of the bottom line becomes selected (Figure 8.13).

7. Press the second mouse button or the Enter key to hatch the left side. Notice that the pattern on the left side spills over the left and right sides of the rectangle (Figure 8.14). The problem is that the top and bottom lines are too long. We need to break these two lines.

Erasing Hatching

Let us erase the incorrect hatching on the left side so we can correct the lines and then fill in with hatching again.

1. Type U for Undo to erase the hatching, and press Enter.

2. Move the selection box to the center of the left hatch area and press the pick button. The hatch pattern should turn spotty to show that it is selected for the Erase command.

3. Press the right mouse button or the Enter key to erase the right hatch pattern.

How to Break Lines with the Break Command

You used the Break command in previous chapters to remove a portion of a line or arc. This command can also be used to break a line or

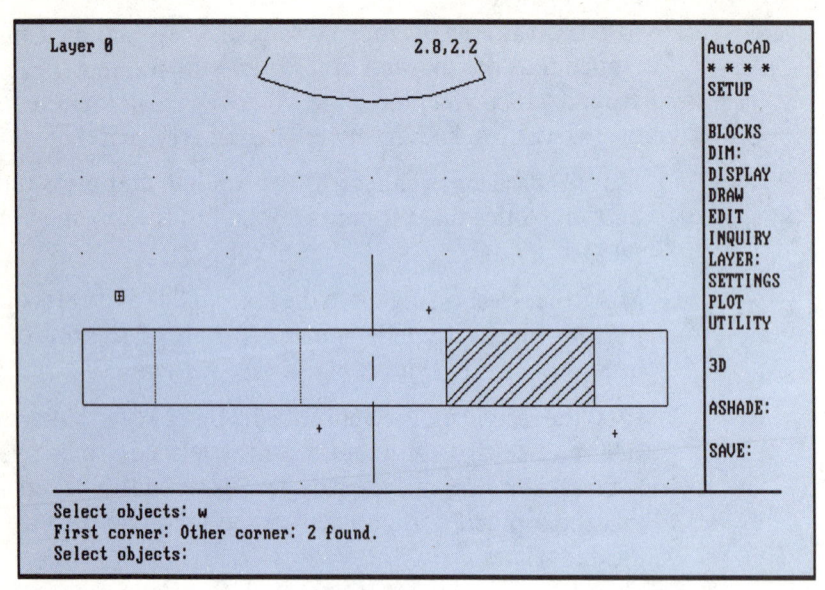

Figure 8.12: Selecting left hatch boundary

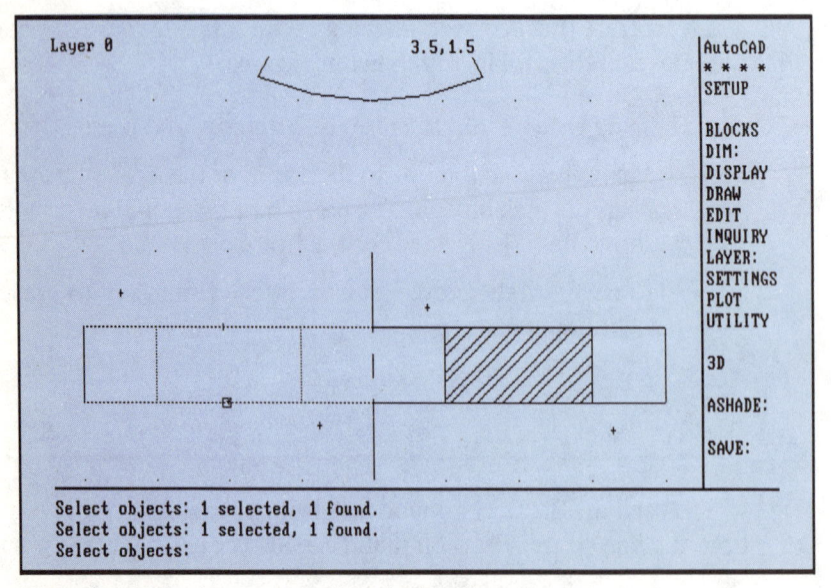

Figure 8.13: Selecting two more lines for hatching

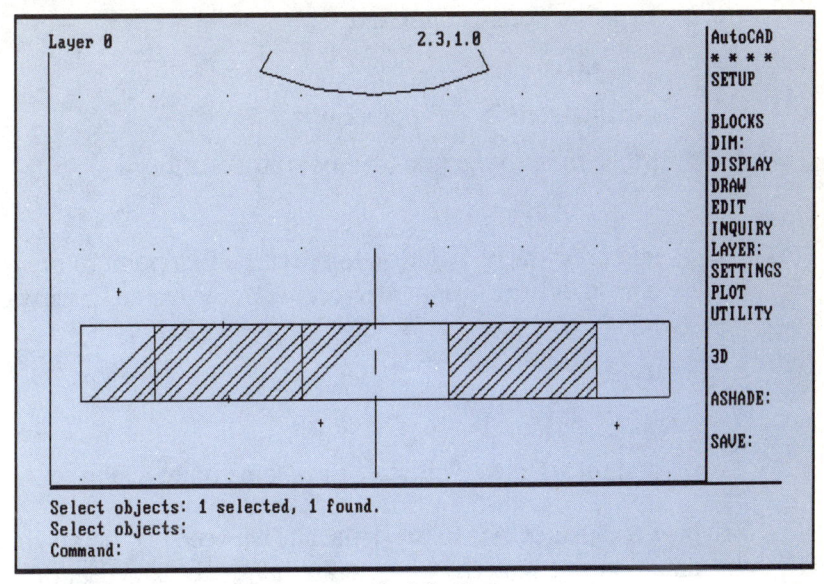

Figure 8.14: Incorrect hatch pattern for left side

arc at a point without removing anything. Let us do that, starting with the upper-left corner.

1. Type the command

    break

    and press Enter.

2. Move the selection box to the upper-left corner of the front view at location

    2.5, 2.0

    Then move a little to the right. Press the pick button. This step merely selects the line we want to break. It does not select the position of the break.

3. Type

    f

    for First point and press Enter to tell AutoCAD that you want to use the three-point method.

4. Type the Osnap command

    int

    for Intersection and press Enter.

5. Move right to the next grid point to location

    3.0, 2.0

    and press the pick button to select the first point to break. Of course, this is the upper-left corner of the rectangle we want to hatch.

6. Type

    @

    and press Enter. This selects the same point again.

You have told AutoCAD to break the line between two points that are the same. Thus no material will be erased. We need to repeat this operation for the other three corners of the rectangle. We will break the upper-right corner next.

1. Press Enter to repeat the Break command.
2. Move the selection box somewhere along the top line, away from other lines, and press the pick button.
3. Type

    f

    and press Enter to tell AutoCAD that you just selected the line.

4. Type the Osnap command

    int

    and press Enter.

5. Move right to the grid point at location

    4.0, 2.0

    and press the pick button to select the first point to break.

6. Type

    @

    and press Enter.

Now we must break the bottom line in the lower-left corner.

1. Press Enter to repeat the Break command.
2. Move the selection box to the lower-left corner of the front view at location

    2.5, 1.5

    Then move a little to the right. Press the pick button. This step selects the bottom line to be broken.
3. Type

    f

    and press Enter to tell AutoCAD that you have selected the line, not the point to be broken.
4. Type the Osnap command

    int

    press Enter.
5. Move right to the next grid point to location

    3.0, 1.5

    and press the pick button to select the first point to break.
6. Type

    @

    and press Enter.

There is one more corner to break—the lower-right corner.

1. Press Enter to repeat the Break command.
2. Move the selection box somewhere along the bottom line, away from other lines, and press the pick button.
3. Type

    f

    and press Enter.
4. Type the Osnap command

    int

    and press Enter.

5. Move right to the grid point at location

    4.0, 1.5

    and press the pick button to select the first point to break.

6. Type

    @

    and press Enter.

How to Add More Hatching

1. Type the command

    hatch

    and press Enter.

2. In response to the prompt

    Pattern (?or name/U,style)<STEEL>:

    press Enter to accept the current pattern.

3. In response to the prompt

    Scale for pattern <1.000>:

    press Enter to accept the default. (Steel is shown as the default because you previously chose it.)

4. In response to the prompt

    Angle for pattern <0>:

    press Enter to accept the default.

5. When the prompt

    Select objects

    appears, move the selection box to the top line at location

    3.5, 2.0

    and press the pick button. This time only the middle third of the line is selected because you broke this into three parts.

6. Move straight downward one grid point to the bottom line

and press the pick button. Again, only the middle third of the line is selected.

7. Move to the vertical line to the left of the center rectangle at location

    3.0, 1.7

    and press the pick button.

8. Move right two grid points and select the right edge of the middle rectangle. The middle rectangle should now be selected (Figure 8.15).

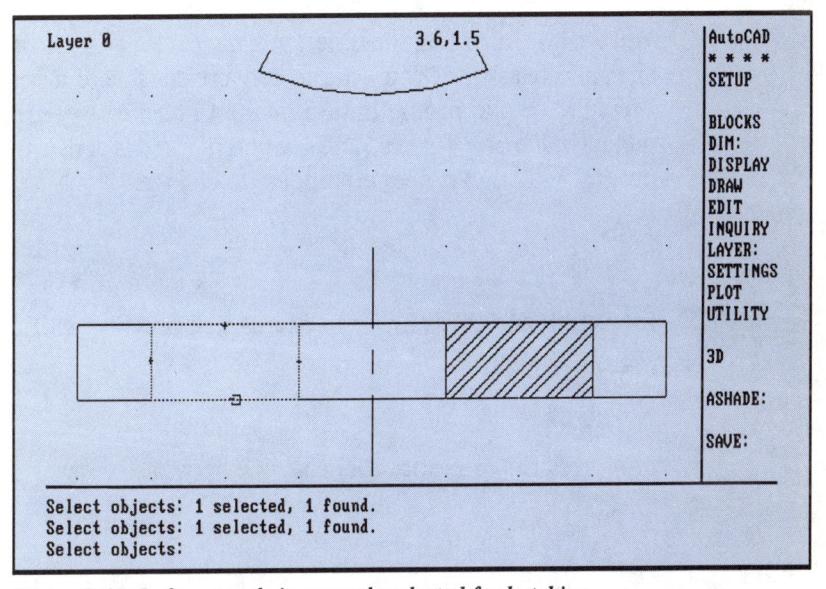

Figure 8.15: Left rectangle is correctly selected for hatching

9. Press the second mouse button or the Enter key to fill in the left area with the Steel hatching pattern.

How to Widen the Object Lines

In this step we will convert the object lines to polylines so we can widen them. (We also did this in Chapter 6.) Let's widen the perimeter of the front view first.

1. Type the command

    pedit

    and press Enter.

2. AutoCAD responds with the prompt:

    Select polyline:

    Move the selection box to the left edge of the front view, near location

    2.5, 1.7

    and press the pick button.

3. You are informed that the object you have selected is not a polyline and are asked if you want to convert this line to a polyline. Press the second mouse button or the Enter key to accept the default value of Y for yes. The line you marked is converted to a polyline although it does not appear to change.

4. Type

    w

    for Width and press Enter to change the polyline width.

5. Give the value

    0.02

    and press Enter. Notice that this line becomes wider.

6. Type

    j

    for Join and press Enter so you can convert the rest of the perimeter into a polyline.

7. In a previous chapter, you used a window to select additional lines for joining to the polyline. However, there are so many lines here that the result would be unpredictable. Therefore, we will select each line segment individually. Move the selection box to the upper-left corner of the front view. Then move a little to the right. Press the pick button to select the left end of the top line. This line becomes spotty.

8. Move to the right to the middle of the next segment. Be careful not to select the hatch pattern. Press the pick button to select the middle third of the upper left line. This line also becomes spotty. (If you accidentally select the hatch pattern, it will turn spotty. Then type **r** for Remove and select the hatch pattern again. Type **a** for Add to return to Add mode so you can select the remaining lines.)

9. Move to the right to the next segment. Press the pick button again. There are 13 perimeter lines to be converted. Continue in this way, moving to each part of the perimeter and pressing the pick button.

10. When the entire perimeter has been selected, press the second mouse button or the Enter key to complete the selection step. The entire perimeter is converted to a wide polyline (Figure 8.16).

11. Press Enter to complete the P-Edit command.

Now we must convert the four vertical interior lines. Because the perimeter polyline is a closed polygon, we cannot join other lines to it. Therefore, we must individually convert the four remaining lines with separate P-edit commands.

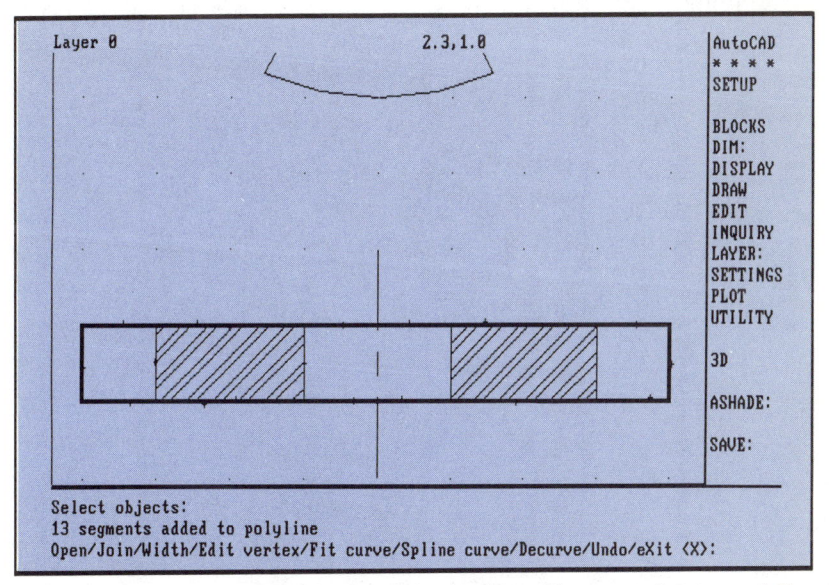

Figure 8.16: The perimeter of the front view is widened by conversion to a polyline

1. Press the second mouse button or the Enter key to restart the P-edit command.
2. Move the selection box to the left interior vertical line. Press the pick button to select this line.
3. Press the pick button to accept the default value of Y to convert this line to a polyline.
4. Type

    w

    and press Enter to set the polyline width.
5. Give the value

    0.02

    and press Enter. Notice that this line becomes wider.
6. Press the second mouse button or the Enter key to complete the P-edit command.
7. Repeat the above six commands for the other three interior lines to convert them to wide polylines.

Let us change the top view next. We have to convert both the outer circle with its six bolt slots and the interior circle. We begin with the bottom arc of the top view.

1. Return to the full view by typing

    zoom

    and pressing the space bar.
2. Type

    a

    for All and press Enter.
3. Type

    pedit

    and press Enter.

4. When AutoCAD responds with the prompt:

   Select polyline:

   move the selection box to the arc at the bottom of the top view where the coordinate location is

   4.5, 3.5

   Press the pick button.

5. As before, you are informed that the object you have selected is not a polyline and then asked if you want to convert this line to a polyline. Press the second mouse button or the Enter key to accept the default value of Y for yes.

6. Type

   w

   for Width and press Enter so you can change the polyline width.

7. Give the value

   0.02

   and press Enter. Notice that this bottom line becomes wider.

8. Type

   j

   for Join and press Enter to convert the remainder of the perimeter to a polyline.

9. We will use a window this time. Type

   w

   and press Enter.

10. To put a window around the entire top view, move to the lower-left side of the top view, near position

    2.0, 3.0

    and press Enter.

11. Move to the upper-right side, near location

    7.0, 8.0

and press Enter. The entire top view except the polyline becomes spotty to show that it is selected.

12. Press the second mouse button or the Enter key to complete the selection step. The entire perimeter, including the bolt slots, is converted to a wide polyline (Figure 8.17).

There remains one object line that is not drawn with a wide line — the medium-size circle at the center of the top view. Let us widen this now. This will be easy because we drew the circle with the Ellipse command and so it is already a polyline.

1. Type

    pedit

    and press Enter.

2. When AutoCAD responds with the prompt:

    Select polyline:

    move the selection box to the perimeter of the medium-size circle at the center of the top view. Press the pick button.

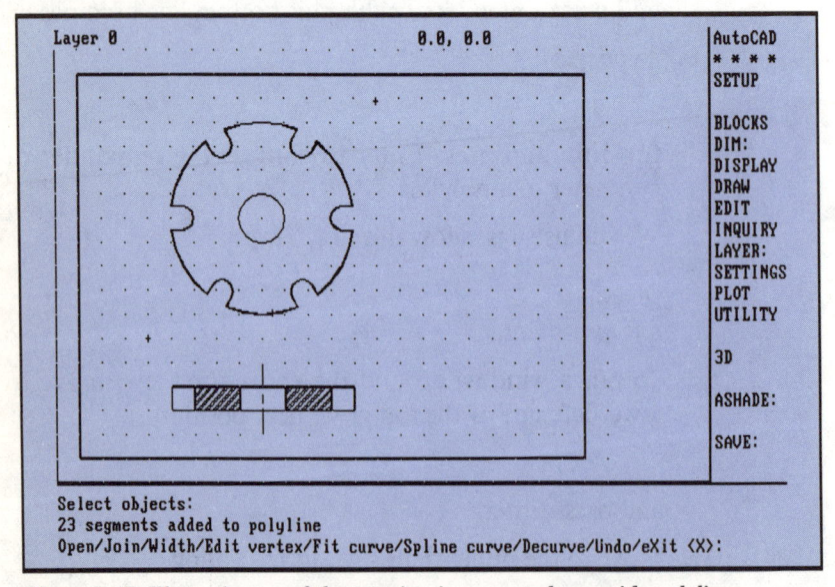

Figure 8.17: The perimeter of the top view is converted to a wide polyline

3. Since this circle is already a polyline, you are given options for changing the polyline. Type

    w

    for Width and press Enter to change the polyline width.

4. Give the value

    0.02

    and press Enter. Notice that the circle becomes wider.

5. Press Enter to complete the P-Edit command.

6. Type

    End

    and press Enter to complete the drawing.

In the following chapter you will add center lines and a cutting-plane line, along with dimensions to the drawing.

9

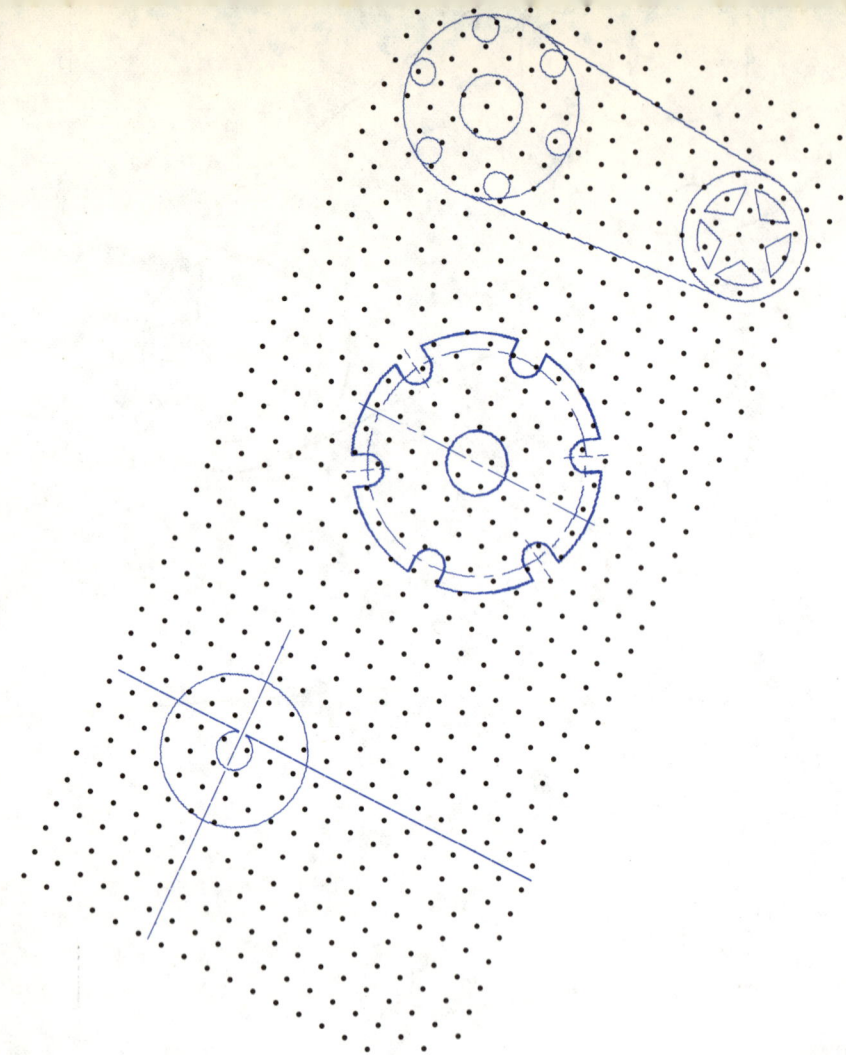

Inserting Labels, Notes, and Legends

Featuring:
- *Changing typefaces*
- *Creating a new layer*
- *Making text disappear*

Technical drawings usually require some type of text, or lettering. AutoCAD enables you to add such text quickly and easily. You have many type styles and sizes to choose from, which enhance the professional quality of your work. Though you may routinely use only a few type styles, as your expertise with AutoCAD increases, you may find other uses for this versatile feature. For example, you could create your own logo to appear on each of your drawings.

In this chapter you will add *legends* to your drawings of a bracket and a flange.

The legend gives information such as the name of the object that is described, the material it is to be made from, the scale, the name of the company responsible for the drawing, the name of the person making the drawing, and the date the drawing was made. In this chapter you'll add a legend along the lower edge of the bracket drawing. First you'll copy the bracket file, then work from the new file, called bracketd. Then if something goes wrong with your work, you can discard it and make another copy from the original.

New commands introduced in this chapter are

- Dtext to write characters on the screen
- Style to change the typeface and size
- Qtext to temporarily change text to boxes
- Layer to create and change layers

Let's copy the file and set up the drawing area now.

1. Start AutoCAD, select option 1, and press Enter to start a new drawing.
2. Type the line

    bracketd = bracket

    and press Enter.
3. If the heavy border around your drawing is not visible, or if the border does not fill the screen, give the command

    zoom

    and press the space bar.

4. Type

    a

    for All and press Enter. The drawing will just fill the screen.

5. Move the mouse and see if the coordinate readout on the top line changes. If not, press the F6 key to turn on the coordinate readout.

6. If the grid is not visible, press the F7 key to turn it on.

7. If the word *Snap* does not appear on the top line, press the F9 key to turn it on.

8. Move the mouse and see if the cursor snaps in increments of 0.5. If not, set Snap to 0.5.

How to Define the Legend Border

Since the legend will be placed along the bottom of the drawing, we can use the bottom and sides of the drawing border for part of the legend border.

Let us draw the top line of the legend border using the polyline command.

1. Type the command

    pline

    and press Enter to start a polyline.

2. Move the cursor to location

    0.5, 1.5

    on the lower-left edge of the border. Press the pick button to start a polyline.

3. Type

    w

    and press Enter to change the line width.

4. Type

   0.03

   and press Enter to set the beginning line width.

5. Press Enter again to set the ending line width to the beginning width.

6. If the word Ortho does not show on the top line, press the F8 key.

7. Move the cursor across the drawing to the right edge. When the coordinate readout shows

   11.0 <0

   press the pick button to establish the top of the legend border.

8. Press the second mouse button or the Enter key to complete the P-line command.

9. Press the F8 key to turn off Ortho mode.

10. Press F9 to turn off Snap mode.

11. Press F7 to turn off the grid.

How to Use AutoCAD Typefaces

You can easily add lettering to your AutoCAD drawings with the Dtext and Text commands. Several different typefaces or fonts are available. The standard or default font is called Txt. Like most of the AutoCAD fonts, Txt is a proportional typeface; that is, some letters such as uppercase M and W are wide, while lowercase letters such as i and l are thin. The advantage of Txt is that because it is simple, it can be rapidly drawn. This can be important for a drawing that has a lot of text. Each time the drawing is regenerated, the lettering must be redrawn. However, Txt is angular and drawn with a single-width line, and so is not as professional looking.

Another AutoCAD typeface is called Monotxt. It is similar to Txt except that all characters have the same width. That is, the letters are not proportionally spaced. This typeface is useful for creating tables in which you need to align columns vertically. Otherwise, you probably will not want to use this font.

Since Txt and Monotxt are angular and plain, it's likely you will want to choose a better-looking typeface. For example, the typeface called Simplex has a smoother appearance. It too is drawn with a constant-width line and so can be drawn almost as quickly as Txt, but it is more professional looking.

Because our drawings are small, we will choose a more complicated font named Complex. This typeface is particularly attractive because it uses variable-width lines. Consequently, it takes longer for AutoCAD to draw this typeface. If you create a drawing that has a large amount of lettering, there are two methods you can use to eliminate the time-consuming regeneration of text along with the rest of the drawing. We will consider these methods shortly. First let us change the typeface to Complex.

Changing the Typeface

Before we write the legend, let us change the typeface from the default Txt to Complex.

1. Give the command

    style

    and press Enter. AutoCAD responds with the prompt:

    Text style name (or?) <STANDARD>:

    telling you the name of the current typeface.

2. Press Enter to keep this name.

3. To the next prompt

    Font file <txt>:

    type

    complex

    or if you have AutoCAD release 9 or later, type

    romanc

    (for Roman-style complex), then press Enter.

4. The next prompt is

   Height <0.0>:

   requesting the text height. You can specify a height now, but if you want to change it later, you must run the Style command again. Since we want to use two sizes in the legend, give the answer

   0

   (zero) and press Enter. When text height is set to zero, you will always be asked for a value. Then you can easily change the height.

5. Press the Enter key five times to accept the current values for the remaining questions. Do not press ^C to skip this part.

Selecting the Typeface from the Screen

If you have AutoCAD release 9 or later, you can display the typefaces on the video screen. Then you can change the typeface by selection directly from the screen. If your version is earlier than release 9, skip over this section.

1. To display the typefaces on the screen, move the cursor to the top line. The top line changes to show several menu items.

2. Move the cursor to the right until the item *Options* changes.

3. Press the pick button to pull down a menu.

4. Move down the menu until the item *Fonts* changes (Figure 9.1).

5. Press the pick button to show the first seven fonts (Figure 9.2). You can select any of these fonts by putting the cursor on the corresponding box and pressing the pick button. However, there are two more screens.

6. Move the cursor to the box for *Next* and press the pick button to see the next screen.

7. Seven more fonts are displayed, including Greek letters. Move the cursor to the box for *Next* and press the pick button.

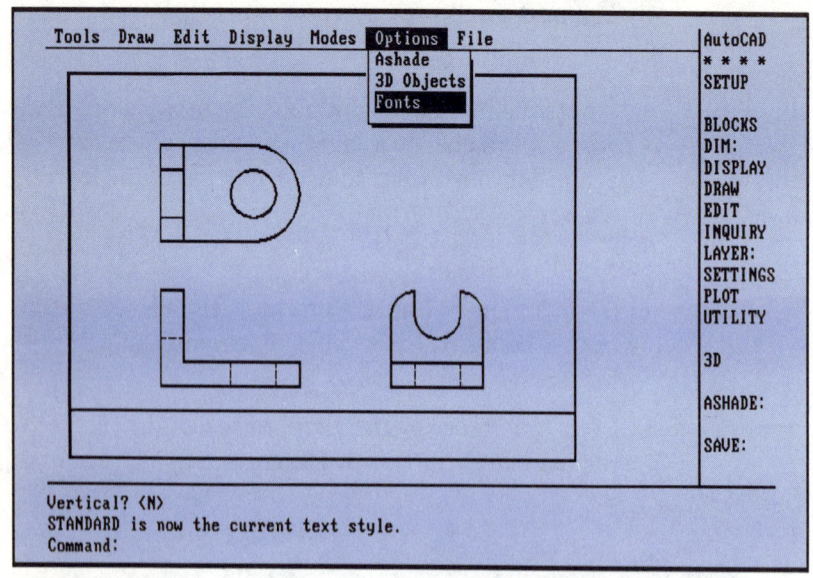

Figure 9.1: The Options pull-down menu for changing fonts

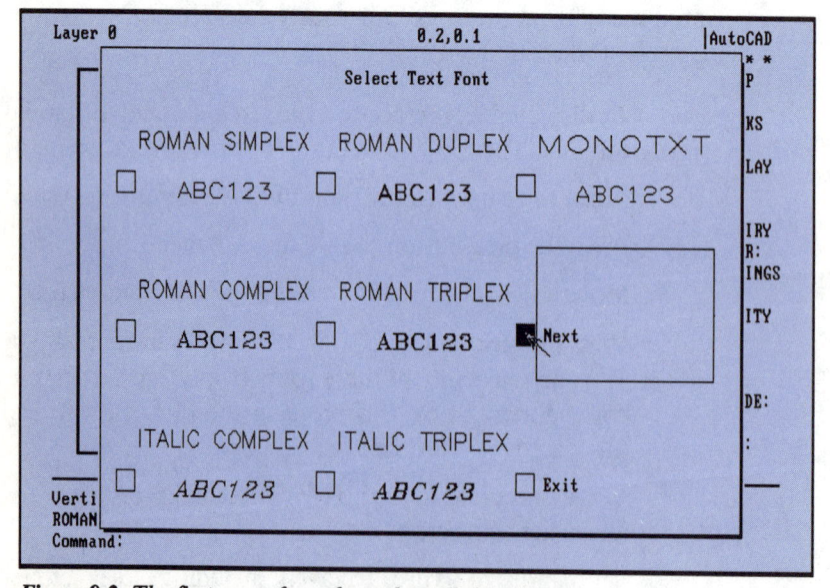

Figure 9.2: The first seven fonts from the pull-down menu

8. The third screen shows sets of special symbols for astronomy, mapping, and music.
9. Move the cursor to the *Exit* box and press the pick button to return to the drawing screen.

How to Write Text in the Legend Border

Let us write the legend next. The bracket legend will include the company name, the drawing name, and a few details about the drawing. There are two AutoCAD commands for writing text—Text and Dtext. With the Text command, you do not see the results of your typing until you have completed a line and pressed Enter. By contrast, with the Dtext (dynamic text) command, each letter appears on the screen as you type it.

1. Give the command

    dtext

    and press Enter.

2. Move to the location

    0.8, 0.8

    and press the pick button to specify where the letters will begin.

3. To the prompt for height, type

    0.25

    and press Enter.

4. The next prompt asks for rotation. Press Enter to accept the default value of zero. The next characters you type will appear on the screen.

5. Press the CapsLock key to enter text in all capital letters.

6. Type the word

    COMPANY

and see that each letter appears on the screen as you type it. If you type an incorrect letter, press the Backspace key to erase it.

7. Type three spaces.
8. Type the word

   BRACKET

   and press Enter. Notice that the cursor moves down one line. AutoCAD is waiting for another line of text.
9. Press Enter a second time to compete the Dtext command.
10. Press the CapsLock key to turn off uppercase.

The remaining text describing the drawing will be smaller.

1. Press the second mouse button or the Enter key to restart the Dtext command. The letters you just wrote temporarily become spotty.
2. Move to the position

   5.9, 1.1

   and press the pick button to start the next line of text.
3. Set the text height to the value

   0.2

   a little smaller this time.
4. Press Enter to accept the current rotation.
5. Type the line

   Make one, Use CRS, Full scale

   and watch the letters appear as you type them. (CRS stands for cold-rolled steel.)
6. Press Enter to continue with text on the next line.
7. Type the line

   (the date), Dr. by (your name)

8. Press Enter twice to complete the Dtext command. Your drawing should look like Figure 9.3.

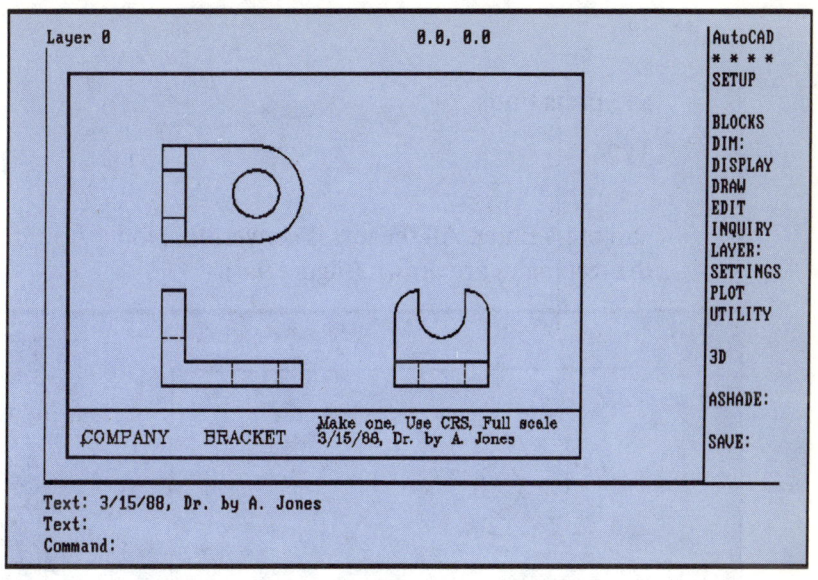

Figure 9.3: A legend is added to the drawing of the bracket

How to Speed Up Text Regeneration

You changed the text style from the initial Txt to the more pleasing Complex. However, AutoCAD takes a considerable amount of time to redraw, or regenerate, the letters. You can use two methods to speed up text regeneration—using the QText command and using Layers. Let's look first at QText.

Using the QText Command

One way to speed up regeneration is to temporarily replace each line of text with a rectangle. You can do this using the Quiet Text, or QText, command. Of course, you cannot read the text in this form. However, you may wish to trade this inconvenience for speed since you do not need to see the legend while you are working on other parts of the drawing. Let us use QText to change the legend to rectangles.

1. Give the command

    qtext

    and press Enter.

2. Type

   on

   and press Enter.

3. Type

   regen

   and press Enter. All the text is converted. Notice how quickly the rectangles are drawn (Figure 9.4).

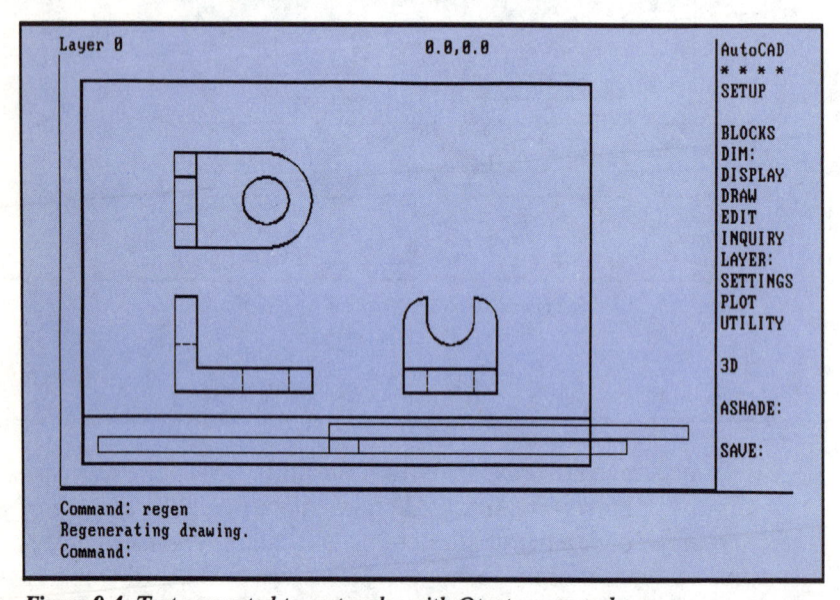

Figure 9.4: Text converted to rectangles with Qtext command

4. To reverse the effect, type

   qtext

   and press Enter.

5. Type

   off

   and press Enter.

6. Type

   regen

   and press Enter. This time, it takes longer to regenerate the screen because the letters have to be drawn.

Let us consider another method for speeding up text regeneration.

Speeding Up Text Regeneration with the Layer Command

While working with AutoCAD, you may have noticed that the words *Layer 0* appear on the upper-left corner of the screen. AutoCAD allows you to organize your drawings on more than one *layer,* or level. You can think of these layers as transparent overlays. The number of layers you can create for each drawing is unlimited, and you can choose to display them in any combination. As your drawings become more complex, you will want to show different aspects on separate layers. For example, you can put all text on one layer, which will make modification easier. You can use layers in AutoCAD for many different uses. In this chapter we will use layers to display text.

All of your work so far has taken place in layer 0. Let us create a new layer named Legend, and then move the legend text to it.

1. Give the command

    layer

    and press Enter.

2. Type

    n

    for New and press Enter.

3. To the prompt

    New layer name(s):

    type

    legend

    and press Enter.

4. Press Enter again to complete the Layer command. This creates a new layer.

5. Type

    change

    and press Enter.

6. To the prompt

    Select objects:

    move the selection box to each row of lettering and then press the pick button. The entire row is selected.

7. When all the lettering is spotty, press the second mouse button to complete the selection step.

8. Type

    p

    for Properties and press Enter.

9. Type

    la

    for Layer and press Enter.

10. Type

    legend

    and press Enter.

11. Press Enter again to complete the Change command. You have just moved all the legend text to the new layer. Now we can make the letters disappear by turning off the layer.

How to Turn Off a Layer

In this section you turn off, that is, make invisible, the text in the legend by turning off a layer. Before you turn off a layer, you must be sure that layer is not current. Let us first change to the Legend layer and then change back to layer 0.

1. Give the command

    layer

    and press Enter.

2. Type

    s

    for Set and press Enter.

3. Type

   legend

   and press Enter.

4. Press Enter again. Notice that the words *Layer LEGEND* appear in the upper-left corner.

5. To change back to layer 0, press Enter to repeat the Layer command.

6. Type

   s

   for Set and press Enter.

7. Type

   0

   (zero) and press Enter.

8. Press Enter again to complete the Layer command. Notice that layer 0 is current.

9. Press Enter to restart the Layer command.

10. Type

    off

    and press Enter.

11. Type

    legend

    and press Enter.

12. Press Enter to complete the Layer command.

The legend lettering disappears from the screen because the Legend layer is off. Now screen regeneration will be faster.

How to Turn a Layer Back On

Let's turn the lettering back on so it will be visible.

1. To turn on the Legend layer, type

    layer

    and press Enter.

2. Type

    on

    and press Enter.

3. Type

    legend

    and press Enter.

4. Press Enter to complete the Layer command.

How to Reset the Text Height

In the previous section you set the text height to zero so you could adjust it as you went along. However, in the next chapter, we are going to use a constant height. Therefore, let us set the text height to the value we need before we save the drawing.

1. Give the command

    style

    and press Enter. AutoCAD responds with a prompt that identifies the current typeface.

2. Since we want to continue with the current typeface, press Enter.

3. Press Enter again to accept the current font file.

4. The next prompt is

    Height <0.0>:

    requesting the text height. This time, type

    0.2

    and press Enter.

Inserting Labels, Notes, and Legends 227

5. Press the Enter key five times to accept the default response for the remaining questions. As before, do not press ^C to skip this part.

6. Type

   end

   and press Enter to save your drawing and return to the Main menu.

How to Create the Legend for the Flange

In this section you create the legend for the flange you drew previously. First copy your drawing; then if something goes wrong with your work, you can discard it and make another copy from the original.

1. Select the AutoCAD option 1 and press Enter to start a new drawing.

2. Type

   flanged = flange

   and press Enter. This will create a new file named flanged that is identical to the original file named flange.

3. If the heavy border around your drawing is not visible, or if the border does not fill the screen, give the command

   zoom

   and press the space bar.

4. Type

   a

   for All and press Enter. The drawing will just fill the screen.

5. Move the mouse and see that the coordinate readout on the top line changes. If it does not, press the F6 key.

6. If the grid is not visible, press the F7 key to turn it on.

7. If the word *Snap* does not appear on the top line, press the F9 key to turn it on.

8. Move the mouse and see if the cursor snaps in increments of 0.5. If not, set Snap to 0.5 as you did previously.

Drawing the Legend Border

Let us draw a small legend box in the lower-right corner using the polyline command.

1. Type the command

   pline

   and press Enter to start a polyline.

2. Move the cursor to the border at the bottom, near the right side. Stop at the location

   7.5, 0.5

   Press the pick button to start a polyline.

3. Type

   w

   and press Enter to change the line width.

4. Type

   0.03

   and press Enter to set the beginning line width.

5. Press Enter again to set the ending line width to the beginning width.

6. If the word *Ortho* does not show on the top line, press the F8 key.

7. Move the cursor up five grid points until the coordinate readout shows

   2.5 <90

   Press the pick button to establish the left edge of the legend border.

8. Move right to the drawing border. The coordinate readout shows

   4.0 <0

   Press Enter to establish the top line of the legend box.

9. Press the second mouse button or the Enter key to complete the P-line command.

Drawing an Interior Line

Let us add an interior line to the legend box.

1. Type the command

   line

   and press Enter.

2. Move to the left edge of the legend border, to the location

   7.5, 2.0

   Press the pick button to start a line.

3. Move right until you reach the drawing border. When the coordinate readout shows

   4.0 <0

   press the pick button.

4. Press the second mouse button or the Enter key to complete the Line command.

5. Press the F8 key to turn off Ortho mode.

6. Press the F9 key to turn off Snap mode.

Setting the Variable Text Height

Let us set the text style to Complex and the text height to zero so we can change it as we work.

1. Give the command

   style

and press Enter. AutoCAD responds with a prompt that identifies the current typeface.

2. Press Enter to use the current name.

3. Type

    complex

    and press Enter.

4. The next prompt requests the text height. Type

    0

    (zero) and press Enter.

5. Press the Enter key five times to accept the default response for the remaining questions. As before, do not press ^C to skip this part.

Writing Text in a Separate Layer

For the previous drawing you created a new layer, then moved the legend text to that layer using the Change command. In this section you will also create a new layer named Legend. However, you will make that layer current before writing text. Then the text will automatically be placed in the new layer.

1. Give the command

    layer

    and press Enter.

2. Type

    m

    for Make and press Enter.

3. Type

    legend

    and press Enter.

4. Press Enter again to create a new layer and make it current.

Notice the words *Layer LEGEND* in the upper-left corner of the screen. Now the next items you create on the screen will be placed in layer Legend. Don't forget to change back to layer 0 before you turn off layer Legend. (We will do this later in the chapter.)

Writing Text in the Legend Border

Let us add text to the legend using the Dtext command.

1. Give the command

    dtext

    and press Enter.

2. Move to the location

    8.0, 2.5

    and press the pick button to specify where the letters will begin.

3. To the prompt for height, type

    0.25

    and press Enter.

4. The next prompt asks for rotation. Press Enter to accept the current value of zero.

5. Press the CapsLock key.

6. Type the word

    COMPANY

    and see that each letter appears on the screen as you type it. If you type an incorrect letter, press the Backspace key to erase it.

7. Press Enter and see that the cursor moves down under the first letter.

8. Type the word

    FLANGE

    and press Enter.

9. Press Enter a second time to complete the Dtext command.

10. Press the CapsLock key to turn off uppercase.

You will make the remaining text smaller.

1. Press the second mouse button or the Enter key to restart the Dtext command.
2. Move to the position

    7.8, 1.6

    and press the pick button to start the next line of text.
3. Set the text height to the value

    0.2

    a little smaller this time.
4. Press Enter to accept the current rotation.
5. Type the line

    Make one, Use HRS

    and press Enter. (HRS stands for hot-rolled steel.)
6. Type in the next three lines

    Full scale
    Dr. by (your name)
    (the date)

    pressing Enter at the end of each line.
7. Press Enter a second time to complete the Dtext command. Your drawing should look like Figure 9.5. Notice the words *Layer LEGEND* in the upper-left corner of the screen.

Changing to a Different Layer

Now that you have written the legend text into a separate layer, let us change back to layer 0. Then you can turn off the Legend text.

1. Type

    layer

    and press Enter.

Inserting Labels, Notes, and Legends 233

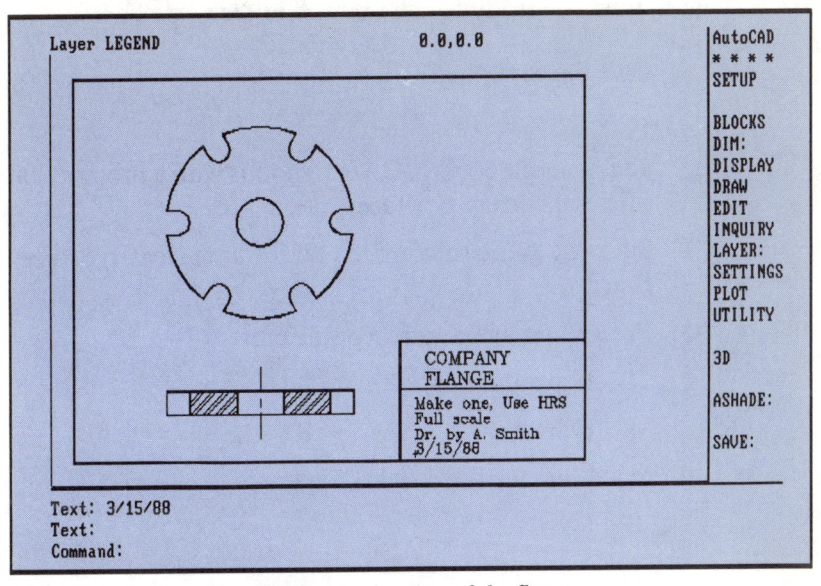

Figure 9.5: A legend is added to the drawing of the flange

2. Type

    s

    for Set and press Enter.

3. Type

    0

    (zero) and press Enter.

4. Press Enter to complete the Layer command. Look for the word *Layer 0* in the upper-left corner of the screen. Now you can turn off the text in layer Legend.

*F*ixing the Text Height

In the previous section you set the text height to zero so you could adjust it as you went along. Let us now set the height to a constant value so it will be ready for an exercise in the next chapter.

1. Give the command

    style

    and press Enter. AutoCAD responds with a prompt that identifies the current typeface.

2. Since we want to continue with the current typeface, press Enter.

3. Press Enter again to accept the current font file.

4. The next prompt is

    Height <0.0>:

    requesting the text height. Type

    0.2

    and press Enter.

6. Press the Enter key five times to accept the default response for the remaining questions. As before, do not press ^C to skip this part.

7. Type

    end

    and press Enter to save your drawing and return to the Main menu.

10

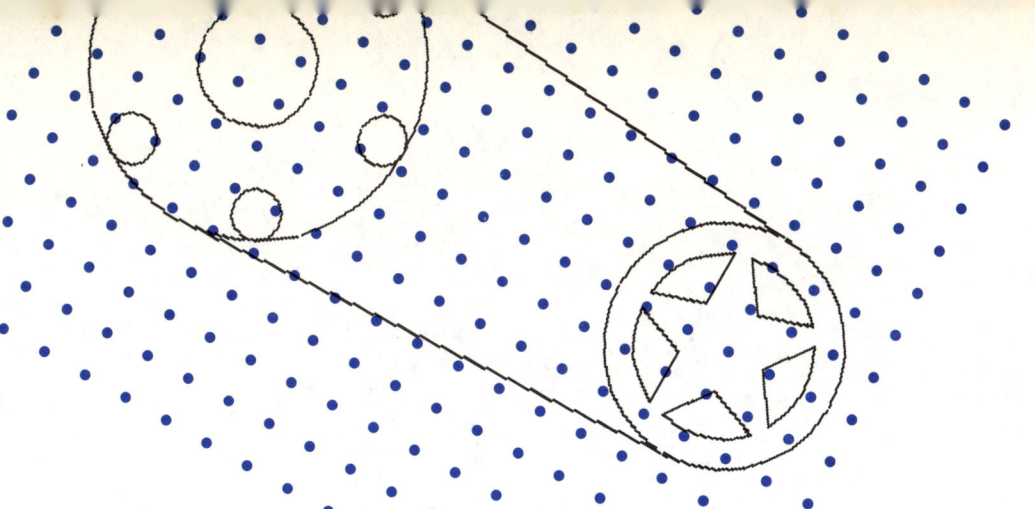

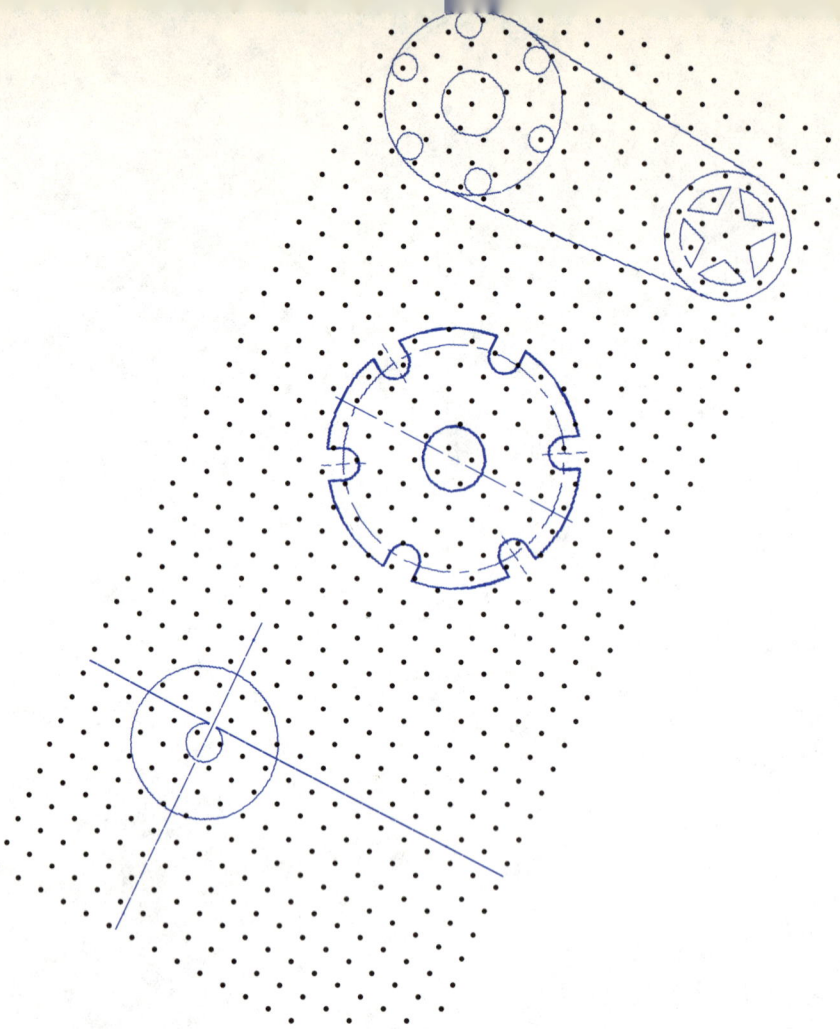

Adding the Dimensions to Your Drawings

Featuring:
    Using the one-point method
    Using the two-point method

You have created several scale drawings, which could be called *shape descriptions,* in the previous chapters. Before these drawings can be used to construct an object, you must include specific information about their size. That is, dimension information must be added to the drawing.

In this chapter you will use several different methods to add dimensions to the drawings you made in the previous chapters. Commands introduced in this chapter are

- Dim to enter the dimension subcommands including
  - Hor for a horizontal dimension
  - Ver for a vertical dimension
  - Dimcen to set the center line style
  - Rad to dimension a radius
  - Dia to dimension a diameter
  - Leader to construct a leader
  - Align to align a dimension with an object

Before we begin, let us review the principles of dimensioning.

Principles of Dimensioning

The *dimension* for each part of a drawing is given as a number that represents the linear distance between two points. The *dimension line* shows the orientation and extent of the dimension. For a machine drawing, a dimension line is a thin line drawn on both sides of the number or dimension. Arrowheads are placed at each end of this line. Thus, the dimension appears in the center of the broken dimension line. By contrast, a dimension line on an architectural drawing is continuous and the dimension is placed above the line. Furthermore, circles or shapes other than arrows might mark the ends of the dimension lines. AutoCAD follows the conventions of machine drawings. However, you can change AutoCAD so it will follow the architectural convention.

Sometimes a *leader* is used instead of a dimension line. The leader is a thin line that connects the dimension or other note to the object being referenced. Leaders are commonly used for dimensioning a diameter or a radius.

Dimension lines do not normally touch the object referenced. Rather, an *extension line,* a thin line extending from the object, meets the dimension line at a right angle.

A *center line* is a thin line that marks the center of circular symmetry. This line is not continuous; it is drawn with alternate long and short dashes. Sometimes, it is convenient to use a center line as an extension line.

An important principle in dimensioning machine drawings is to avoid redundancy. (Of course, there must be enough information to completely describe the object.) For example, if you give the overall dimensions for a rectangular item, then you must not give a sequence of dimensions along a direction that can be added up to the overall length. That is, you must omit one of the dimensions in the series when the overall length is given. On the other hand, the overall length is often omitted where there is circular symmetry.

Let us begin with the bracket you drew in Chapters 6 and 9.

Continuing with the Bracket Drawing

In the previous chapter you copied your bracket drawing to a file named bracketd. Then you added a legend. We will continue our work with this drawing by creating a new layer for the dimensions.

1. Select option 2 to continue with an existing drawing and press Enter.
2. Type

    bracketd

    and press Enter. Your drawing will appear on the screen.
3. Give the command

    layer

    and press Enter.

4. Type

   m

   for Make and press Enter.

5. Type

   dim

   and press Enter.

6. Press Enter a second time. Notice that the words *Layer DIM* appear on the top line.

How to Dimension Using the One-Point Method

Let us dimension the front view first. AutoCAD can automatically calculate the length of each part. However, there are two ways to tell AutoCAD which part to dimension. With the one-point method, you select a point somewhere along a line and AutoCAD calculates the length. With the two-point method, you select the two end points of a part and AutoCAD calculates the corresponding distance. You'll use the simpler one-point method first. You'll use the second method when a single dimension spans more than one line segment or has a gap.

1. Enlarge the front view by giving the command

   zoom

   and pressing the space bar.

2. Type

   w

   for Window and press Enter.

3. Move the cursor to the left edge to position

   1.2, 5.7

   and press the pick button to start a window.

4. Move to location

   7.3, 1.5

   and press the pick button to complete the Zoom command. The entire front view and part of the top should be visible.

To start the dimensioning procedure, you'll use the Dim command. This command switches over to a set of dimensioning commands. After you complete each dimension command, you are returned to the Dim: prompt so you can give additional dimension commands. (You can return to regular commands by giving the ^C command.)

5. Type the command

    dim

    and press Enter to start the dimension subcommands. Notice that the prompt *Dim:* appears on the bottom line.

Good. Now you're ready to specify your first dimension.

Specifying a Vertical Dimension

You will dimension a vertical edge of the front view first.

1. Next to the Dim: prompt, type

    ver

    for Vertical dimension, and press Enter. The prompt asks you to specify either the location of the first extension line (the two-point method) or to type **return** to select the line to be dimensioned (the one-point method).

2. Press the second mouse button (of course, you can also press Enter or the space bar) to choose the one-point method. The cursor changes to a selection box.

3. Move the cursor to the left edge of the front view, to location

    2.5, 2.5

    and press the pick button to select the left edge.

4. The next prompt asks for the dimension line location. Move the selection box to location

    1.8, 3.0

    to the left of the left edge and press the pick button.

5. The next prompt is

    Dimension text <2.0>:

    telling you AutoCAD has calculated the value 2.0 for this dimension. Press the second mouse button or Enter to accept this value (Figure 10.1).

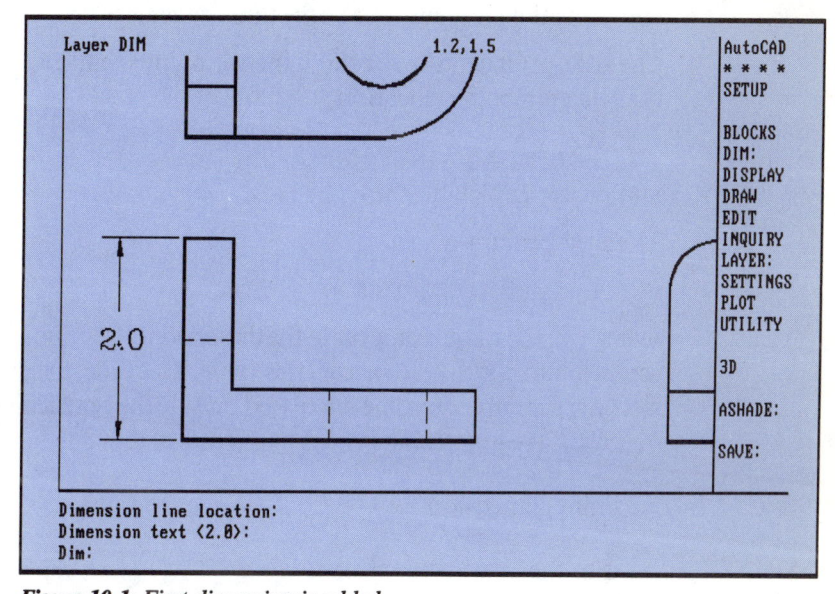

Figure 10.1: First dimension is added

Notice that the Vertical command has been completed. However, the familiar Command: prompt does not appear on the bottom line of the screen. Instead, the Dim: prompt is there. You will remain in the dimension commands until you press ^C.

Specifying a Horizontal Dimension

You will dimension a horizontal edge next.

1. Next to the Dim: prompt, type

    hor

    for Horizontal dimension, and press Enter.

2. Press the second mouse button or Enter to choose the one-point method. As before, the cursor changes to a selection box.

3. Move the cursor to the top line of the front view to location

    2.7, 4.0

    and press the pick button to select this edge.

4. The next prompt asks for the dimension line location. Move the selection box to location

    2.7, 4.3

    and press the pick button.

5. The next prompt is

    Dimension text <0.5>:

    telling you the value to appear in the dimension. Press the second mouse button or Enter to accept this value. This time, the dimension and the dimension line are placed outside the extension lines because there is no room inside.

The remaining dimension for the front view is the right edge.

1. Next to the Dim: prompt, type

    ver

    for Vertical dimension and press Enter.

2. Press Enter to choose the one-point method. The cursor changes to a selection box.

3. Move the cursor to the right edge of the front view to location

    5.5, 2.2

    and press the pick button to select this edge.

4. The next prompt asks for the dimension line location. Move to location

    6.0, 2.7

    and press the pick button.

5. Press the second mouse button or Enter to accept the dimension of 0.5. As with the previous example, the dimension and the dimension line are placed outside the extension lines because there is no room inside (Figure 10.2).

6. Press ^C to leave the Dimension subcommands.

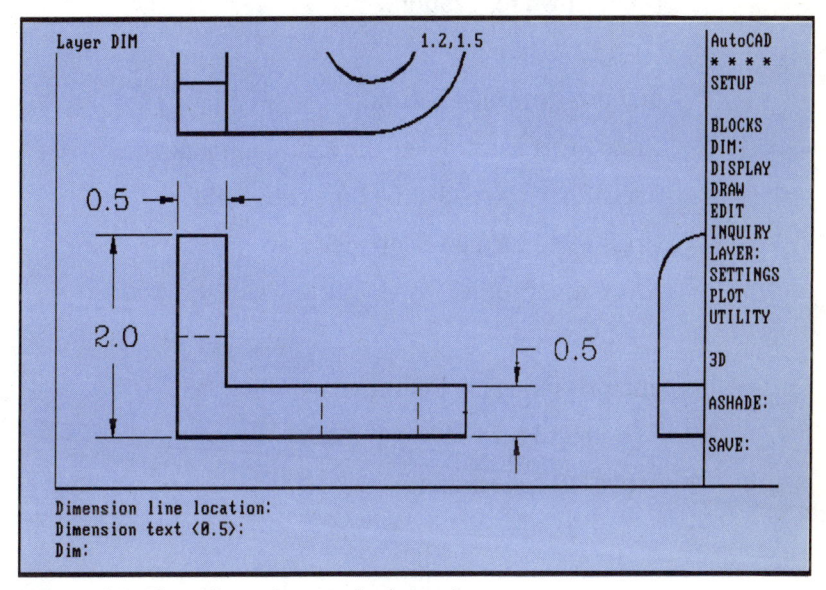

Figure 10.2: Three dimensions on the front view

Adding Center Lines

We add two center lines to complete the front view.

Press F8 to turn on Ortho mode.

2. Press F7 to turn on the grid.

3. Press F9 to turn on Snap mode.

If the grid points are separated by 1 unit rather than 0.5, set snap spacing to 0.5 and then set the grid spacing to the snap spacing.

4. Type

line

and press Enter.

5. Move to coordinate position

    4.5, 3.0

    and press the pick button.
6. Press F9 to turn off Snap mode.
7. Move down to location

    1.4 <270

    and press the pick button.
8. Press Enter to complete the Line command.
9. Press Enter to restart the Line command.
10. Press F9 to turn on Snap mode.
11. Move to location

    3.5, 3.5

    and press the pick button.
12. Press F9 to turn off Snap mode.
13. Move left to location

    1.4 <180

    and press the pick button.
14. Press Enter to complete the Line command.
15. Press F7 to turn off the grid.
16. Press F8 to turn off Ortho mode.
17. Give the command

    change

    and press Enter.
18. Move the selection box to the line you just drew and press the pick button.
19. Move the selection box to the other new line and press the pick button.
20. Press Enter to complete the selection.

21. Press Enter to complete the selection.
22. Type

    p

    for Property change and press Enter.
23. Type

    Lt

    for Line Type and press Enter.
24. Type

    center

    for Center line and press Enter.
25. Press Enter to change the lines.

Let us dimension the top view next.

How to Use Other Dimensioning Techniques

The screen currently shows the enlarged front view and part of the top view. You can fill the screen with an enlarged top view by giving the Zoom command twice. First zoom back to the full view and then zoom to the top view. However, it is easier to do this with the Dynamic Zoom command.

Dynamic Zooming to the Top View

The AutoCAD Dynamic Zoom command allows you to easily move from one enlarged view to another. When you give this command, the screen changes from the first zoomed view to show the entire drawing. The first zoomed view is outlined in a dotted box. You can move a second box anywhere on the screen to select the next zoomed view.

1. Give the command

    zoom

    and press the space bar.

2. Type

   d

   for Dynamic and press Enter. The screen shows the entire drawing, with a dotted box around the front view (Figure 10.3).

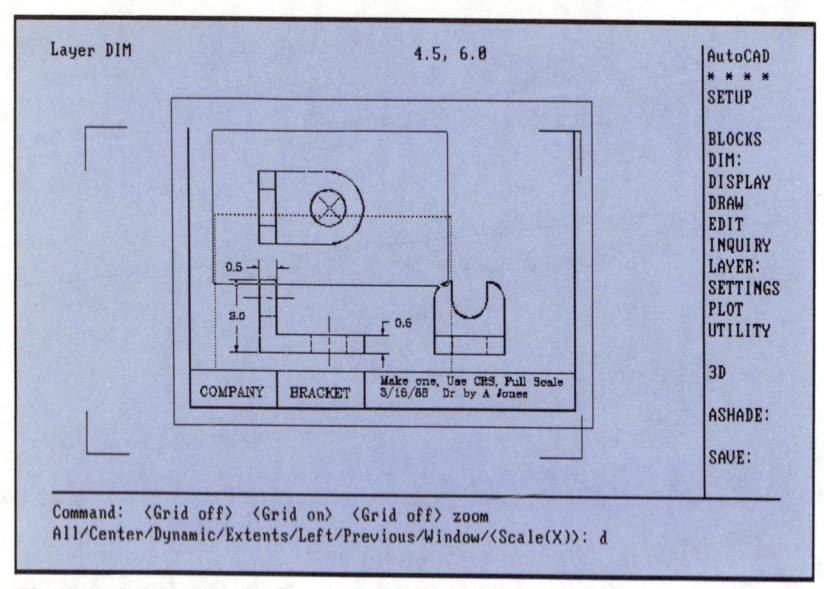

Figure 10.3: The Dynamic Zoom command lets you change views

3. Move the cursor and watch a second box, with an X in the center, move on the screen.

4. Move the box over the top view until the X is centered on the circle. When the coordinate readout shows approximately

   4.5, 6.0

   press Enter. The top view now fills the screen.

Establishing the Center Line Form

Before we dimension the top view, let us change the way center lines are shown. As you have seen, center lines are drawn with alternating long and short dashes. When two center lines cross at the center of a circle, it is customary to place a plus sign at the center. Then long dashes are drawn from the plus in each of the four directions. Thus the two center lines cross at their short dashes. AutoCAD can draw center lines in this way. However, this is not the default setting. Initially, AutoCAD marks circle centers with just a plus mark. Let us change that.

1. Type

    dim

    and press Enter to change to the dimension subcommands.

2. Type

    dimcen

    for Dimension center of circle, and press Enter.

3. The prompt gives the current value of 0.1. When this value is positive, a plus mark is placed at the center of a circle. If we make the value negative, AutoCAD will then place crossed center lines on the circle. Type the value

    -0.1

    and press Enter. Notice that the Dim: prompt returns to the bottom line.

How to Dimension a Radius

In this section you dimension the semicircular arc at the right side of the top view. As with the previous linear dimensioning, AutoCAD can automatically write the dimension and place the dimension line. AutoCAD will also add crossed center lines. For the previous dimensions, we accepted the value that AutoCAD calculated. This time, however, we will change it slightly.

1. If the word *Ortho* appears on the top line, press the F8 key to turn it off.

2. Check that the prompt *Dim:* appears on the bottom line. On the other hand, if *Command:* appears, type

   Dim

   and press Enter.

3. To dimension the arc at the right side of the top view, type

   rad

   for Radius, and press Enter.

4. The prompt asks you to select the arc or circle. Move the selection box to the upper-right edge of the arc, near location

   5.2, 6.7

   and press the pick button.

5. The next prompt shows the calculated radius of the circle:

   Dimension text <1.0>:

   If you accept this value by pressing Enter, AutoCAD prefixes the number with the letter *R* to denote a radius. However, we will change this so the letter *R* appears at the end of the number. Type

   1.0R

   and press Enter. This overrides AutoCAD's value.

6. Finally, the prompt

   Text does not fit. Enter leader length for text:

   appears. AutoCAD is telling you that the dimension text will not fit inside the circle. We will tell AutoCAD to place the dimension outside the circle. Type the value

   0.5

   and press Enter. Alternatively, you can move upward and to the right to location

   0.5 <45

   and press the Enter key. The screen should look like Figure 10.4. Notice that crossed center lines were automatically added along with the leader and dimension because you changed Dimcen to a negative value.

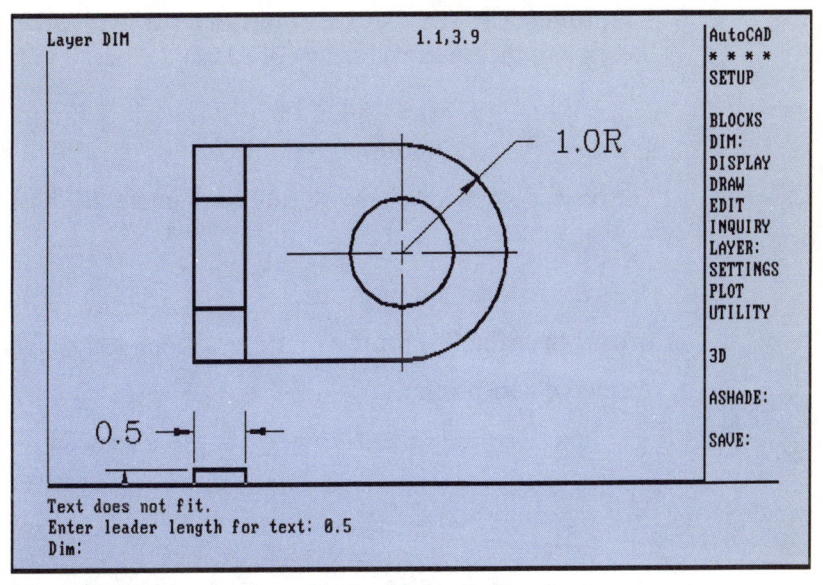

Figure 10.4: Dimension for radius is added to the top view

How to Dimension a Diameter

In this section you use the Diameter command to dimension the circle in the top view that is concentric with the semicircle. Unfortunately, because the circle and the arc share the same center, the two sets of center lines will overlap to produce continuous lines, and thus will no longer look like center lines. Therefore, we will remove this dimension with the U command. In the next section, we will dimension the diameter another way.

1. Check that the prompt *Dim:* appears on the bottom line. On the other hand, if *Command:* appears, type

    dim

    and press Enter.

2. To dimension the circle in the top view type

    dia

    for Diameter, and press Enter.

3. The prompt asks you to select the arc or circle. Move the selection box to the lower-right edge of the circle, near location

    4.9, 5.7

   and press the pick button.

4. The next prompt shows the calculated diameter of the circle:

    Dimension text <1.0>:

   Press Enter to accept this value.

5. Record the value 1.0 for use in the next step.

6. When the next prompt

    Text does not fit. Enter leader length for text:

   appears, Type

    0.9

   and press Enter. AutoCAD adds a second set of crossed center lines and the caption ϕ1.0 to designate a diameter.

7. Let us remove this last dimension and redo it another way. Type

    u

   for Undo and press Enter to remove the dimension.

8. Press F7 twice to restore the erased center lines.

How to Dimension with the Leader Command

In this section you dimension the circle in the top view using the Leader command. In the previous section you dimensioned the circle in the top view using the Diameter command. Then you erased this dimension with the U command. The Leader command lets you draw your own sequence of line segments for dimensioning a radius or diameter. Furthermore, it does not add center lines.

1. Check that the prompt *Dim:* appears on the bottom line. If not, type

    dim

   and press Enter.

2. To dimension the circle in the top view, type

   leader

   and press Enter.

3. The prompt asks you to select the starting position of the leader. Move the cursor to the lower-right edge of the circle, at location

   4.9, 5.7

   and press the pick button.

4. The next prompt asks for the To point. Move the cursor in the lower-right direction, to location

   0.9 <315

   Notice that a new line follows your cursor. (If the new line is horizontal or vertical, turn off Ortho mode with F8.) Press the pick button to fix this part of the leader.

5. You can continue in this way, adding more segments to the leader, pressing the pick button each time you move. Then, AutoCAD will automatically add a horizontal segment for you if your last segment is not horizontal. However, we just need one line segment. Therefore, press Enter to complete the leader. AutoCAD adds a short horizontal segment.

6. AutoCAD next requests the dimension text. Type

   1.0DIA

   and press Enter to define the diameter of the circle. The view should look like the right side of Figure 10.5.

Good. Continue to the next exercise to add the third and last dimension to the top view.

1. Check that the prompt *Dim:* is shown on the bottom line.
2. Type

   hor

   for Horizontal dimension and press Enter.

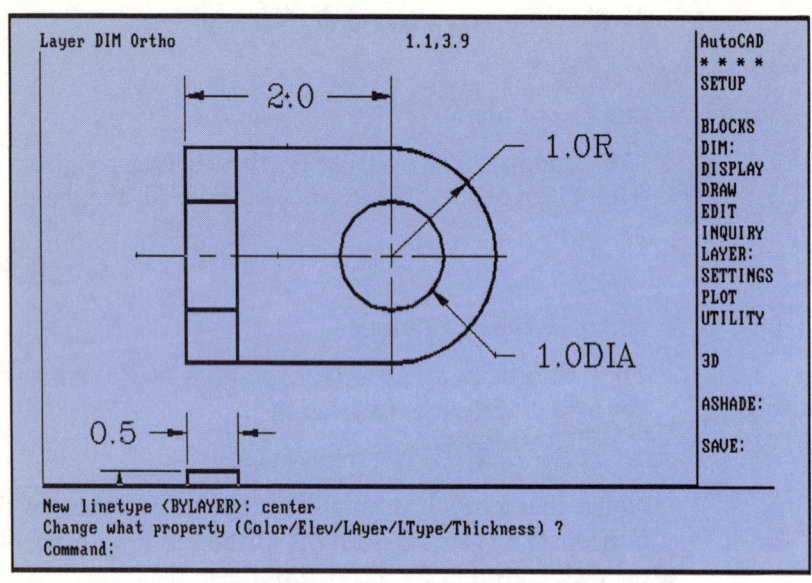

Figure 10.5: The dimension for the diameter is added to the top view

3. Press Enter to choose the one-point method. The cursor changes to a selection box.

4. Move the cursor to the top edge of the top view to location

    3.5, 7.0

    and press the pick button to select the top edge.

5. The next prompt asks for the dimension line location. Move to location

    3.5, 7.5

    and press the pick button.

6. The next prompt is

    Dimension text <2.0>:

    telling you the value that will appear in the dimension. Press Enter to accept this value. Notice that the right extension is connected to the vertical center line (Figure 10.5).

7. Type ^C to exit the dimension subcommands.

*E*xtending the Center Line

Let us extend the horizontal center line to the left edge.

1. Press F8 to turn on Ortho mode.
2. Type

    line

    and press Enter.
3. Type the Osnap command

    end

    and press Enter to start the new line.
4. Move to the approximate coordinate position

    3.4, 6.0

    and press the pick button. This locks the new line to the left end of the horizontal center line.
5. Move the cursor left to the coordinate position

    1.4<180

    and press the pick button.
6. Press the second mouse button to complete the Line command.

*C*onverting a Line to a Center-Line Style

The center line you just drew is solid. Let us convert it to the style of a center line—alternating long and short segments.

1. Give the command

    change

    and press Enter.
2. The cursor changes to a selection box and the prompt asks you to select the objects to change. Type

    L

    for Last line drawn and press Enter.

3. Press the second mouse button to complete the selection step.
4. For the next prompt, type

    p

    for Property change and press Enter.
5. To the next prompt:

    Change what property:

    type

    lt

    for Line type and press Enter.
6. The next prompt requests the line-type name. Answer

    center

    and press Enter.
7. Press Enter to the next prompt. The new line changes to a center line (Figure 10.5).

Let us move on to the right view.

How to Dimension the Right View

We have to add two dimensions and some center lines to the right view. Let us use the Dynamic Zoom command to move that view.

1. If the word *Command:* does not appear on the bottom line of the screen, give the ^C command.
2. Give the command

    zoom

    and press the space bar.
3. Type

    d

for Dynamic and press Enter. As before, the screen shows the entire drawing, with a dotted box around the previous view.

4. Move the cursor until the box with an X in it moves to the right view. When the coordinate readout shows approximately

   8.5, 3.5

   press Enter. The right view fills the screen.

*A*dding a Center Line to the Slot

In this section, you will add crossed center lines to the circular part of the slot.

1. Type

   dim

   and press Enter.

2. Give the command

   center

   and press Enter.

3. Move to the circular part of the slot at coordinate position

   8.9, 3.2

   and press the pick button. Crossed center lines appear in the slot. (If a plus appears, remove it with the U command. Then change Dimcen to -0.1 as you did previously.)

*D*imensioning the Slot

1. Next to the Dim: prompt, type

   hor

   for Horizontal dimension, and press Enter. Previously, we used the one-point method to identify a length. However, this time we are dimensioning an opening. Therefore, we must use the two-point method.

2. Type the Osnap command

    int

    for Intersection, and press Enter.

3. Move the cursor to the upper-left opening of the slot at coordinate position

    8.1, 4.1

    and press the pick button.

4. Type the Osnap command

    int

    again and press Enter.

5. Move the cursor to the upper-right opening of the slot at coordinate position

    9.0, 4.1

    and press the pick button.

6. Move the cursor to

    8.5, 4.2

    to select the location of the dimension.

7. The next prompt is

    Dimension text <1.0>:

    telling you the value to appear in the dimension. Press the second mouse button or Enter to accept this value. The dimension and the dimension line are placed outside the extension lines because there is not enough room inside (Figure 10.6).

Notice that the last dimension was placed outside the extension lines on the right side. When you use the two-point method, you can choose the end at which the dimension is placed. Thus, in this example, the dimension was placed on the right because the right end was chosen after the left end.

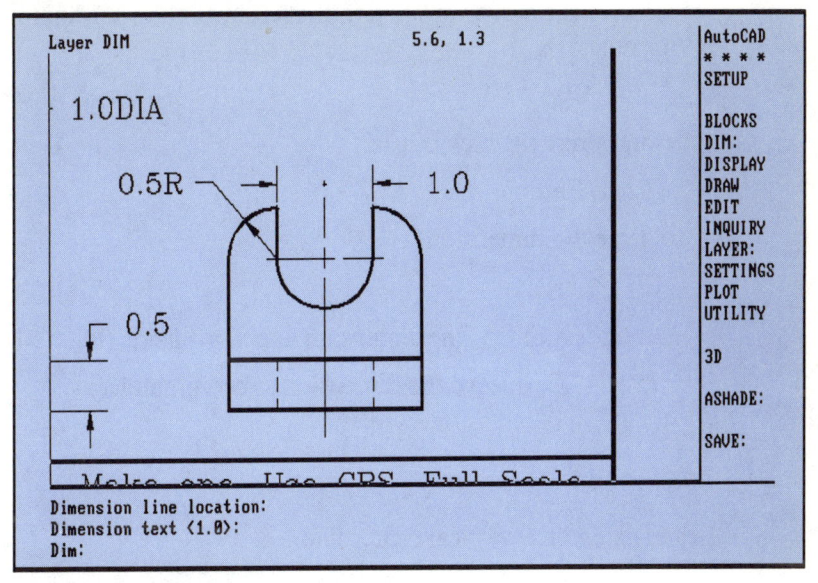

Figure 10.6: Dimensions for the right view

Dimensioning the Corner

In this section you dimension the upper-left arc with the Leader command.

1. At the Dim: prompt, type the command

    lead

    for Leader, and press Enter.
2. Press F9 to turn on Snap mode.
3. Move the cursor to the center of the arc at coordinate position

    8.0, 3.5

    and press the pick button.
4. Press F9 to turn off Snap mode.
5. Check that Ortho mode is off.

6. Move the cursor upward to the left until the coordinate read-out shows

    1.0 <130

    and press the pick button.
7. Press Enter.
8. Type the dimension

    0.5R

    and press Enter. The dimension appears outside (Figure 10.6).
9. Press ^C to leave the dimension subcommands.

Extending the Vertical Center Line

Let us extend the vertical center line.

1. Press F8 to turn on Ortho mode.
2. Type

    line

    and press Enter.
3. Type the Osnap command

    end

    and press Enter to start the new line.
4. Move to the bottom end of the center line at coordinate position

    8.5, 2.9

    and press the pick button. This locks the new line to the end of the horizontal center line.
5. Move the cursor down below the bottom edge to the coordinate position

    1.2 <270

    and press the pick button (Figure 10.6).
6. Press the second mouse button to complete the Line command.

Converting to a Center-Line Style

Let us convert the center line you just drew from a solid line to a center line.

1. Give the command

    change

    and press Enter.

2. The cursor changes to a selection box and the prompt asks you to select the objects to change. Type

    L

    for Last item drawn and press Enter.

3. Press Enter again to complete the selection step.

4. For the next prompt, type

    p

    for Property change and press Enter.

5. To the prompt:

    Change what property:

    type

    lt

    for Line type and press Enter.

6. The next prompt requests the line type. Answer

    center

    and press Enter.

7. To the next prompt, type Enter to complete the command.

You have now completed the dimensioning of the bracket.

1. Type

    zoom

    and press the space bar.

2. Type

   a

   for All and press Enter to see the complete view of the bracket (Figure 10.7).

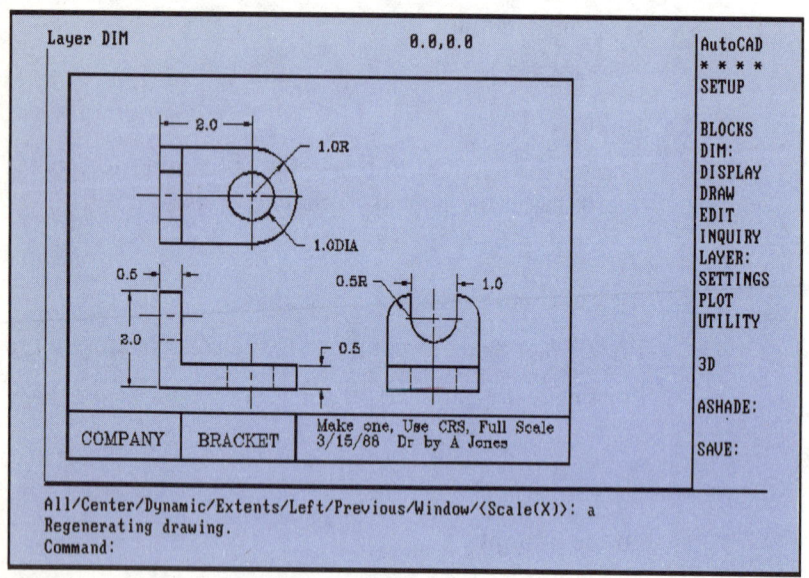

Figure 10.7: Completed drawing of bracket

3. Type

   end

   and press Enter. This saves your drawing and returns you to the Main menu.

Let us dimension the flange next.

How to Dimension the Flange

In the previous chapter you copied your flange drawing to a file named flanged. Then you added a legend. We will continue with this drawing.

1. Select option 2, to continue with an existing drawing, and press Enter.

2. Type

    flanged

and press Enter. Your drawing will appear on the screen.

3. If the drawing does not fill the screen, type

    zoom

and press the space bar.

4. Type

    a

for All and press Enter.

5. Give the command

    layer

and press Enter.

6. Type

    m

for Make and press Enter.

7. Type

    dim

and press Enter.

8. Press Enter again and check for the words *Layer DIM* on the top line.

Specifying a Vertical Dimension for the Front View

You will dimension a left edge of the front view first.

1. Type the command

    dim

and press Enter. Check that the prompt *Dim:* appears on the bottom line.

2. Next to the Dim: prompt, type

    ver

for Vertical dimension, and press Enter. The prompt asks you to specify either the location of the first extension line (the two-point method) or to type **return** to select the line to be dimensioned (the one-point method).

3. Press the second mouse button or Enter to choose the one-point method. The cursor changes to a selection box.

4. Move the cursor to the left edge of the front view, to location

   2.5, 1.8

   and press the pick button to select the left edge.

5. The next prompt asks for the dimension line location. Move the selection box to the left to location

   2.0, 1.8

   and press the pick button.

6. The next prompt is

   Dimension text <0.5>:

   telling you the value AutoCAD has calculated for this dimension. Press the second mouse button or Enter to accept this value and complete the command.

Remember that although the Vertical command has been completed, the Dim: prompt remains on the bottom line of the screen. You will be working with dimension commands until you give the ^C command.

*S*pecifying a Horizontal Dimension for the Front View

You will dimension the top edge of the front view next.

1. Next to the Dim: prompt, type

   hor

   for Horizontal dimension, and press Enter.

2. Because the top edge of this view is not a single entity, but is

composed of several line segments, we must use the two-point method. Therefore, type the Osnap command

int

for Intersection and press Enter.

3. Move the cursor to the upper-left corner at coordinate position

   2.5, 2.0

   Press the pick button to select this corner.

4. When AutoCAD asks for the second point, type

   int

   again and press Enter.

5. Move to the upper-right corner at position

   6.5, 2.0

   and press the pick button.

6. The next prompt asks for the dimension line location. Move the selection box just above the center line at location

   4.5, 2.8

   and press the pick button.

7. The next prompt is

   Dimension text <4.0>:

   giving you the value to appear in the dimension. Press the second mouse button or Enter to accept this value. The screen should look like Figure 10.8.

Let us dimension the top view next.

Dimensioning the Top View

Before we begin with the top view, let us enlarge it.

1. Type ^C to terminate the dimension subcommands.

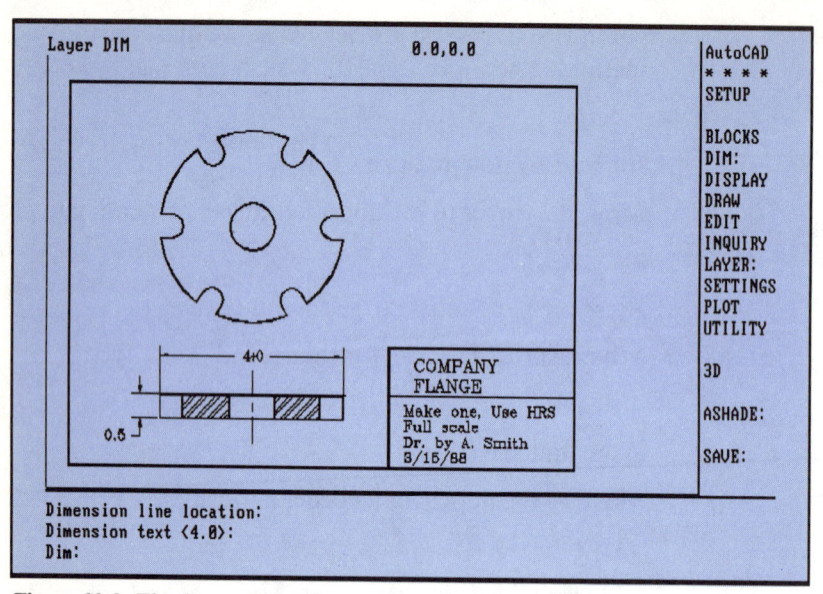

Figure 10.8: The dimensioned front view

2. Type the command

   zoom

   and press the space bar.

3. Type

   w

   for Window and press Enter.

4. Move the cursor to the upper-left corner to position

   1.6, 8.3

   and press the pick button to start a window.

5. Move to location

   8.5, 3.1

   and press the pick button to complete the Zoom command. The top view will fill the screen.

Adding Center Lines to One Bolt Slot

In this section you will add center lines to the bolt slots in the top view. After you create one crossed pair of center lines, you will erase the vertical center line. Then you will replicate the horizontal line for the remaining slots.

1. Give the command

    dim

    and press Enter to start the dimension subcommands.

2. Give the command

    cen

    for Center and press Enter to dimension the center of a circle.

3. Move the cursor to location

    6.0, 5.6

    and press the pick button. A small pair of crossed center lines appears (Figure 10.9). Notice that there are three segments in each direction.

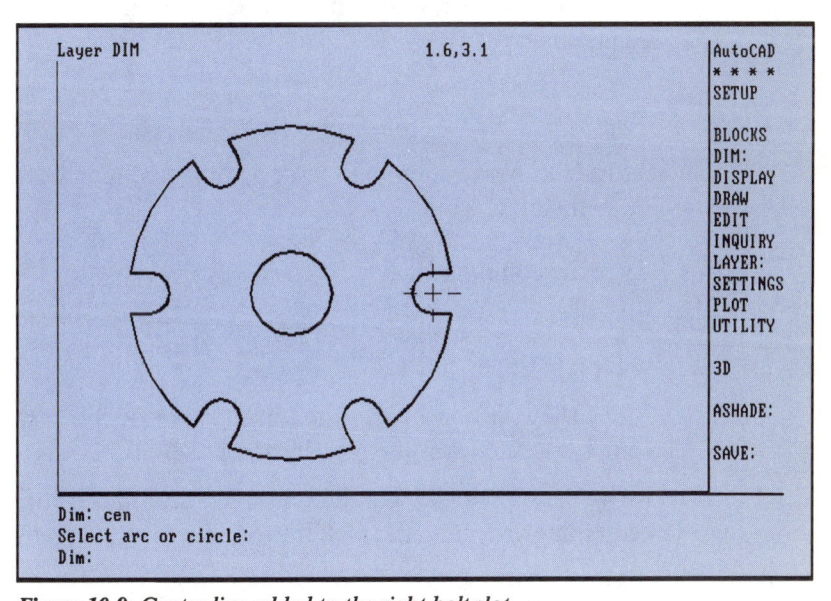

Figure 10.9: Center line added to the right bolt slot

4. Give the ^C command to complete the dimension subcommand.

5. Remove the vertical center line by typing

    erase

    and press Enter.

6. Move the selection box to the top segment of the vertical center line and press the pick button to select this segment. If you select the polyline perimeter around the top view by mistake, type **r** for Remove and press Enter to reverse the selection procedure. Select the polyline again, then type **a** for Add and press Enter to continue with the selection.

7. Move the selection box to the center segment of the vertical center line and press the pick button to select this segment. Be careful not to select the horizontal center line.

8. Move the selection box to the bottom segment of the vertical center line and press the pick button to select this segment. The entire vertical center line should be spotty to show that it is selected.

9. Press the second mouse button or Enter to erase the vertical center line.

Replicating the Center Line for the Bolt Slot

We next use the Array command to copy the remaining horizontal center line to the other slots.

1. Type the command

    array

    and press Enter.

2. Move the selection box to the left segment of the horizontal center line and press the pick button to select this segment.

3. Move the selection box to the center segment of the horizontal center line and press the pick button to select this segment.

Adding the Dimensions to Your Drawings **267**

4. Move the selection box to the right segment of the horizontal center line and press the pick button to select this segment. The entire horizontal center line should be spotty to show that it is selected.

5. Press the second mouse button or Enter to complete the selection process.

6. Type

    p

    for Polar and press Enter.

7. To designate the center of the polar array, type the Osnap command

    cen

    for Center and press Enter.

8. Move the cursor to the edge of the large circle, at location

    6.2, 6.6

    and press the pick button.

9. To the prompt requesting the number of items, type

    6

    and press Enter.

10. Press Enter to the next two questions. The center line is copied to each of the other bolt slots.

Removing Two Horizontal Center Lines

Let us remove two of the center lines, those for the left and right slots.

1. Type

    erase

    and press Enter.

2. Type

    w

    for Window and press Enter.

3. Move the cursor to the left center line at

   2.3, 5.6

   and press the pick button.

4. Move to location

   3.3, 5.4

   and press the pick button again. The three parts of the left center line become spotty.

5. Type

   w

   again for Window and press Enter.

6. Select the right center line next. Move the cursor to the location

   5.8, 5.6

   and press the pick button.

7. Move to location

   6.7, 5.4

   and press the pick button again. The three parts of the right center line become spotty.

8. Press the second mouse button or Enter to erase the two horizontal center lines.

Let us add center lines for the large circle next.

Adding Center Lines to the Large Circle

In this section you will add regular crossed center lines to the top view. Then you will delete the horizontal center line so you can replace it with a section line.

1. Type

   dim

   and press Enter to start the dimension subcommands.

2. Type

   cen

   for Center and press Enter.

3. Move the selection box to the edge of the large circle at location

   6.2, 6.6

   and press the pick button. Crossed center lines appear on the top view. (If a plus appears, remove it with the U command. Then change Dimcen to −0.1 as you did previously.)

4. Press ^C to terminate the dimension subcommand.

5. Type

   erase

   and press Enter so you can erase the horizontal center line.

6. Move the selection box to the left segment of the horizontal center line and press the pick button to select this segment.

7. Move the selection box to the center segment of the horizontal center line and press the pick button to select this segment. Be careful not to select the vertical center line.

8. Move the selection box to the right segment of the horizontal center line and press the pick button to select this segment. The entire horizontal center line should be spotty to show that it is selected.

9. Press the second mouse button or Enter to erase the horizontal center line.

Drawing the Bolt-Circle Center Line

We draw the center line for the bolt circle next. We start with a regular line type. Then using the Change command, we convert it to a center line type.

1. Give the command

   circle

   and press Enter.

2. Type the Osnap command

    cen

    for Center and press Enter.
3. Move the cursor to the edge of the large circle to location

    6.2, 6.6

    and press Enter to establish the center.
4. Type

    d

    for Diameter and press Enter to override the expected radius input.
5. Type the value

    3.5

    and press Enter to create a circle with a diameter of 3.5.

Changing the Circle to a Center Line

In this section you change the solid circle to a center line.

1. Type

    change

    and press Enter.
2. When asked to select objects, type

    L

    for Last item drawn and press Enter. The circle becomes spotty. Of course you can also select this circle by moving the selection box to it and pressing the pick button.
3. Press Enter to complete the selection step.
4. Type

    p

    for Property and press Enter to select property change.

5. Type

   lt

   for Line type and press Enter.

6. Type

   center

   for Center line and press Enter twice to change the solid line to a center line (Figure 10.10).

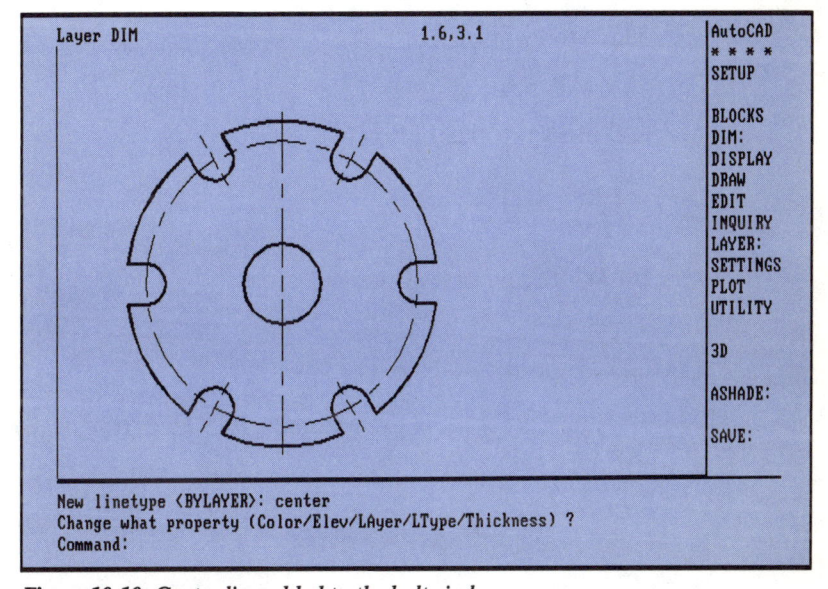

Figure 10.10: Center line added to the bolt circle

Adding a Cutting-Plane Line

In this part you add a cutting-plane line across the middle of the top view. This line marks the cutting plane that matches the adjacent view, the front view in this example. The cutting plane is marked with a wide broken line. One long segment alternates with two short segments. Furthermore, the ends of the cutting-plane line are marked with arrows that point away from the corresponding sectioned view. We will first draw the cutting-plane line as a regular polyline. Then we will convert it to a cutting-plane line with the Change command.

1. Press F7 to turn on the grid if it is off.
2. Press F9 to turn on Snap mode.
3. If Ortho mode is off, press F8 to turn it on.
4. Type

    pline

    and press Enter.
5. Move to location

    2.0, 6.0

    and press the pick button.
6. Type

    w

    for Width and press Enter.
7. Type

    0

    and press Enter to set the beginning line width (the head of the first arrow).
8. Type

    0.12

    and press Enter again to set the ending width of the arrow.
9. Turn off Snap mode by pressing the F9 key.
10. Move the cursor downward about halfway to the next grid point. When the coordinate reads

    0.2 <270

    press the pick button to create an arrow on the left side.
11. Type

    w

    and press Enter to reset the width.

12. Type

    0.03

    and press Enter for the beginning width.

13. Press Enter to set the ending width to the beginning width.

14. Turn Snap mode back on by pressing the F9 key.

15. Move down to the next grid point that marks the horizontal axis of the top view. Press the pick button to establish the next segment.

16. Move right across the center of the top view until you are one grid point past the right edge. The coordinate position shows

    5.0 <0

17. Press the pick button to establish the horizontal segment.

18. Turn off Snap mode by pressing the F9 key.

19. Move upward about halfway to the next grid point, until the horizontal cursor meets the bottom of the arrow on the left side. When the coordinate reads

    0.3 <90

    press the pick button to create the next segment.

20. Type

    w

    for Width and press Enter.

21. Type

    0.12

    and press Enter to set the tail of the second arrow.

22. Type

    0

    and press Enter to set the arrowhead width to zero.

23. Turn on Snap mode by pressing the F9 key.

24. Move upward to the next grid point and press the pick button to complete the section line with a second arrowhead.

25. Press F9 to turn off Snap mode.
26. Press F8 to turn off Ortho mode.
27. Press Enter to complete the P-line command.

Converting the Polyline to a Cutting-Plane Line

In the previous section you drew a cutting-plane line as a wide polyline. However, the line is solid, rather than broken as is required of a cutting-plane line. Therefore, in this section you use the Change command to convert this polyline into a cutting-plane line.

1. Type

    change

    and press Enter.

2. Type

    L

    to select the last item drawn. The polyline becomes spotted to show that it is selected.

3. Press Enter to complete the selection step.
4. Type

    p

    for Property and press Enter to select property change.

5. Type

    lt

    for Line type and press Enter.

6. Type

    phantom

    and press Enter two times to change the solid line to a cutting-plane line (called *phantom* in AutoCAD). You now have a complete cutting-plane line (Figure 10.11).

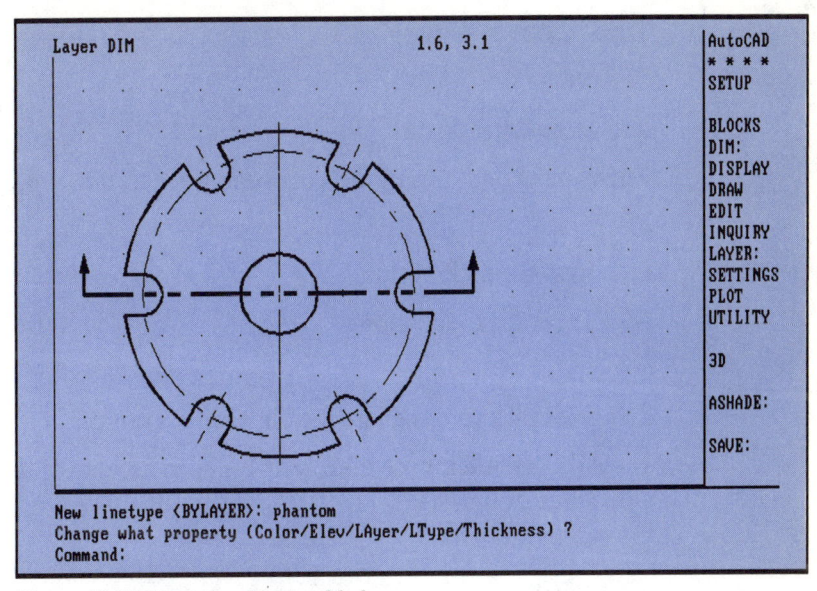

Figure 10.11: A section line is added

Dimensioning a Bolt Slot

We dimension the upper-right bolt slot next. Since this is an opening, we must use the two-point method.

1. Type

    dim

    and press Enter to start the Dimension subcommands.

2. Type

    align

    and press Enter to select an aligned dimension. (You can abbreviate the Align command to *ali*.)

3. Type the Osnap command

    int

    for Intersection and press Enter.

4. Move to the coordinate position

    5.3, 7.4

    at the upper-right slot and press the pick button.

5. Type

    int

    and press Enter again.

6. Move to the right side of the slot opening at coordinate position

    5.8, 7.1

    and press the pick button.

7. Move upward to location

    5.7, 7.6

    and press pick to designate the dimension location.

8. Press the second mouse button or Enter to accept the dimension value of 0.5.

Dimensioning the Bolt Circle

We will now dimension the bolt circle using the Leader command.

1. Check that *Dim:* is shown on the bottom line.
2. Type

    lead

    for Leader and press Enter to start a leader for the bolt circle.

3. Move to location

    6.0, 4.5

    on the bolt circle and press the pick button.

4. Move downward and to the right until the coordinate readout shows

    0.8 <326

    and press the pick button. Alternatively, you can type

    @0.8 <326

    at the keyboard.

5. Press Enter to complete the leader. AutoCAD adds a short horizontal segment.

6. AutoCAD next requests the dimension text. Type

   3.5DIA

   and press Enter to define the diameter of the bolt circle.

Dimensioning the Inner Circle

We also dimension the inner circle using the Leader command.

1. Check that *Dim:* is shown on the bottom line.
2. Type

   lead

   and press Enter to start a leader for the bolt circle.
3. Move to location

   5.0, 5.7

   on the inner circle and press the pick button.
4. Move upward and to the right until the coordinate readout shows

   2.1 <18

   and press the pick button. Again, you can type

   @2.1 <18

   at the keyboard.
5. Press Enter to complete the leader.
6. AutoCAD next requests the dimension text. Type

   1.0DIA

   and press Enter to define the diameter of the bolt circle.
7. Type ^C to leave the dimension subcommands.
8. Type

   zoom

   and press the space bar.

9. Type

   a

   for All and press Enter. You have now completed the drawing. It should look like Figure 10.12.

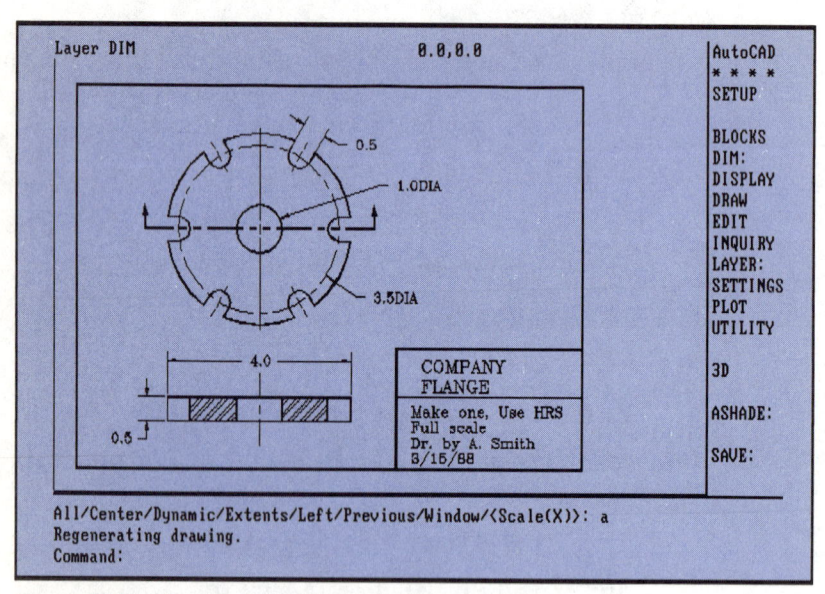

Figure 10.12: Completed drawing of flange

10. Type

    end

    and press Enter to complete the drawing and return to the Main menu.

11

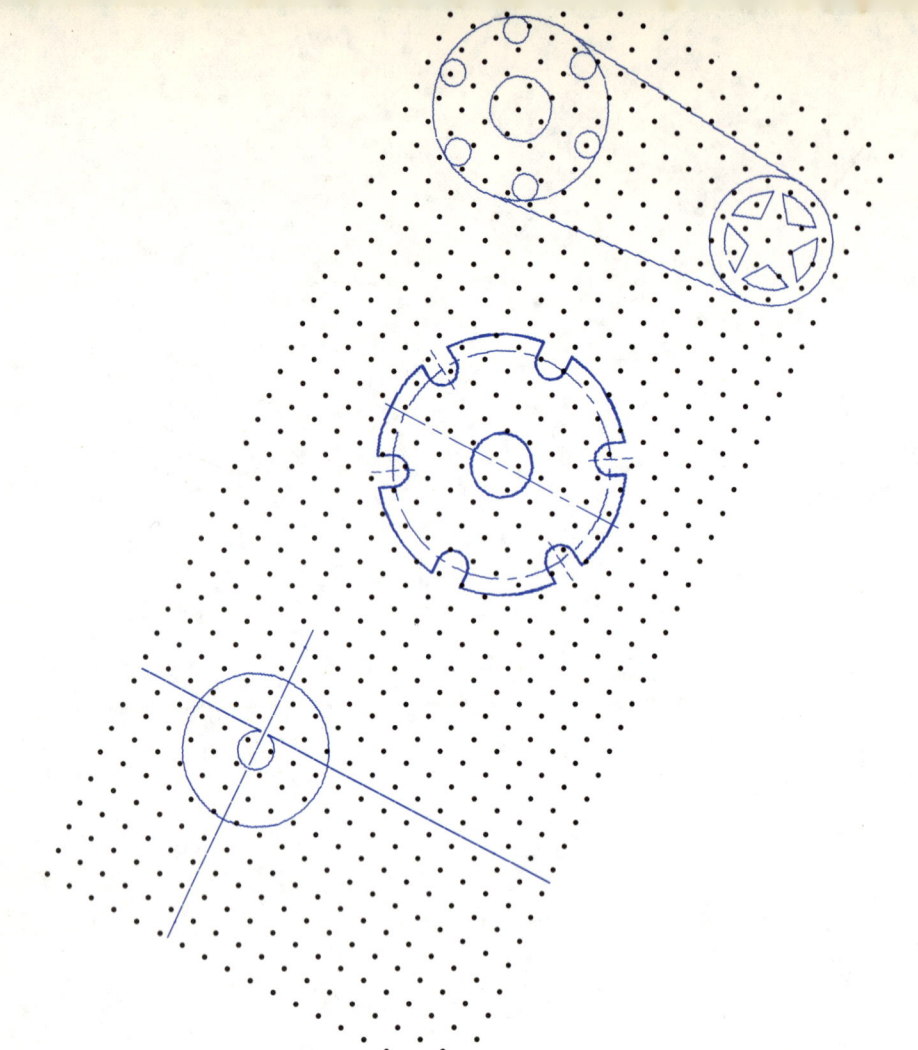

Drawing in
Three Dimensions

Featuring:
　Drawing an
　　isometric view of a cube
　Drawing an isometric circle

In this chapter we explore the *isometric view,* a style of drawing that gives a three-dimensional effect. In the previous chapters, our viewpoint was perpendicular or orthogonal to the front, top, and right faces of the object. In this system, two axes of each view are perpendicular to each other. Thus, a cube drawn in the orthogonal style appears to be a square in each of the three views.

Another method of drawing is known as *isometric* or equal measure. An isometric drawing of a cube is shown in Figure 11.1. It appears that we are looking down one corner of the cube. Now, instead of just two axes, we can see three axes. Although they are actually 90 degrees, we draw them 120 degrees apart.

Figure 11.1: Isometric view of a cube

The orthogonal views we drew in previous chapters show the true shape. That is, both the lengths and angles in the orthogonal views are correct. By contrast, the lengths and angles of the isometric view are generally incorrect. For example, the three axes in Figure 11.1 actually meet at 120 degrees on the drawing instead of the correct 90 degrees. Thus, in an isometric view, the square faces are drawn as parallelograms and a circle is drawn as an ellipse. Your mind, however, makes the necessary correction so that an ellipse appears to be a circle. Nevertheless, this is an illusion.

AutoCAD can help us draw isometric views by changing the usual 90-degree axes to 120 degrees. The grid and snap points also change to a 120-degree, or *hexagonal orientation*. When AutoCAD is operating in isometric mode, only two axes are active at a time as with the regular orthographic mode.

To gain experience with isometric drawing, you'll first draw a cube and three circles. Then you'll draw an isometric view of the bracket you drew in Chapter 6.

New commands used in this chapter are

- Isometric Snap style to shift the grid from square to hexagonal
- Isoplane command ^E to change cursor shape
- Isometric ellipse to draw circles in the isometric view
- Open option of P-edit command to remove part of an ellipse

How to Set Up an Isometric Drawing

Let us set up the isometric drawing mode. You begin an isometric drawing in the usual way, setting the Units, Snap, and Grid.

1. Start AutoCAD and choose option 1 to begin a new drawing.
2. Type the name

    brack3d =

    and press Enter.
3. Give the command

    units

    and press Enter.
4. Press Enter again to accept the current system of units.
5. Type

    1

    and press Enter to choose the display of one digit past the decimal point.

6. Type ^C to complete the Units command.
7. Type F1 to return to the drawing screen.
8. Type

    snap

    and press Enter.
9. Type

    0.5

    and press Enter to set the snap spacing.
10. Type

    grid

    and press Enter.
11. Type

    s

    and press Enter to set the grid spacing to the snap spacing. The grid now appears on the screen.
12. Press F6 to turn on the coordinate readout.
13. Type

    snap

    and press Enter.
14. Type

    s

    for Style and press Enter. AutoCAD gives the prompt

    Standard/Isometric<S>:

    The S in angle brackets shows that Standard style (that is, rectangular grid) is the current mode.
15. Type

    i

    for Isometric style and press Enter. The next prompt gives the vertical spacing (0.5) and requests a new value.

16. Press Enter to accept the current spacing. The grid now changes from orthogonal to hexagonal and the crossed lines of the cursor change from 90 degrees to 120 degrees (Figure 11.2).

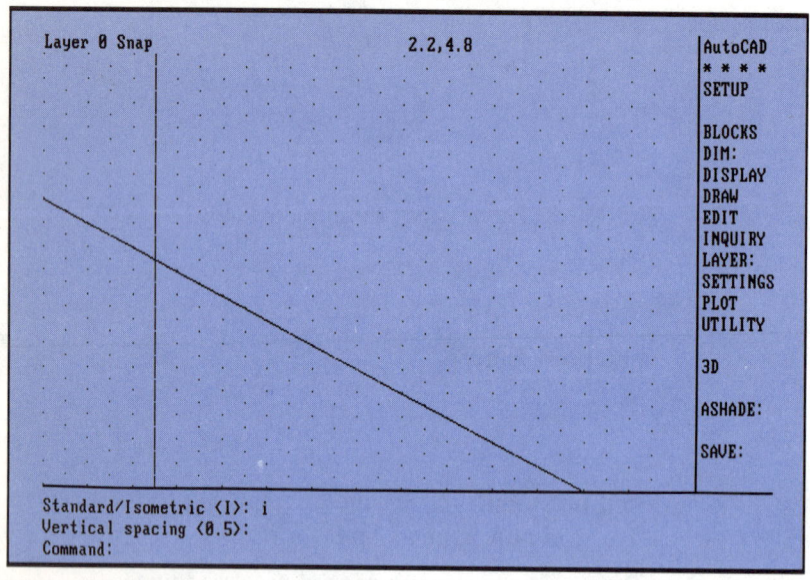

Figure 11.2: Isometric grid and cursor

How to Identify the Three Isometric Views

Look at the three faces of the cube shown in Figure 11.1. The faces are labeled Left, Top, and Right. When you draw an isometric view with AutoCAD, you imagine that you are drawing on one of these cube faces. These three faces are known as isoplane left, isoplane top, and isoplane right.

Notice that the appearance of the cursor has changed: one line is vertical while the other line slopes from the upper-left corner to the lower-right corner of the screen. This cursor is used to draw on the left side of the cube, because the crossed lines of the cursor align with the left and bottom edges on the left face of the cube. This mode of cursor is called *isoplane left*.

Follow these steps to draw on the top face of the cube:

1. Press ^ E. The vertical line of the cursor rotates to the right to match the edges on the top of the cube. The message <Isoplane Top> appears on the bottom line of the screen. Notice that neither line of the cursor is vertical.

2. When you want to draw on the right face of the cube, press ^ E again. The upper-left line of the cursor changes to vertical. The lines of the cursor now match the right face of the cube. The message <Isoplane Right> appears on the bottom line of the screen.

3. Type ^ E a third time to complete the cycle. The cursor again matches the left face of the cube and the message <Isoplane Left> appears on the bottom line of the screen.

How to Draw an Isometric View of a Cube

In this section you will draw an isometric view of a cube like the one shown in Figure 11.1. Then you will draw ellipses representing circles on the three faces. Let us enlarge the grid before beginning.

1. Press F9 to turn off Snap mode.
2. Type

    zoom

    and press the space bar.

3. Type

    w

    for Window and press Enter.

4. Move the cursor to coordinate position

    1.0, 7.6

    and press the pick button. Alternatively, you can type the coordinates from the keyboard and press Enter.

5. Move the cursor down and to the right to coordinate position

    7.7, 2.9

    and press the pick button to enlarge the view.

Now you're ready to draw the faces of the cube. You'll start in the upper-right corner of the left face and go around in a counterclockwise direction. Be sure that the left isoplane cursor, the one shown in Figure 11.2, is current. Press ^E if it is not.

1. Type the command

    line

    and press Enter.

2. Move the cursor to the center of the screen, near the coordinate position

    4.3, 5.5

    then press F9 to make the cursor snap to the exact location.

3. Press the pick button to start a line. Alternatively, you can type the coordinates from the keyboard and press Enter.

4. Move four grid points to the upper left, along the direction of the slanted cursor line. Stop at the coordinate location

    2.0 <150

    Press the pick button to establish the top edge of the left face.

5. Move four grid points straight down. Stop at the coordinate location

    2.0 <270

    Press the pick button to establish the left edge of the left face.

6. Move four grid points to the lower right, along the direction of the slanted cursor line. Stop at the coordinate location

    2.0 <330

    Press the pick button to establish the bottom edge.

7. Move four grid points straight up to the original point. Stop at the coordinate location

   2.0 <90

   Press the pick button to complete the left face of the cube.

Now draw the right face of the cube. You will go around this face in a clockwise direction. Be sure to change to the right isoplane cursor.

1. Press ^E to change to isoplane top.
2. Press ^E again to change to isoplane right. One line of the cursor should be vertical and the other should go from the lower-left corner to the upper-right corner of the screen.
3. The Line command is still active. Move four grid points to the upper right, along the direction of the slanted cursor line. Stop at the coordinate location

   2.0 <30

   Press the pick button to establish the top edge of the right face.

4. Move four grid points straight down, stopping at the coordinate location

   2.0 <270

   Press the pick button to establish the right edge of the face.

5. Move four grid points to the lower left, along the direction of the slanted cursor line. Stop at the coordinate location

   2.0 <210

   Press the pick button to establish the bottom edge and complete the right face.

6. Press the second mouse button or the Enter key to complete the Line command.

Good. You now have two faces of the cube. Continue to the next exercise to to complete the top face of the cube by adding two more lines.

1. Press ^E to change to isoplane left.

2. Press ^E again to change to isoplane top. Both lines of the cursor should be angled.
3. Press the second mouse button or Enter to start the Line command.
4. Move to the upper-left corner of the left face to coordinate position

    2.6, 6.5

    and press the pick button to start a new line segment.
5. Move four grid points to the upper right, stopping at the coordinate location

    2.0 <30

    Press the pick button to establish the left edge of the top face.
6. Move four grid points to the lower right, stopping at the coordinate location

    2.0 <330

    Press the pick button to complete the top view.
7. Press the second mouse button or Enter to complete the Line command.

Good. You've completed the isometric view of the cube.

How to Draw an Isometric Circle

In this section you will draw isometric circles on the faces of the cube you drew in the previous section. AutoCAD will actually draw an ellipse rather than a circle. However, your eye will interpret this ellipse as a circle if it is oriented in the correct way. In the following steps, you will want to choose locations with Snap mode turned on so AutoCAD can precisely locate the positions. Unfortunately, the hexagonal grid will often make the cursor snap to the wrong place. Therefore, you may find it easier to temporarily turn off Snap mode until you are nearly to the correct position, then turn on Snap mode.

Let's first draw a circle in the left face of the cube.

1. Because the cursor was previously set for isoplane top, press ^E two times to change to isoplane left.

2. Type the command

    ellipse

    and press Enter.

3. Type

    i

    for Isometric circle and press Enter.

4. Move the cursor to the center of the left face of the cube, to coordinate location

    3.5, 5.0

    Press the pick to establish the center.

5. Move the cursor straight upward two grid points to the cube edge. The coordinate readout shows

    1.0 <90

    Notice that the edge of the ellipse touches the edge of the left face at four places (Figure 11.3).

6. Press ^E to change to isoplane top. Notice that the shape of the ellipse changes. It no longer matches the cube face.

7. Press ^E again to change to isoplane right. Again, the shape of the ellipse changes and no longer matches the cube face.

8. Press ^E a third time to return to isoplane left. Check that the ellipse matches the cube face.

9. Press the pick button to fix the shape.

Now draw an isometric circle in the top face of the cube using the same technique.

1. Press ^E to change to isoplane top. Both cursor lines are angled.

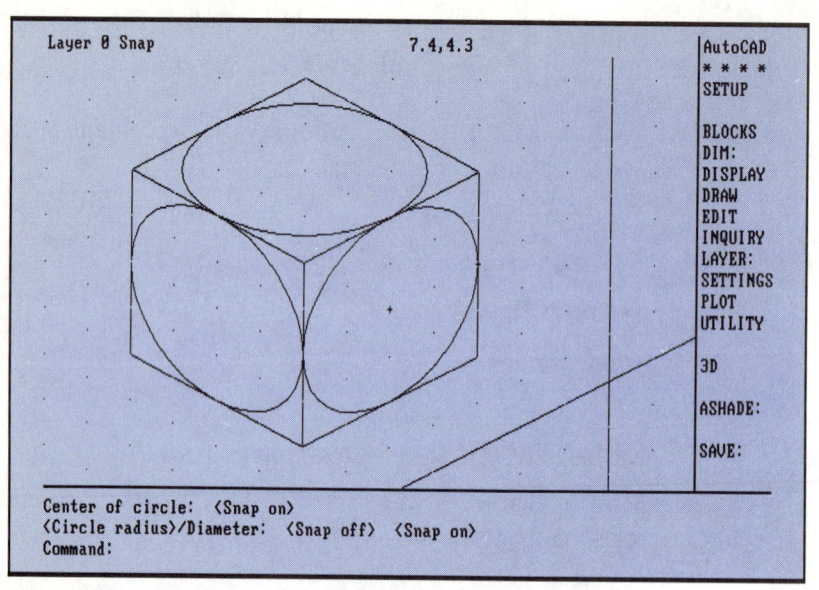

Figure 11.3: Isometric view of cube and isometric circles

2. Press Enter to repeat the Ellipse command.
3. Type

    i

    for Isoplane ellipse and press Enter.

4. Move the cursor to the center of the top face of the cube, to coordinate location

    4.3, 6.5

    Press Enter to establish the center.

5. Move the cursor upward and to the right two grid points to the cube edge. The coordinate readout shows

    1.0 <30

    Notice that the edge of the ellipse touches the four edges of the top face.

6. Press the pick button to fix the shape.

Good. You have one more ellipse to draw—the one in the right face of the cube.

1. Press ^E to change to isoplane right.
2. Press Enter to repeat the Ellipse command.
3. Type

    i

    for Isoplane ellipse and press Enter.
4. Move the cursor to the center of the right face of the cube, to coordinate location

    5.2, 5.0

    Press the pick button to establish the center.
5. Move the cursor upward and to the right two grid points to the cube edge. The coordinate readout shows

    1.0 <30

    Check that the edge of the ellipse touches the four edges of the right face.
6. Press the pick button to fix the shape. Your screen should look like Figure 11.3.

How to Erase Parts of an Ellipse

Later in this chapter you will need to remove parts of ellipses. Let us explore the nature of an AutoCAD ellipse. As you know, an AutoCAD ellipse is a polyline. Unlike a circle, which is complete, an ellipse has a beginning and an end. If you want to erase a part of an ellipse, you must be careful not to include the beginning and ending point in the part you want to erase. However, the beginning and ending point is not apparent. Therefore, let us learn how to locate it.

1. Press F9 to turn off Snap mode.

2. Type

   pedit

   and press Enter to start the Polyedit command. The cursor changes to a selection box.

3. Move to the ellipse in the left face to location

   4.1, 5.4

   and press the pick button. The cursor changes back to crossed lines. This command is unusual because the appearance of the object does not change when it is selected.

4. Type

   o

   for Open and press Enter. This command opens the ellipse by removing a line segment at the ending point. For the isoplane left face, this is always at the lower-left or 8 o'clock position (Figure 11.4).

5. Press Enter to complete the P-edit command.

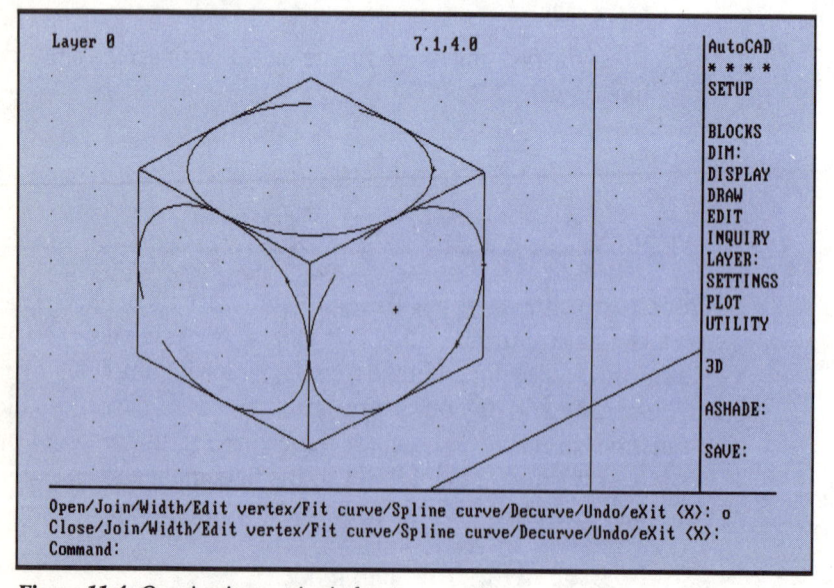

Figure 11.4: Opening isometric circles

6. Let us now open the top ellipse. Press Enter to restart the P-edit command. The cursor changes to a selection box.

7. Move to the ellipse in the top face, to location

    4.3, 5.8

    and press the pick button. The cursor changes back to crossed lines.

8. Type

    o

    for Open and press Enter. A line segment is removed from the 1 o'clock position of the top edge (Figure 11.4).

9. Press Enter to complete the P-edit command.

10. To open the right ellipse, press Enter to restart the P-edit command. The cursor changes to a selection box.

11. Type

    L

    for Last item drawn and press Enter. Although no change is apparent, the ellipse in the right face is selected. The cursor changes back to crossed lines.

12. Type

    o

    for Open and press Enter. A line segment is removed from the upper-left or 11 o'clock position of the right face (Figure 11.4).

13. Press Enter to complete the P-edit command.

When you work with an isometric ellipse, you may want to refer to Figure 11.4 to help you remember the location of the isocircle end points.

You are finished with this drawing, but you will use a portion of it to draw an isometric view of the bracket you drew in Chapter 6. But first, let's save a copy of the drawing in the usual way. Type **save** and press Enter, then type **isocube** and press Enter.

Now, let's prepare to draw the rectangular parts of the bracket by first erasing some unwanted lines from the current drawing.

1. Type

    erase

    and press Enter.

2. Type

    c

    for Crossing window and press Enter.

3. Move to the upper-left part of the screen at location

    2.4, 7.3

    and press the pick button.

4. Move to the lower-right part of the screen at location

    6.2, 3.8

    and press the pick button. The entire figure becomes spotty. We now want to remove three lines from the selection set so they will not be erased.

5. Type

    r

    for Remove and press Enter.

6. Move to the upper-left edge of the top face at location

    3.0, 6.8

    and press the pick button. This line returns to normal.

7. Move to the far-left edge at location

    2.6, 6.2

    and press the pick button. This line also returns to normal.

8. Move to the lower edge of the left face at location

    2.8, 4.4

    and press the pick button.

9. Press the second mouse button or Enter to complete the selection step and erase the unwanted lines.

10. Press the F7 key two times to remove the plus marks from the screen.

How to Draw the Isometric View of the Bracket

In the remainder of this chapter you will draw an isometric view of the bracket you drew in Chapter 6; an isometric view is shown in Figure 6.1. First you will draw the rectangular portion, then the ellipses. You will refine your drawing and add detail by copying, connecting, and trimming parts of your drawing.

Drawing the Rectangular Parts

Let us draw the rectangular parts first. Figure 11.5 shows the lines you will draw.

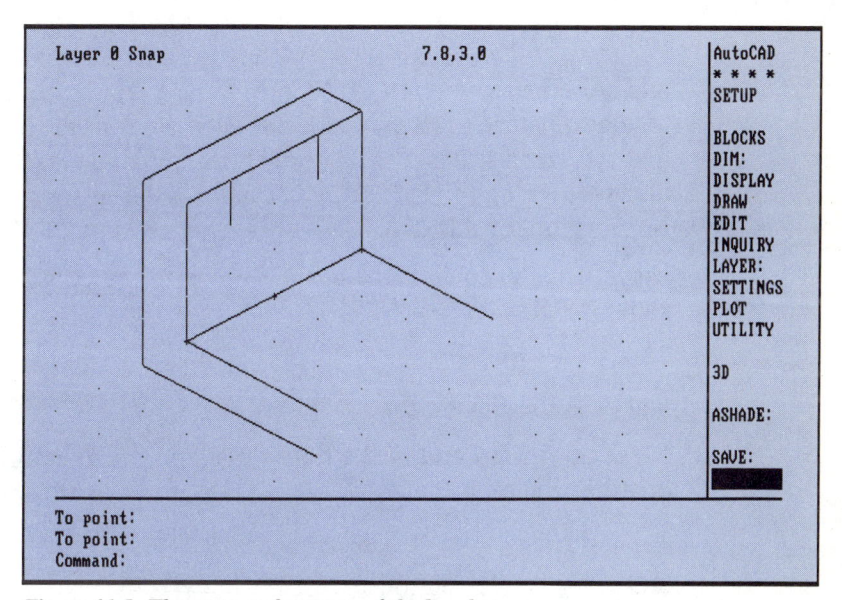

Figure 11.5: The rectangular parts of the bracket

1. The cursor should still be set for isoplane right. Therefore, press ^E two times to change to isoplane top. If it has not changed to isoplane top, press ^E.

2. Type

    line

    and press Enter.

3. Move to the right end of the top line to location

   4.3, 7.5

4. Press F9 to turn on Snap mode.
5. Press the pick button to start a line.
6. Move downward and to the right to the next grid point. The coordinate shows

   0.5 <330

7. Press the pick button to fix a line segment.
8. Move downward and to the left four grid points until the coordinate shows

   2.0 <210

   and press the pick button. As before, you may find it easier to temporarily turn off Snap mode until you are near the point, and then turn it back on. Although the next line is drawn along the left and right faces, you can leave the cursor set for isoplane top for this step.

9. Move straight down three grid points until the coordinate shows

   1.5 <270

   and press the pick button.

10. Move downward and to the right three grid points until the coordinate shows

    1.5 <330

    and press the pick button.

11. Press the second mouse button to complete the Line command.
12. Press the second mouse button to restart the Line command.
13. Move back to the previous point, the beginning of the last line. The coordinate shows

    3.0, 4.8

14. Press the pick button to start a new line segment.
15. Move upward and to the right four grid points. The coordinate shows

    2.0 <30

    Press the pick button to fix the line segment.
16. Move downward and to the right three grid points to coordinate

    1.5 <330

    and press the pick button.
17. Press the second mouse button to complete the Line command.
18. Press the second mouse button to restart the Line command.
19. Move back to the previous point, the beginning of the last line. The coordinate shows

    4.8, 5.8

    Press the pick button to start a line segment.
20. Move straight up three grid points until the coordinate shows

    1.5 <90

    and press the pick button.
21. Press the second mouse button to complete the Line command.
22. Press the second mouse button to restart the Line command.
23. In the next steps, we draw two short lines. Move to the coordinate position

    3.5, 6.5

    and press the pick button.
24. Move straight downward one grid point. When the coordinate shows

    0.5 <270

    press the pick button.
25. Press Enter to complete the Line command.
26. Press Enter to restart the Line command.

27. Move upward and to the right two grid points. Stop at location

    4.3, 6.5

    and press the pick button.

28. Move straight upward one grid point. When the coordinate shows

    0.5 <90

    press the pick button.

29. Press Enter to complete the Line command.

Good. You've completed the first part of the drawing. Your screen should look like Figure 11.5. Now you're ready to draw the second part of the isometric view—the ellipses.

Drawing the Ellipses

In this section you will draw an isometric circle with the isoplane top mode, then remove a portion of the circle.

1. Check that both lines of the cursor are angled, indicating isoplane top. Press ^E if not.

2. Type the command

    ellipse

    and press Enter.

3. Type

    i

    for Isometric circle and press Enter.

4. Move the cursor midway between the two lines at the lower-right side. The coordinate location is

    5.2, 4.5

    Press the pick button to establish the center.

5. Move the cursor upward and to the right two grid points to the end of one of your lines. The coordinate readout shows

    1.0 <30

Notice that the edge of the ellipse touches both lines.

6. Press the pick button to establish the isocircle.

Good. Now remove some of the ellipse with the P-edit and Break commands.

1. Press F9 to turn off Snap mode.
2. Type

    pedit

    and press Enter. As before, the cursor changes to a selection box.

3. Type

    L

    for Last and press Enter to select the most recently drawn isocircle. (The isocircle does not change appearance.)

4. Type

    o

    for Open and press Enter to remove a section of the ellipse (Figure 11.6).

5. Press Enter to complete the P-edit command.

The remaining half of the ellipse will be removed using the Break command. You must erase the two pieces adjacent to the opening. One piece is long and one is short.

6. Type

    break

    and press Enter.

7. Move the selection box to the left side of the opening in the ellipse. The coordinate position is

    5.2, 5.2

    Press the pick button.

8. Press F9 to turn on Snap mode.

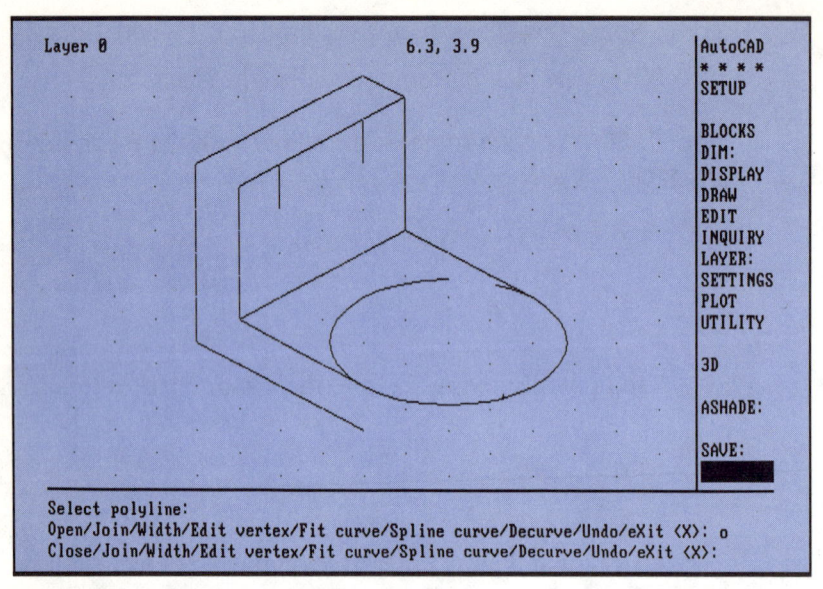

Figure 11.6: A piece is removed from the ellipse

9. Move left to the intersection of the ellipse and the line. The coordinate position is

    4.3, 4.0

    Press the pick button to trim the ellipse back to the line.

10. Press Enter to restart the Break command.
11. Press F9 to turn off Snap mode.
12. Move the selection box to the right side of the opening in the ellipse. The coordinate position is

    5.7, 5.1

    Be careful not to include the nearby line in the selection box. Press the pick button.

13. Press F9 to turn on Snap mode.
14. Move right to the intersection of the ellipse and the line. The coordinate position is

    6.1, 5.0

    Press the pick button to trim the other side of the ellipse back to the second line.

See how your isometric view is taking shape? Your screen should look like Figure 11.7. Continue to the next section to draw the second ellipse.

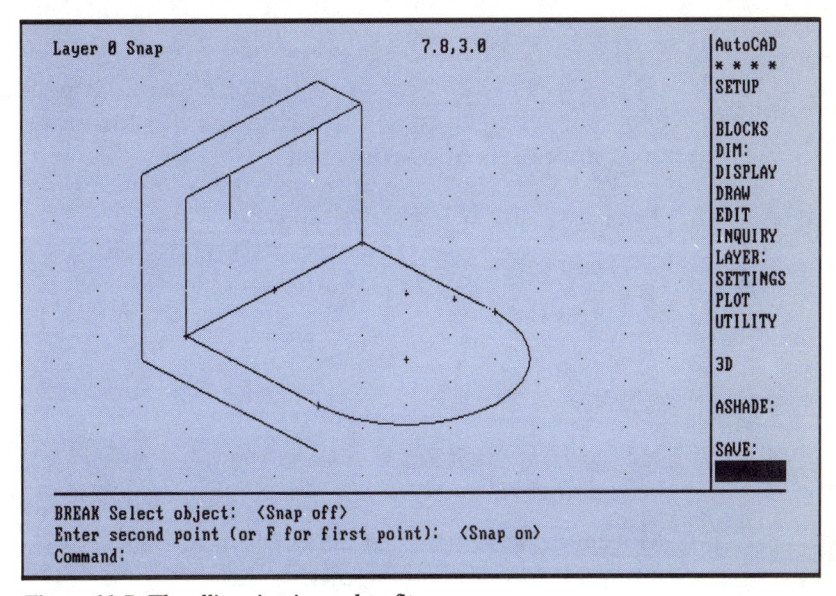

Figure 11.7: The ellipse is trimmed to fit

1. Type the command

    ellipse

    and press Enter.

2. Type

    i

    for Isometric circle and press Enter.

3. Move the cursor to the center of the large ellipse. The coordinate location is

    5.2, 4.5

    Press the pick button to establish the center.

4. Move the cursor upward and to the right one grid point. The coordinate readout shows

    0.5 <30

5. Press the pick button to establish the isocircle.
6. Turn off Snap mode with F9.

Copying the Two Ellipses

The two ellipses you just drew are on the top edge of the bracket. In this section you will make copies of each ellipse for the lower edge, then remove some parts of one of them.

1. Type

    copy

    and press Enter.

2. Type

    L

    for Last and press Enter to select the small ellipse. It should become spotty.

3. Move the selection box to the large ellipse and press the pick button. It too should be spotty.

4. Press the second mouse button to complete the selection step.

5. AutoCAD requests the base point or displacement. We want to place the duplicate ellipses one grid point straight downward. One way to do this is to pick any point on the screen, then move down one grid point and pick that point. However, this time it is easier to enter the information from the keyboard. Type

    0,0

    and press Enter.

6. Type

    @0.5 <-90

    and press Enter. Copies of the ellipses now appear (Figure 11.8).

Now erase the hidden parts of the small lower ellipse. Of course, we could show the hidden parts with dashed lines. However, the resulting

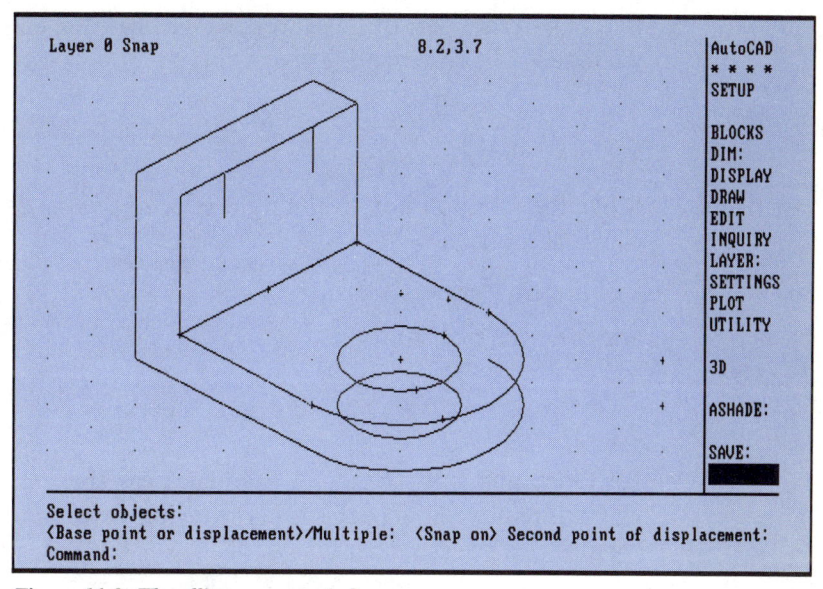

Figure 11.8: *The ellipses are copied*

picture will be clearer if we remove the hidden parts instead. But first, enlarge the ellipses.

1. Type

    zoom

    and press the space bar.

2. Type

    w

    for Window and press Enter.

3. Move the cursor to location

    4.5, 5.0

    and press the pick button.

4. Move to location

    6.8, 3.4

    and press the pick button again to enlarge the view.

5. Before we erase part of the ellipse, let us locate the end point with the P-edit command. Type

    pedit

    and press Enter.

6. Move the selection box to the right edge of the small lower ellipse at location

    5.8, 4.1

    and press the pick button.

7. Type

    o

    for Open and press Enter. A segment near the top of the ellipse is removed. Since this is in the region we want to keep, we must put the piece back.

8. Type

    c

    for Close and press Enter. The ellipse is restored.

9. Press Enter to complete the P-edit command.

10. Type

    break

    and press Enter.

11. The selection box should still be at location

    5.8, 4.1

    Press the pick button to select this ellipse.

12. Type

    f

    for First and press Enter to switch to the three-point method you used previously. Now you must select the beginning and ending points to be erased.

13. There are snap points at each end of the piece we want to erase. Therefore, press F9 to turn on Snap mode.

14. Move to the right intersection of the two small ellipses. The coordinate readout is

    5.6, 4.3

    Press the pick button.

15. Move one grid point left to the other intersection of the two small ellipses. The coordinate readout is

    4.8, 4.3

    Press the pick button. The lower part is erased because the opening is in the upper part (Figure 11.9).

16. Press F9 to turn off Snap mode.

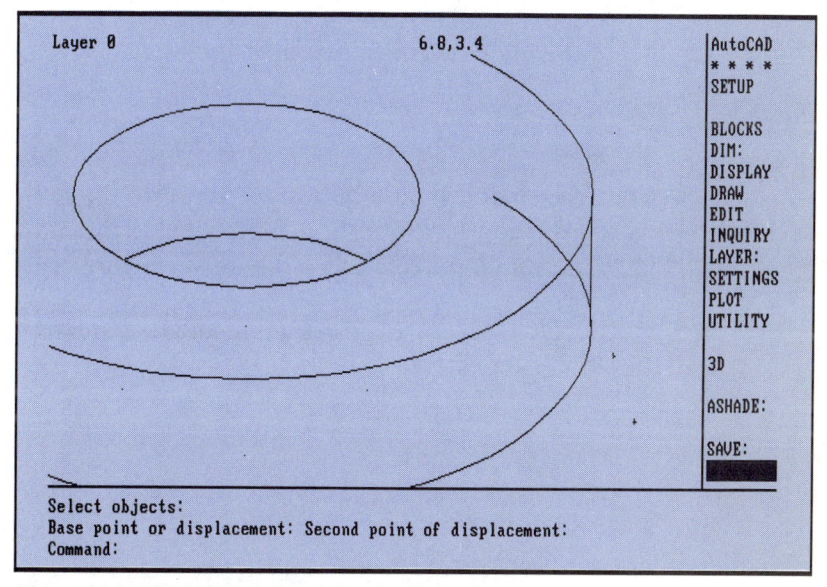

Figure 11.9: The hidden part of the ellipse is erased

Connecting the Ellipses

In this section you will connect the two large ellipses with a short line using the Tangent Osnap command. You will then remove parts of the lower ellipse.

1. Type

    line

    and press Enter.

2. Type the Osnap option

    tan

    for Tangent and press Enter.

3. Move to the right edge of the upper large ellipse to coordinate position

    6.4, 4.5

    Press the pick button to start a line.

4. Type

    tan

    again and press Enter.

5. Move straight down to coordinate location

    6.4, 4.0

    and press the pick button.

6. Press the second mouse button to complete the Line command. You now have a vertical line tangent to the ends of the large ellipses. Your screen should look like Figure 11.9.

In this section you will use the Break command to erase the hidden part of the large lower ellipse.

1. Type

    break

    and press Enter.

2. Move the selection box to the end of the lower ellipse sticking out in the upper-left direction. When the coordinate readout shows

    6.1, 4.5

    press the pick button.

3. Type the Osnap option

    int

    for Intersection and press Enter.

4. Move the cursor down the ellipse to the point where it meets the lower end of the short line. The coordinate readout shows

   6.4, 4.0

   Press the pick button to erase the segment.

5. Type

   zoom

   and press the space bar.

6. Type

   p

   for Previous and press Enter.

Good. The whole bracket should now look like Figure 11.10. You've completed the isometric view of one end of the bracket. Now we will work on the elliptical part for the other end. First you will enlarge the left side, then you'll draw the center ellipse that represents the slot in the bracket and open it at the top.

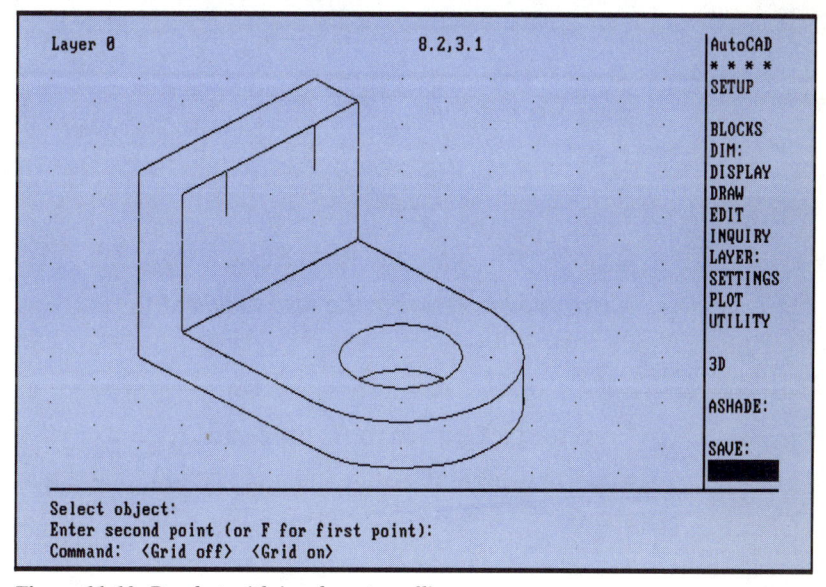

Figure 11.10: Bracket with isoplane-top ellipses

1. Type

    zoom

    and press the space bar.
2. Type

    w

    for Window and press Enter.
3. Move to the upper left to position

    2.2, 7.6

    and press the pick button.
4. Move to the lower right to position

    5.0, 5.5

    and press the pick button.
5. Press ^E to change the cursor to isoplane right.
6. Press F9 to turn on Snap mode.
7. Type

    ellipse

    and press Enter.
8. Type

    i

    for Isometric circle and press Enter.
9. Move midway between the lower ends of the two short vertical lines at location

    3.9, 6.3

    Press the pick button to fix the center.
10. Move upward and to the right one grid point until the readout shows

    0.5 <30

    Press the pick button to establish the ellipse.

Next you will open the ellipse with the P-edit command.

11. Type

    pedit

    and press Enter.

12. Type

    L

    for Last and press Enter to select the ellipse.

13. Type

    o

    and press Enter to open a segment at the top of the ellipse.

14. Press Enter to complete the P-edit command.

15. Press F9 to turn off Snap mode.

Now you will use the Break command and the two-point method of selection to erase parts of the center ellipse.

1. Type

    break

    and press Enter.

2. Move the selection box to the left side of the opening in the ellipse. The coordinate position is

    3.6, 6.4

    Press the pick button.

3. Type the Osnap option

    int

    for Intersection and press Enter.

4. Move left and down to the intersection of the ellipse and the line. The coordinate position is

    3.5, 6.0

    Press the pick button to trim the ellipse back to the line.

5. Press Enter to restart the Break command.
6. Move the selection box to the upper-right edge of the ellipse at location

    4.2, 6.8

    and press the pick button.
7. Type **f** and press Enter to select the three-point method.
8. Type

    end

    and press Enter.
9. Move the selection box to the right side of the opening in the ellipse. When the coordinate readout shows

    3.7, 6.6

    press the pick button.
10. Type

    int

    and press Enter.
11. Move right to the intersection of the ellipse and the line. The coordinate position is

    4.3, 6.5

    Press the pick button to trim the other side of the ellipse back to the second line. Your screen should look like Figure 11.11.

Drawing the Bracket Corners

In this section you draw the left and right corners. First you will draw two ellipses, then you will modify both of them to create the curved corners.

1. Type

    ellipse

    and press Enter.

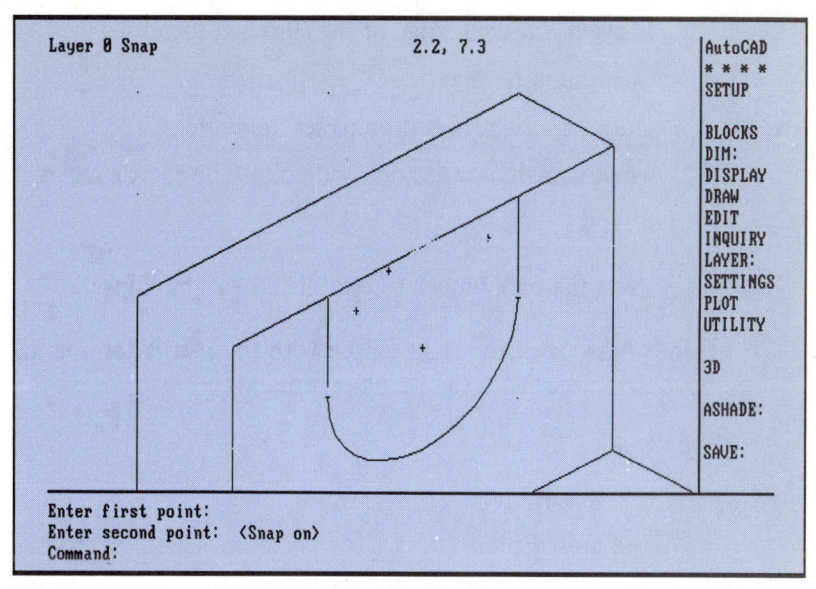

Figure 11.11: Upper half of the ellipse is opened

2. Type

    i

    for Isometric circle and press Enter.

3. Turn on Snap mode with F9.
4. Move to the left edge of the ellipse at location

    3.5, 6.0

    and press the pick button to fix the center of the new ellipse.

5. Move straight upward one grid point. The coordinate readout is

    0.5 <90

6. Press the pick button to establish the left ellipse.
7. Press Enter to restart the Ellipse command.
8. Type

    i

    for Isometric circle and press Enter.

9. Move to the right edge of the ellipse at location

    4.3, 6.5

    and press the pick button to set the center.

10. Move straight upward one grid point. The coordinate readout is

    0.5 <90

11. Press the pick button to establish the right ellipse.

Good. Now open the right ellipse with the P-edit command, then remove two pieces with the Break command.

1. Type

    pedit

    and press Enter.

2. Type

    L

    for Last and press Enter to select the ellipse you just drew.

3. Type

    o

    and press Enter to open a segment at the top of the ellipse.

4. Press Enter to complete the P-edit command.
5. Press F9 to turn off Snap mode.
6. Type

    break

    and press Enter.

7. Move the selection cursor to the left side of the opening at location

    4.0, 6.7

    and press the pick button.

8. Press F9 to turn on Snap mode.

9. Move to the right edge by the vertical line. The coordinate is

    4.8, 6.8

    Press the pick button to erase one part of the ellipse.

10. Press F9 to turn off Snap mode.

11. Press Enter to restart the Break command.

12. Move to the upper end of the ellipse at coordinate readout

    4.2, 6.9

    Press the pick button.

13. Type the Osnap option

    int

    for Intersection and press Enter.

14. Move a little to the right to the grid point at coordinate position

    4.3, 7.0

    Press the pick button to remove the remaining part or the right ellipse.

Now you're ready to remove a piece of the left ellipse with the Break command. We do not have to open the left ellipse with the P-edit command because the opening is not in the region we need to remove.

1. Type

    break

    and press Enter.

2. Move to position

    3.8, 6.5

    and press Enter.

3. Type **f** and press Enter to select the three-point method.

4. Type

    int

    and press Enter.

5. Move to the top edge at coordinate position

    3.5, 6.5

    Press the pick button.

6. Type

    int

    and press Enter.

7. Move to the left edge at coordinate position

    3.0, 5.8

    and press the pick button. You now have curved corners at both sides (Figure 11.12).

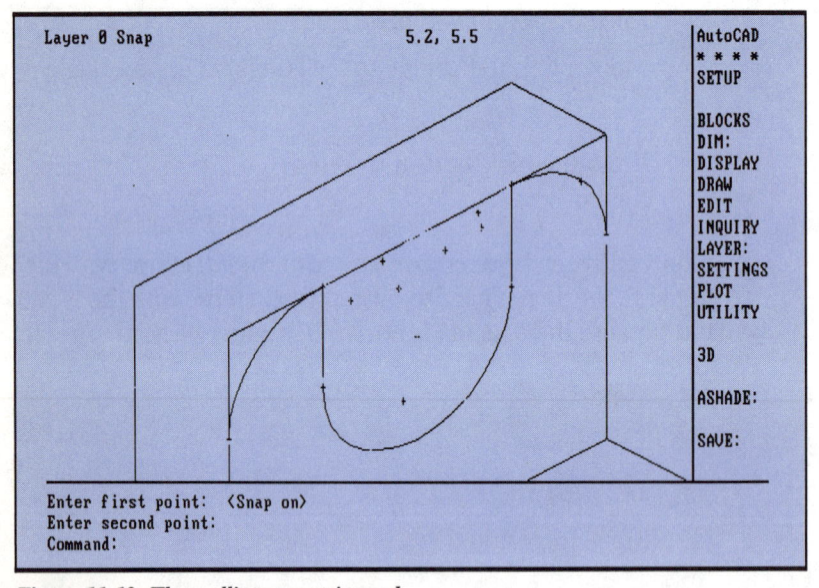

Figure 11.12: Three ellipses are trimmed

Trimming the Openings

In this section you trim away the straight line from the ellipses.

1. Type

    erase

    and press Enter.

2. Move the selection cursor to the center of the line across the top of the ellipses. The coordinate position is

   4.0, 6.8

   Press the pick button to select this line.

3. Move upward and to the left one grid point to select the parallel line at location

   3.5, 7.0

   and press the pick button.

4. Press the second mouse button to erase these two lines.

5. Press F9 to turn on Snap mode.

6. Type

   break

   and press Enter.

7. Move the selection box to the top of the upper-left corner by the left ellipse. When the coordinate readout shows

   3.0, 6.3

   press the pick button.

8. Move down to the next grid point to location

   3.0, 5.8

   and press the pick button to remove the stub.

9. Press F9 to turn off Snap mode.

10. Press Enter to restart the Break command.

11. Move right across the bracket to the upper-right corner. Move down a little from the corner to location

    4.8, 7.1

    Press the pick button.

12. Type

    f

    for First and press Enter to switch to the three-point method.

13. Press F9 to turn on Snap mode.
14. Move up to the corner at coordinate position

    4.8, 7.3

    and press the pick button.
15. Move down one grid point to coordinate position

    4.8, 6.8

    and press the pick button.
16. Press F9 to turn off Snap mode.

Replicating the Three Ellipses

In this section you will copy the three ellipses to the back face. You need to select the three ellipses and the two connecting lines. Since the left ellipse has an opening in it, each half must be separately selected. Thus there are six objects to be selected. You could select them one at a time. However, we will use a Crossing window.

1. Type

   copy

   and press Enter.
2. Type

   c

   for Crossing window and press Enter.
3. Move to coordinate location

   2.9, 7.2

   and press the pick button.
4. Move to coordinate location

   4.7, 5.9

   and press the pick button.
5. When all parts are selected, press the second mouse button to complete the selection step.

6. Now you must give the base and offset. Press F9 to turn on Snap mode.

7. Type the coordinates

    0, 0

    and press Enter.

8. Type

    @0.5 <150

    press Enter to replicate the ellipses and connecting lines. Your screen should look like Figure 11.13.

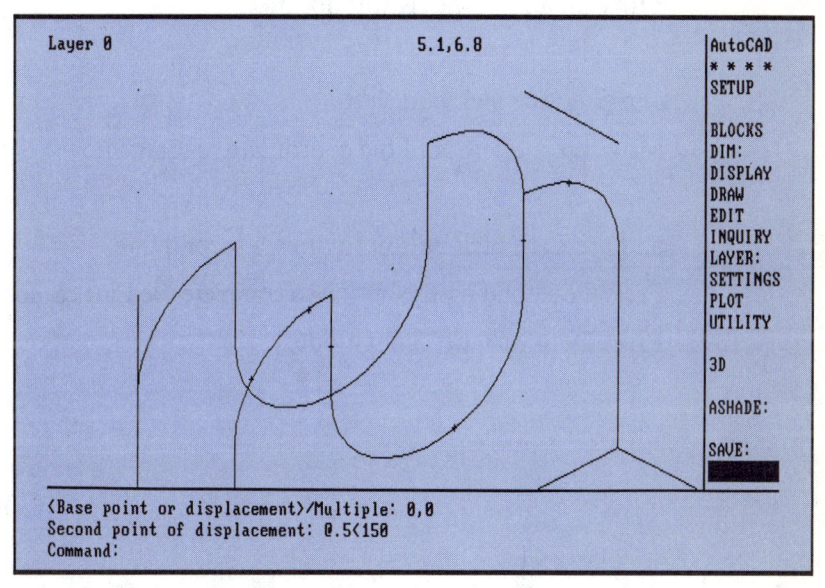

Figure 11.13: The ellipses are copied

Adding Connecting Lines to the Ellipses

In this section you add two connection lines between the two sets of ellipses.

1. Type

    line

    and press Enter.

2. Move to the left rear ellipse and snap to the location

    3.0, 6.8

    Press the pick button.

3. Move downward and to the right to the front ellipse. When the coordinate readout shows

    0.5 <330

    press the pick button to add a line.

4. Press the second mouse button to complete the Line command.

5. Press the second mouse button to restart the Line command.

6. Move up and to the right to location

    4.3, 7.0

    and press the pick button.

7. Move up and left until the coordinate readout shows

    0.5 <150

    and press the pick button to draw a second line.

8. Press the second mouse button to complete the Line command.

9. Press F9 to turn off Snap mode.

Trimming the New Ellipses

1. Type

    erase

    and press Enter.

2. Move the selection box to the vertical line at location

    3.0, 6.5

    and press the pick button.

3. Move the selection box to the short line at location

    4.5, 7.4

    and press the pick button.

4. Press the second mouse button to delete these lines.
5. Press F9 to turn on Snap mode.
6. Type

    break

    and press Enter.
7. Move to the end of the ellipse at location

    3.0, 6.3

    and press the pick button.
8. Move down and right to the crossing of the two ellipses at location

    3.5, 6.0

    and press the pick button to remove another part.

You have nearly completed the isometric view of the bracket. The last steps are to trim one line, add a tangent line, and trim an ellipse.

1. Type

    break

    and press Enter.
2. Move to the end of the upper-left line at location

    2.6, 6.5

    and press the pick button.
3. Move down one grid point to the intersection with the ellipse. When the coordinate position shows

    2.6, 6.0

    press Enter.
4. Press F9 to turn off Snap mode.
5. Type

    line

    and press Enter.

6. Type the Osnap option

    tan

    for Tangent and press Enter.

7. Move the selection box to the ellipses in the upper-right corner at location

    4.2, 7.3

    and press the pick button.

8. Type

    tan

    again and press Enter.

9. Move right and down to the ellipse at location

    4.7, 7.0

    and press the pick button to draw a tangent connector.

10. Press Enter to complete the Line command.
11. To trim the remaining ellipse, type

    break

    and press Enter.

12. Move to location

    4.3, 7.1

    and press the pick button.

13. Type

    f

    for First and press Enter to switch to the three-point method.

14. Press F9 to turn on Snap mode.
15. Move to location

    4.3, 7.0

    and press the pick button.

16. Press F9 to turn off Snap mode.

17. Type

    int

    and press Enter.

18. Move to location

    4.2, 7.3

    and press the pick button to trim the last piece. Your screen should look like Figure 11.14.

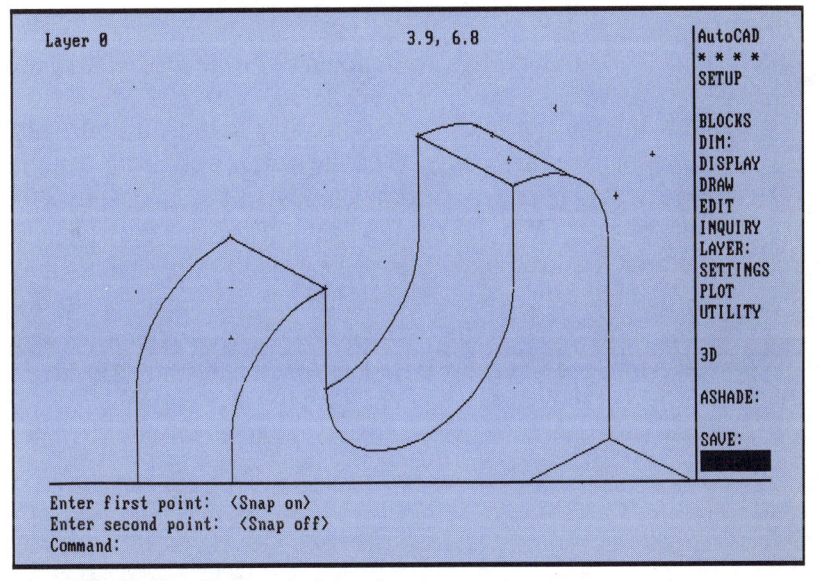

Figure 11.14: The ellipses are trimmed

19. Press F7 to remove the plus marks.

You have completed the isometric view. Take a look at the full view of the bracket with the Dynamic Zoom command.

1. Type

    zoom

    and press the space bar.

2. Type

    d

for Dynamic and press Enter. The scale changes to show the entire bracket.

3. Move the zoom box until the coordinate readout shows

    3.4, 5.2

    and press the pick button. The X in the cursor box changes to an arrow.

4. Move the box until it surrounds the bracket. The coordinate readout shows

    5.2, 5.3

    Press Enter. The screen should show the bracket in Figure 6.1.

Now that you have explored some of the most useful AutoCAD commands, you are ready to create larger and more complicated drawings. As a next step, you could draw a set of layouts for drawings of various sizes. You could complete parts of the legend giving your name and organization. Then you can load these layouts into each new drawing using the Insert command. Another possibility is to explore some of the AutoCAD commands and options not discussed in this book. See Appendix B for a list of all the AutoCAD commands.

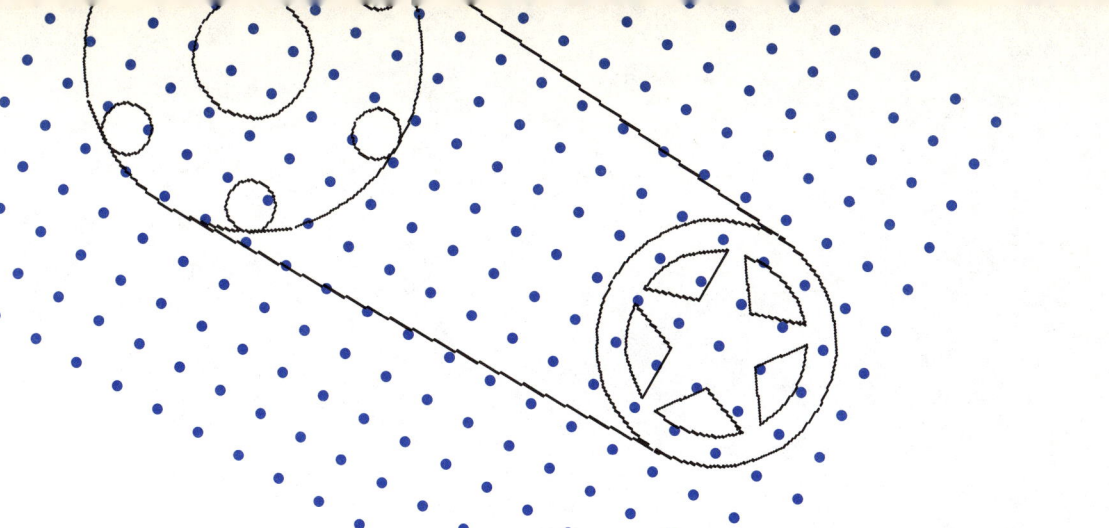

A

Installing AutoCAD

In this appendix you will learn how to install AutoCAD on your computer. The first section gives you some pointers on working with floppy disks. The required and recommended equipment is listed next. Then, the steps for starting your computer and setting it up for AutoCAD are given. AutoCAD then is copied to the hard disk of your computer. Finally, AutoCAD is started and configured for your system.

Working with Floppy Disks

This section contains some important information about using and handling disks. The simple safeguards given here will help you protect your disks from many common dangers.

How to Write-Protect Your Disks

Five-inch disks are equipped with a *write-protect* notch. When this notch is covered with a piece of tape, the disk drive can no longer record or write on the disk. However, when the notch is exposed, that is, when the tape is not in place, the disk can be written on. The 3.5-inch disk has a write-protect window with a built-in tab. When the window is closed with the tab, information can be written on the disk. When the window is open, the disk is write-protected. Write-protection safeguards important information. For example, the original DOS disks that came with your computer and your AutoCAD disks should be write-protected. Of course, you must not write-protect a disk when you want to record information on it.

Handling Disks

Five-inch disks are delicate and can be easily damaged. Always treat them with care. Put each disk in its protective sleeve and place it into a box when you're not using it. You can grasp a disk by its outer cover, but do not touch the exposed magnetic surfaces, especially the slotted opening for the magnetic heads. The grease from your fingers can ruin both the disk and the drive head.

Do not expose a disk to dust, smoke, or liquids, and be especially careful to keep the disk away from magnetic fields or metal that might be magnetized. Do not write on a 5-inch disk with a ball-point pen or a pencil because the impression of the writing instrument can damage the underlying surface. Mark the disk only with a felt-tipped pen or write on a separate label and then affix the label to the disk.

Inserting a Disk into the Disk Drive

Hold the disk with your right thumb on the label as you insert it into the drive. The write-protect notch is on the left side. Insert the 3.5-inch disk with the arrow on the upper-left side pointing inward. When the 5-inch disk is in position, turn or press the drive handle to close the drive and position the magnetic heads. The 3.5-inch disk is automatically seated.

You should never remove or insert a disk, or turn off the computer when the computer is reading or writing on the disk. There is an indicator light on each drive that is turned on when the disk is in use. To be safe, always check that the light is off before inserting or removing a disk or turning off the computer. You can, however, safely turn off the computer while a disk is still in the drive if the computer is not using that drive.

AutoCAD is such a large program that it will not fit on a single floppy disk. Therefore, it is awkward to run AutoCAD with floppy disks. It is a good idea to copy AutoCAD from the original floppy disks to a hard disk. A hard disk can store many times more information than a floppy disk, and it operates much faster, too. However, you must remember that all the information on a hard disk can be accidentally erased. Therefore, it is important to make backup copies of your work onto floppy disks. (Of course, it is not necessary to copy the AutoCAD or DOS disks.)

Required and Recommended Equipment to Run AutoCAD

The following equipment is needed to run AutoCAD:

- IBM PC, XT, AT, or compatible computer

- A minimum of 512K bytes of main memory, but 640K bytes is recommended
- Hard disk and floppy disk
- An 8087, 80287, or 80387 math coprocessor (starting with Release 9)
- Graphics video screen (Hercules, EGA, or VGA)
- Dot-matrix or laser printer
- PC-DOS or MS-DOS (version 2 or later)

The following equipment is recommended, but not essential, to run AutoCAD:

- Mouse, tablet, or other input device
- Expanded or extended memory up to 4M bytes
- Plotter
- Surge suppressor

How to Configure Your Computer for AutoCAD

The following section gives directions for turning on and configuring your computer. For more information, consult your DOS manual or *The ABC's of PC-DOS* (1987), another excellent Sybex publication.

Each time you turn on your computer, several features are automatically set to default values. However these original values are not best for running AutoCAD; you can greatly improve AutoCAD's performance by changing them. Furthermore, you can make the changes in such a way that they are automatically put into effect each time you turn on your computer. Before you change these default settings, follow these steps to turn on your computer.

1. Make sure that there is no floppy disk in the disk drive.
2. Check that the main switch on the computer and on the video screen (if present) are on.

3. Turn on the surge suppressor switch to start up the computer. (If you do not have a surge suppressor, you should consider getting one to protect your computer and the information stored there.)

Good. First you'll set the prompt.

How to Set the Prompt

In this section you will set the prompt to display the subdirectory name as well as the drive name.

The prompt

C>

or

C:\>

should be present on the screen. This is the DOS prompt and indicates that the root directory of drive C is current. If the lines

Current date is Tue 01-01-1980
Enter new date (mm-dd-yy)

appear instead, your computer needs more extensive set-up. See your DOS manual or *The ABC's of PC-DOS* for details.

1. At the C> prompt, type the command

    set

    and press Enter.

2. Look for a line that begins with

    PROMPT =

    If that line is not present, type the command

    prompt = pg

    and press Enter. This will help you find your way around the hard disk.

3. The prompt should be

    C:\>

If the prompt begins with another letter, type

c:

and press Enter.

4. If the prompt begins with the letter C, but is not

C:\>

type

cd

and press Enter. The root directory of the hard disk is current.

*H*ow to Set the Number of Files and Buffers

In this section you will set the number of files and the amount of working space (called memory buffers) to the optimum values. There is an upper limit to the number of disk files and memory buffers that you can use. Unfortunately, the default values are so small that they cause AutoCAD to run slowly. Therefore, you should increase the number of files and buffers that can be used. The changes are made to a DOS file named CONFIG.SYS.

1. To check the number of files and buffers, give the command

    type config.sys

    and press Enter.

2. Look at the display on the video screen. If the words

    File not found

    appear, it means that there is no file named CONFIG.SYS and you will need to create one. Complete steps 3, 4, and 5, then go to step 9. If that message does not appear, go to step 6.

3. To create a CONFIG.SYS file from the keyboard, type the command

    copy con config.sys

    and press Enter. Be sure to put a space after *copy* and after *con*.

4. Type the two lines

    buffers = 20
    files = 15

   pressing Enter at the end of each line.

5. Give the command ^ Z and press Enter.

6. If there is a file named CONFIG.SYS, look for a message that shows the number of buffers and files. If it reads

    buffers = 20
    files = 15

   then the default values have already been increased. Go on to the next section. If you do not see these lines, or if the numbers are smaller than the ones shown, you should add the above lines to the CONFIG.SYS file. Complete steps 7-9.

7. To add the two lines to your CONFIG.SYS file, type the command

    copy config.sys + con

   and press Enter.

8. Type the two lines

    buffers = 20
    files = 15

   pressing Enter at the end of each line.

9. Give the command

    ^ z

   and press Enter.

Good. You've set the number of files and buffers. Go to the next section to set up another DOS file.

How to Set Up the AUTOEXEC.BAT File

Each time your computer is turned on, the disk file named AUTOEXEC.BAT is automatically read for instructions. There are several instructions you should place in this file, if they are not already present. To check what is already there, follow these steps:

1. Give the command

    type autoexec.bat

    and press Enter.

2. Look at the display on the video screen. If the words

    File not found

    appear, it means that there is no file by that name and you will need to create one. Complete steps 3-5. If that message does not appear, go to step 6.

3. To create an AUTOEXEC.BAT file from the keyboard, type the command

    copy con autoexec.bat

    and press Enter. Be sure to put a space after *copy* and *con*.

4. Type the lines

    verify on
    path c:\;c:\acad
    prompt pg
    mouse

    pressing Enter at the end of each line.

5. Give the command ^ Z and press Enter.

6. If there is a file named AUTOEXEC.BAT, look for the following commands:

    PATH C:\;C:\ACAD
    VERIFY ON
    PROMPT PG
    MOUSE

    If these commands are not in the AUTOEXEC.BAT file, you should add them. Follow steps 7-9.

7. To add lines to your AUTOEXEC.BAT file, type the command

    copy autoexec.bat + con

    and press Enter.

8. Type the lines

   verify on
   path c:\;c:\acad
   prompt pg
   mouse

   as needed, pressing Enter after each line.

9. Give the command ^Z and press Enter.

How to Set Up Mouse-Driver Software

If you have a mouse, you need to install mouse-driver software in order to use it. Several different drivers may be provided, but let's install the one called MOUSE.COM.

1. If the prompt is not

   C:\>

   type

   cd

   and press Enter to make the root directory current.

2. Type

   dir mouse*

   and press Enter. Look for the name

   MOUSE COM

   on the screen.

3. If you cannot find this line, put the floppy disk that came with your mouse in drive A. Type the command

   copy a:mouse.com

   and press Enter.

4. Type

   mouse

   and press Enter.

Your mouse driver is now installed and ready to use each time you turn on your computer.

How to Reset the Computer

The changes you make to the CONFIG.SYS and AUTOEXEC.BAT files do not take effect until you reset your computer.

1. Make sure that there is no floppy diskette in drive A.
2. Press simultaneously the three keys Ctrl, Alt, and Del and the computer will be reset.

How to Set Up the AutoCAD Subdirectory

The AutoCAD program should be in a subdirectory named ACAD. (A subdirectory is a partition of the disk devoted to one subject.) Let us check to see if you have such a subdirectory, and then create one if you do not.

1. Be sure that the root directory is current. Look for the *C:\>* prompt. Give the command **cd** if you don't see this prompt.
2. Give the command

    dir ac*.

    and press Enter. The dot at the end of the command selects subdirectories.
3. If the line

    file not found

    appears on the screen, there is no AutoCAD directory. Go to steps 4 and 5 to create one. If the line

    ACAD <DIR>

    appears on the screen, you already have an AutoCAD directory. Skip steps 4 and 5 and go to the next section.

4. To create an AutoCAD directory, type

   md\acad

   and press Enter. (MD is the Make Directory command.)

5. Type

   cd\acad

   to make this subdirectory current. The prompt now should be

   C:\ACAD>

*H*ow to Copy AutoCAD to Your Hard Disk

In this section you will copy some of the AutoCAD files from the original floppy disks to your hard disk. Then you can put the original disks away in a safe place. There are six disks to copy if you have 5-inch floppies, fewer if you have 3½-inch disks.

1. Put the disk named

   EXECUTABLE & OVERLAYS

   in drive A.

2. Check that the prompt is

   C:\ACAD>

3. Type

   copy a:*.*

   and press Enter. The name of each file is listed on the screen as it is copied from the floppy disk to the hard disk.

4. When all files have been copied, remove the disk from drive A and replace it with the disk named

   OVERLAYS 1

5. Type

   copy a:*.*

(or press F3 to repeat the previous command) and press Enter. Again, the name of each file is listed on the screen as it is copied from the floppy disk to the hard disk.

6. When all files have been copied, remove the disk from drive A and replace it with the disk named

    OVERLAYS 2

7. Type

    copy a:*.*

    (or press F3 to repeat the previous command) and press Enter.

8. When all files have been copied, remove the disk from drive A and replace it with the disk named

    OVERLAYS 3

9. Type

    copy a:*.*

    (or press F3 to repeat the previous command) and press Enter.

10. When all files have been copied, remove the disk from drive A and replace it with the disk named

    SUPPORT DISK 1

11. Type

    copy a:*.*

    (or press F3 to repeat the previous command) and press Enter.

12. When all files have been copied, remove the disk from drive A and replace it with the disk named

    SUPPORT DISK 2

13. Type

    copy a:*.*

    (or press F3) and press Enter.

If you have room on your hard disk (about 320K bytes) you can also copy the disk named SAMPLE DRAWINGS. This disk contains several interesting drawings, including the Challenger spacecraft and St. Paul's cathedral. However, each of these drawings requires over 100K bytes of disk space.

Configuring AutoCAD for Your Computer

The first step in configuring AutoCAD is to copy the driver disks, which set up the program to work with your hardware. There are two disks containing routines that are needed to ensure that AutoCAD works properly with your hardware, including the video display, the mouse, the printer, and the plotter. These routines are known as *device drivers*. The disks containing the device drivers are named DRIVER DISK 1 and DRIVER DISK 2. There are many files on these disks; however, you will only need a few of them. Furthermore, you only need these routines during the configuration step, when AutoCAD asks you for the location of the device drivers. Therefore, you do not want to put them in the ACAD directory of your hard disk.

We will consider two ways to use the driver routines—using backup floppy disks, and temporarily copying files to a separate hard-disk directory. The floppy-disk method is better if you know where to find the DISKCOPY program, which is used to make backup copies of disks. However, you cannot use the hard-disk method if there is not enough room on the disk. Let us consider the floppy-disk method first.

Copying the Driver Routines to Another Floppy Disk

You can configure AutoCAD from driver routines located in a floppy disk in drive A. However, you should not use the original disks. Rather you should make backup copies and then use only the copies. This is a good method to use if you know how to find the DOS program named DISKCOPY.COM or DISKCOPY.EXE. If you don't know how to find this program, go to the next method.

1. Get two new disks. Write the words DRIVER DISK 1 and DRIVER DISK 2 on labels and place them on the new disks.

2. Give the command

   diskcopy a: a:

   and press Enter.

3. When the prompt

   Insert SOURCE diskette in drive A:
   Press any key when ready . . .

   appears on the screen, put the *original* version of DRIVER DISK 1 in drive A and press Enter.

4. When the prompt

   Insert TARGET diskette in drive A:
   Press any key when ready . . .

   appears on the screen, remove the original disk and replace it with the corresponding new disk. Press Enter.

5. If your computer memory is not large enough, you will be prompted to repeat steps 3 and 4. Switch the disks as instructed.

6. When the message

   Copy another diskette (Y/N)?

   appears, remove the new disk and replace it with the *original* version of DRIVER DISK 2. Type **Y** and press Enter to copy the second driver disk. Follow the instructions as you did for disk 1.

7. When you have copied the driver disks, put the original disks in a safe place.

Temporarily Storing the Driver Routines on the Hard Disk

An easier method for configuring AutoCAD is to create on your hard disk a separate subdirectory for the driver routines. The disadvantage with this method is that you need about 500K (500,000) bytes of disk space. You can then copy these routines from the original floppy disk to the hard disk. Since you need these files only for configuring the program, you can erase the driver routines from your hard disk after configuring AutoCAD to recover the space. The final section in this appendix explains how to erase the routines.

First you must determine if you have enough disk space. Let's do that now.

1. Make the hard disk current by typing the command

    c:

    and pressing Enter.

2. Give the command

    md\acaddrv

    to create a new directory for the driver routines.

3. To change to the new directory, give the command

    cd\acaddrv

    (or type **c** and press F3 to repeat the previous command) and press Enter.

4. Type the command

    dir *.

    and press Enter.

The resulting output on the screen will end with a line such as

1000000 bytes free

telling how much space is left. Check that you have at least 500,000 bytes. If don't have that much space, you cannot use this method and will have to copy the disks to floppy disks, as described previously in this section. If you do have enough space, complete the following steps.

1. Put DRIVER DISK 1 in drive A.

2. Type the command

    copy a:*.*

    and press Enter.

3. When all the routines have been copied, change to DRIVER DISK 2 and give the command

    copy a:*.*

and press Enter to copy the second disk.

Good. You have one more task before you configure AutoCAD for your computer.

Recovering a Routine from Driver Disk 1

There is one routine on the first driver disk that must be copied to the AutoCAD subdirectory. Let us do that now.

1. Make sure that drive C is current and give the command

    cd\acad

    Press Enter to change to the AutoCAD subdirectory.

2. Give the command

    copy   \acaddrv*.ovl

    and press Enter. Be sure to put a space after *copy,* but nowhere else. This will copy the file from the driver disk to the AutoCAD directory.

*C*onfiguring AutoCAD for Your Hardware

In this section you will start AutoCAD and configure it for your hardware.

1. Make sure that the AutoCAD directory is current. Type

    cd\acad

    if it is not.

2. Start AutoCAD by typing

    acad

    and pressing Enter.

3. Press Enter when the opening message appears.

4. AutoCAD automatically determines that it has not been configured. The prompt

   Enter drive or directory containing the display device drivers:

   appears because the driver routines are not located in the current directory.

5. If your AutoCAD device drivers are on a floppy disk, put the driver disk 1 in drive A. Type

   a:

   and press Enter. If you have copied the driver routines into a subdirectory of the hard disk, give the command

   \acaddrv

   and press Enter. AutoCAD will then find the routines it needs.

6. Next, a list of the video screens with corresponding reference numbers appears on the screen (Figure A.1). Look through the list for your screen and record the number. For example, a Hercules screen is 14 and an IBM EGA is 18. The listing stops when the screen is filled. Press Enter to see the next screen.

7. At the prompt

   Select device number or ? to repeat list <1>:

   type the number of your screen and press Enter.

8. Press Enter to accept the default settings for the following questions.

   If you have previously measured the height and width of a "square" on your graphics screen, you may use these measurements to correct the aspect ratio.

   Would you like to do so? <N>

   Do you want a status line? <Y>

   Do you want a command prompt area? <Y>

   Do you want a screen menu area? <Y>

Installing AutoCAD **341**

> **You may select either a dark (black) or a light graphics area background. If you select a light graphics area background, then lines drawn in color 7 will be drawn in black instead. This choice most closely resembles a black ink drawing on paper.**
>
> **Do you want dark vectors on a light background field? <Y>**
>
> **Do you want to supply individual colors for parts of the graphics screen? <N>**
>
> **Press RETURN to continue:**

You may need to repeat this operation later to make changes.

9. AutoCAD now asks you to specify the type of mouse or other pointing device. Type the corresponding number of your device.

10. Now select the type of printer and plotter by typing the number that matches your equipment. Then AutoCAD lists the names of the hardware devices you have selected—the video display, digitizer (mouse), plotter, and printer.

11. Press Enter to return to the Configuration menu.

12. Press Enter again to return to the Main menu.

13. You are asked to verify that you want to save the configuration changes you just made. Press Enter to accept the default value of Y.

AutoCAD is now ready to run. But before you continue, let's check the vertical-to-horizontal aspect ratio by drawing a circle. You need to set this feature if circles are flattened and look like ovals. However, until you begin drawing with AutoCAD, you won't know if circles are flattened and what ratio to choose.

1. At the AutoCAD Main menu, type **1** and press Enter to start a new drawing.

1. ADI display v3.0
2. BNW Precision Graphics Adapter
3. Bell & Howell CDI IV
4. Cambridge Micro-1024
5. Compaq Portable III Plasma Display
6. Conographic Model-40 Color Display
7. Control Systems Artist I & II
8. Control Systems Transformer
9. Cordata 400 Line graphics
10. Cordata Fast Draft 480
11. Frontier CADgraph 2
12. GraphAx 20/20 display
13. HP Enhanced Graphics Adapter
14. Hercules Graphics Card
15. Hewlett-Packard 82960 Graphics Controller
16. Hewlett-Packard Multi Mode Video Adapter
17. IBM Color/Graphics
18. IBM Enhanced Graphics Adapter
19. IBM Personal System/2   8514/A Display
20. IBM Professional Graphics Controller

— Press RETURN for more —

Figure A.1: AutoCAD list of video displays

2. Type the name

    chkcir

    and press Enter.

3. When the drawing screen appears, type

    circle

    and press Enter.

4. Move the cursor to the center of the screen and press Enter or the left mouse button.

5. Move the mouse upward to create a circle that nearly fills the screen. Press Enter or the left mouse button to establish the circle.

6. With a decimal ruler, measure the vertical diameter of the circle and record the number.

7. Measure the horizontal diameter of the circle and record the number. If the two numbers are the same, your aspect ratio is correct. You can skip over the rest of this section. (I have found that the Hercules screen needs to be adjusted but the EGA does not.)

8. Type

    end

    and press Enter to save the program and return to the Main menu.

9. At the Main menu, type **5** and press Enter to reconfigure AutoCAD.

10. The current configuration is displayed on the screen. For example, you might see

    Current AutoCAD configuration
    Video display: Hercules Graphics Card
    Digitizer: Microsoft Serial or Bus Mouse
    Plotter: Hewlett-Packard 7470
    Printer plotter: Epson FX-80

    Press Enter to continue.

11. The Configuration menu appears next (Figure A.2). Type **3** and press Enter to change the video display.

> 0. Exit to Main Menu
> 1. Show current configuration
> 2. Allow I/O port configuration
> 3. Configure video display
> 4. Configure digitizer
> 5. Configure plotter
> 6. Configure printer plotter
> 7. Configure system console
> 8. Configure operating parameters
>
> Enter selection <0>:

Figure A.2: The AutoCAD Configuration menu

12. Your current video display is identified and you are asked if you want to select a different one. Press Enter to accept the default answer of N. You do not need the driver routines this time.
13. Next, you are asked if you want to change the aspect ratio. Type **Y** and press Enter.
14. When the prompt

    Width of square <1.0000>:

    appears, type the horizontal size you measured and press Enter. For example, type 160 if you found 160 mm.
15. When the prompt

    Height of square <1.0000>:

    appears, type the vertical size you measured and press Enter. For example, type 150 if you found 150 mm.

16. Press Enter to the next questions about status line and prompt area.

17. If you see the prompt

    Do you want dark vectors on a light background? <Y>

    (which is only available on some screens and some AutoCAD versions), press Enter. This will draw dark lines on a light screen instead of the usual reverse. If you find that the screen is too bright, reconfigure AutoCAD and type **N** at this point.

18. Press Enter again until the Configuration menu appears.

19. Type **0** and press Enter to return to the Main menu.

20. AutoCAD asks if you want to keep the changes you just made. Press Enter to accept the default value of Y.

21. At the AutoCAD Main menu, type **2** and press Enter to continue with an existing drawing.

22. Type the name

    chkcir

    and press Enter.

23. Measure the height and width of the circle. If they are not equal, repeat the above steps to reset the aspect ratio.

How to Erase the Hard-Disk Drivers

If you copied the device drivers to a subdirectory of your hard disk, you may erase them now, since you will no longer need them. You now can use this space on your hard disk for other files and programs.

1. Give the command

   del c:\acaddrv*.*

   and press Enter.

2. When you are asked for verification, type **Y** and press Enter.

3. To remove the driver subdirectory, type

   rd\acaddrv

   and press Enter.

Now AutoCAD is ready for use.

B

AutoCAD Commands

This appendix lists the AutoCAD commands that can be typed from the keyboard. You can view this list on screen through AutoCAD's Help feature—just type **help** or **?** and press Enter.

An apostrophe in front of a command means that it can be given while another command is running. The symbols +1, +2, and +3 mean that AutoCAD files named ACAD0.OVL, ACAD2.OVL, and ACAD3.OVL are required. At the DOS prompt, type **dir acad?.OVL** and look for these file names in the listing.

APERTURE +2	DIST
ARC	DIVIDE +3
AREA	DONUT +3
ARRAY	DOUGHNUT +3
ATTDEF +2	DRAGMODE +2
ATTDISP +2	DTEXT +3
ATTEDIT +2	DXBIN +3
ATTEXT +2	DXFIN
AXIS +1	DXFOUT
BASE	ELEV +3
BLIPMODE	ELLIPSE +3
BLOCK	END
BREAK +1	ERASE
CHAMFER +1	EXPLODE +3
CHANGE	EXTEND +3
CIRCLE	FILES
COLOR	FILL
COPY	FILLET +1
DBLIST	FILMROLL +3
DDATTE +3	'GRAPHSCR
'DDEMODES +3	GRID
'DDLMODES +3	HATCH +1
'DDRMODES +3	'HELP / '?
DELAY	HIDE +3
DIM/DIM1 +1	ID

IGESIN +3
IGESOUT +3
INSERT
ISOPLANE +2
LAYER
LIMITS
LINE
LINETYPE
LIST
LOAD
LTSCALE
MEASURE +3
MENU
MINSERT
MIRROR +2
MOVE
MSLIDE +2
MULTIPLE
OFFSET +3
OOPS
ORTHO
OSNAP +2
'PAN
PEDIT +3
PLINE +3
PLOT
POINT
POLYGON +3
PRPLOT
PURGE
QTEXT

QUIT
REDEFINE +3
REDO
'REDRAW
REGEN
REGENAUTO
RENAME
'RESUME
ROTATE +3
RSCRIPT
SAVE
SCALE +3
SCRIPT
SELECT
'SETVAR
SHAPE
SHELL/SH +3
SKETCH +1
SNAP
SOLID
STATUS
STRETCH +3
STYLE
TABLET
TEXT
'TEXTSCR
TIME
TRACE
TRIM +3
U
UNDEFINE +3

UNDO	VSLIDE
UNITS +1	WBLOCK
'VIEW +2	'ZOOM
VIEWRES	3DFACE +3
VPOINT +3	3DLINE +3

Index

^ C, 44-45
^ E, 282, 285

A

abbreviating commands, 96
acad command, 10
ACAD command (DOS), 339
ACAD subdirectory, 333
Add command, 50
ADE-1, 33
ADE-2, 33
ADE-3, 33
aligned dimension, 275
Alt key, 4
angle brackets, 20, 37
angled lines, 25, 28
apostrophe, 33-34
applications software, 3
Arc command, 110-111, 139-143
Array command, 81, 106-107, 116-118, 186, 266
arrowheads, drawing, 171
aspect ratio, 344
AutoCAD
  configuring, 336-346
  copying to hard disk, 334-336
  installing, 325-346
  prompt, 13
  required equipment, 326-327
  starting, 9-12
AutoCAD command list, 349-351
AutoCAD commands. *See* individual command names
AutoCAD menus. *See* individual menu names

AUTOEXEC.BAT, 330-332
axes, 15

B

backspace key, 4
backup. *See* Save command
backup copies, 326, 336-337
base point, 64, 91, 93, 302
borders, 124
  making templates for, 127
Break command, 97, 114, 197-201, 299, 306, 309, 312, 313
  three-point method, 103
  two-point method, 98-101, 309
buffers, 329-330

C

CAD, 1
canceling commands, 44-45
cartesian coordinates, 15
CD command (DOS), 10, 334, 338-339
Cen command, 265, 269
Center command (osnap), 67, 91, 93, 107, 110-111, 117, 183-184, 187, 267, 270
center line style, 253
center lines, 188, 190, 238, 243, 246
Change command, 57-58, 60, 150, 189, 224, 244, 253, 259, 270, 274
Change Point option, 60

Circle command, 35, 84-85, 104, 173, 176, 269, 343
circles, 104-105
Close command, 127, 130
command line, 6
commands, giving to AutoCAD, 12-13. *See also* individual command names
completing a drawing, 54
Complex font, 216
computer components, 2-3
concentric circles, 104
CONFIG.SYS, 329
Configuration menu, 341, 344-345
configuring AutoCAD, 336-346
construction line, 110, 115, 182-183, 185
continuous line type, 147, 149
control character, 6
Control key (Ctrl), 4, 6
Control-C, 44-45
Control-E, 282, 285
coordinates, 14, 83
Copy command, 45, 57, 62, 302, 316
COPY command (DOS), 330, 334-335, 338-339
COPY CON command (DOS), 329, 331
copying files, 57
CPU, 2
cross hatching. *See* Hatch patterns
Crossing command, 51
Crossing window, 46, 51, 316
Ctrl key, 4, 6
Ctrl-C, 44-45
Ctrl-E, 282, 285
current layer, 224-225, 230
cursor, 21
  drawing, 9
  in DOS, 5

cutting plane, 171, 271
cutting-plane line, 171, 271, 274

D

data files, 3
default values, 327
DEL command (DOS), 345
Del key, 5
device drivers, 336
  display, 340
Diameter command, 249
Dimcen command, 246-247
Dimension subcommands, 240, 247-250, 255, 261, 265, 268, 275
dimension line, 237
dimension text, 241-242
dimensioning, 237
  horizontal, 241
  one-point method, 239
  two-point method, 256
  vertical, 240
DIR command (DOS), 332-333, 338
disks, 2, 325-326
disk drive, 326
disk file, 155, 157
disk operating system (DOS), 3, 6, 9, 327. *See also* individual DOS command names
disk space, 338
DISKCOPY command (DOS), 336-337
displacement, establishing, 63
display device drivers, 340
displayed digits, 23
DOS, 3, 6, 9, 327
DOS commands. *See* individual command names
DOS prompt, 5, 328

dot-matrix printer, 155, 165
drawing area, setting up, 81–83
drawing cursor, 9, 14
drawing editor, 12–13
drawing limits, 18
driver disks, 336
Dtext command, 215, 219–220, 231
duplicating objects, 62
Dynamic Zoom command, 107–109, 118, 245–246, 254, 321–322

E

ellipses, 288, 301
  erasing part of, 291–293, 299–301
  locating end points, 291–293
Ellipse command, 138–139, 174, 289, 291, 298, 308, 310–311
End command, 54, 119, 260, 278, 343
End command (osnap), 111, 114, 258, 310
enlarging screen images. *See* Zoom
Enter key, 4, 6, 12, 31, 33, 44, 59
equal sign, 11, 58, 125, 172
Erase command, 51, 68, 98, 135, 144, 185, 197, 266–267, 269, 294, 314, 318
  a and r options, 266
Escape key (Esc), 4
exit icon menu item, 217
Explode command, 133–134, 136
Extend command, 114, 179–180
extension line, 238

F

F option, 98
files, 3, 329–330
flat sides in circles, 178

floppy disks, 2
  damage to, 326
  using, 325–326
Font file, 217
fonts, 215
  Monotxt, 215
  Romanc, 216
  Simplex, 216
  Txt, 215
Fonts menu item, 217
function keys, 5
  F1 (flip-screen), 18
  F6 (coordinate display), 14
  F7 (grid system), 20
  F8 (ortho mode), 26
  F9 (snap mode), 21

G

getting help, 34–35
Grid command, 22, 125, 173
grid points, 20
grid spacing, 21–22
grid system, 20

H

hard disk, 2, 326
hardware, 2
hardware configuration, 327
Hatch command, 195–196, 202
hatch patterns, 194–196
Help command, 33–34
hexagonal grid, 288
hexagonal orientation, 282
hidden lines, 146–147, 149, 151, 171
Home key, 5
Horizontal dimension command, 241, 251, 255, 262

I

I/O, 2
icon menu, 217
input/output ports, 2
Inquiry menu, 18
Insert command, 172
Insert (Ins) key, 5
inserting a drawing, 171
installing AutoCAD, 325-346
Int command (osnap), 102-103, 183, 200-201, 256, 263, 275-276, 306, 309, 310, 313-314, 321
interior lines, 188, 191
interrupt commands, 46
isometric circles, 288-289
Isometric ellipse command, 282, 289
isometric grid, 284
isometric mode, 282
Isometric snap command, 282, 283
isometric style, 283
isometric view, 128, 281-282, 284, 295, 307
isoplane ellipse, 290-291
isoplane left and right, 284-285, 287-289
isoplane top, 284-285, 287-289

K

keyboard, 4
keys. *See* individual key names

L

laser printer, 155, 165
Last command, 45
Layer 0, 223
Layer command, 223-226, 230, 232, 238, 261
layers, 223
  changing, 232
  making current, 224-225, 230, 232
  turning off, 224
  turning on, 225
leader, 238
Leader command, 250, 257, 276-277
legend border, 214, 219, 228
legends, 213, 219
limits, 19
Limits command, 20, 82
Line command, 24-25, 27, 32, 58, 83, 110, 112, 128-130, 135, 137-138, 147-149, 178-179, 183, 189-192, 194, 229, 243-244, 253, 258, 286, 295-298, 305, 317, 319
line segment, 27
Line Type command, 150
line types, 145-146, 150. *See also* Continuous line type, Hidden line type, Phantom line type, Scale line type
line widths, 124
lines
  converting to polylines, 159-164, 203-209
  increasing width, 165, 203-209. *See also* individual line names
lowercase letters, 22
Ltscale command, 151-152, 190

M

Main menu, 10-11, 54, 341
Mark option, 97
math coprocessor, 2
MAX plot size, 166
MD command (DOS), 334, 338
memory buffers, 329
Mid command (osnap), 112
Mirror command, 113

Index

monitor, 2
Monotxt font, 215
mouse, 12–14, 341
mouse buttons, 13
mouse command (DOS), 332
mouse driver software, installing, 12, 332
Move command, 42, 45–46, 57, 62, 67, 92

N

number pad, 5
NumLock key, 5

O

object selection, 41–53
　adding objects, 50–51
　with Crossing window, 51, 53
　L option, 45–46
　pointing, 41, 45
　previously drawn, 45–46
　previously selected, 45
　with Regular window, 46–49
　removing objects, 49–50
object snap, 65. *See also* individual Osnap command names
　Open option, 292
operating system. *See* Disk operating system
Options pull-down menu, 217–218
Ortho command, 24
Ortho mode, 26, 28, 58, 60
orthogonal axes, 15
orthogonal view, 281
orthographic projection, 1, 15
orthographic view, 128
osnap, 65
Osnap command, 179
Osnap commands. *See* individual command names
Osnap menu, 65
　displaying with mouse, 66
　Release 9, 66
Osnap options, 65

P

P command, 45
P-edit command, 159, 161, 165, 204, 206, 292, 299, 304, 309, 312
　Open option of, 292
P-line command, 124, 126, 127, 171, 214, 272
　changing line width with, 272–273
path, 331
PgDn key, 5
PgUp key, 5
phantom line type, 171, 274
pick button, 13, 27–28, 58–59
Plot command, 155
Plot Display option, 155
Plot Extents option, 155
Plot Limits option, 156
Plot View option, 156
Plot Window option, 155
plotter, 1, 3, 9, 155, 165, 341
plotting to disk file, 155, 157
plus sign, 25, 31, 52
pointing device, 341. *See also* Mouse
polar array, 106
polar notation, 16
polar reference, 27, 59
Polygon command, 131–132
Polyline command. *See* P-line command
polyline join, 160
polyline width, 159
polylines, 155, 171
　converting from lines, 159, 203–209

ports, 2
Previous command, 45
printers, 3, 9, 155, 341
printouts, obtaining, 155
projection, 1
properties, 150
Prplot command, 156, 166
PrtSc key, 33
pull-down menu, 217

Q

Qtext command, 221
Quad command (Osnap), 67, 105, 176, 179

R

Rad command, 248
radius dimension, 247–248
RD command (DOS), 346
recalling a file, 42
rectangular coordinates, 15
rectangular reference, 25
Redo command, 32, 53
redundancy, 238
reflection line, 113
Regen command, 94–95, 222
regeneration, text, 221
Regular window, 46, 51
Remove command, 49
resetting computer, 333
Return key, 44
Romanc font, 216
root directory, 329
Rotate command, 57, 64, 90, 184
rotate plot, 157

S

Save command, 37, 54, 68, 96, 128, 134, 152, 158, 188, 293
scale factor, 190
scale line type, 151
scaling, 18
scan lines, 165
Screen menu, 13
section lines, 194
sectional view, 171, 188
sectioned view, 271
selecting objects, 41–53
selection box, 41, 49–50
selection cursor, 41
selection set, 49
SET command (DOS), 328
shape descriptions, 237
Shift key, 4–5
Simplex font, 216
Snap command, 82, 125, 173, 283
Snap mode, 21, 28, 84, 288
snap spacing, 21–22
software, 2–3
squares, drawing, 128
standard line types, 145–146
starting AutoCAD, 9–12
Status command, 18–19
Stretch command, 81, 92–94
Style command, 216, 226, 229–230, 234
subdirectory, 333, 337
surge suppressor, 2–3

T

Tab key, 4
Tan command (osnap), 86–89, 305, 306, 320

tangent circles, 104-105
Tangent command (osnap), 86-89, 305
tangent lines, 84, 86
technical drawing conventions, 1
template, border, 127
terminating commands, 44-45
text, 213
   regeneration, 221
   setting height of, 226, 233-234
Text command, 215, 219
Text mode, 23, 156
text screen, 18
three-dimensional drawing, 281-282
toggle key, 20
Tools option, 66
trim boundary, 69
Trim command, 57, 68-75, 81, 101-102, 144, 181-182, 185
   compared to Break, 101-102
   compared to Erase, 76-77
trimming, 73-75
Txt font, 215
TYPE command (DOS), 329
type styles, 213
   changing, 216-217
   displaying, 217

U

U command, 30-32, 53, 101, 250
Undo command, 30-31, 96-97, 158
Units command, 23, 82, 125, 172, 282
uppercase letters, 22
USER plot size, 166

V

verify on, 331

Vertical dimension command, 240, 242, 261-262
vertical spacing, 283
video display list, 342
video screen, 2-3, 9
views
   in engineering drawing, 1
   isometric, 128, 281-282, 284, 295, 307
   orthographic, 128, 281
   sectional, 171, 188, 271

W

Window command, 46
windows
   Crossing, 46, 51, 316
   Regular, 46, 51
write-protect
   notch, 325-326
   window, 325
write-protection, 325

X

X direction, 14
X-axis, 15

Y

Y direction, 14
Y-axis, 15

Z

Zoom command, 57, 61, 81, 94, 124, 134-135, 142, 145, 150-151, 165,

175, 177, 183, 188, 194, 206, 213,
227–228, 239, 259, 261, 264, 277,
285, 303, 307–308

dynamic, 107–109, 118, 245–246,
254, 321–322
Zoom window, 61-62

Selections from The SYBEX Library

COMPUTER-AIDED DESIGN AND DRAFTING

The ABC's of AutoCAD
Alan R. Miller
350pp. Ref. 498-4

This brief but effective introduction to AutoCAD quickly gets users drafting and designing with this complex CADD package. The essential operations and capabilities of AutoCAD are neatly detailed, using a proven, step-by-step method that is tailored to the results-oriented beginner.

Mastering AutoCAD (Second Edition)
George Omura
650pp. Ref. 502-6

Now in its second edition, this tutorial guide to computer-aided design and drafting with AutoCAD is perfect for newcomers to CADD, as well as AutoCAD users seeking greater proficiency. An architectural project serves as an example throughout.

Advanced Techniques in AutoCAD
Robert M. Thomas
410pp. Ref. 437-2

Develop custom applications using screen menus, command macros, and AutoLISP programming—no prior programming experience required. Topics include customizing the AutoCAD environment, advanced data extraction techniques, and much more.

DESKTOP PUBLISHING

Mastering Ventura
Matthew Holtz
546pp. Ref. 427-5

A complete, step-by-step guide to IBM PC desktop publishing with Xerox Ventura Publisher. Practical examples show how to use style sheets, format pages, cut and paste, enhance layouts, import material from other programs, and more.

Mastering PageMaker on the IBM PC
Antonia Stacy Jolles
287pp. Ref. 393-7

A guide to every aspect of desktop publishing with PageMaker: the vocabulary and basics of page design, layout, graphics and typography, plus instructions for creating finished typeset publications of all kinds.

Understanding PostScript Programming
David A. Holzgang
457pp. Ref. 396-1

In-depth treatment of PostScript for programmers and advanced users working on custom desktop publishing tasks. Hands-on development of programs for font creation, integrating graphics, printer implementations and more.

WORD PROCESSING

The ABC's of WordPerfect (Second Edition)
Alan R. Neibauer
300pp. Ref. 504-2

This introduction explains the basics of desktop publishing with WordPerfect 5: editing, layout, formatting, printing, sorting, merging, and more. Readers are shown how to use WordPerfect 5's new features to produce great-looking reports.

The ABC's of WordPerfect
Alan R. Neibauer
239pp. Ref. 425-9

This basic introduction to WordPefect consists of short, step-by-step lessons—for new users who want to get going fast. Topics range from simple editing and formatting, to merging, sorting, macros, and more. Includes version 4.2

Mastering WordPerfect 5
Susan Baake Kelly
475pp. Ref. 500-X

The revised and expanded version of this definitive guide is now on WordPerfect 5 and covers wordprocessing and basic desktop publishing. As more than 100,000 readers of the original edition can attest, no tutorial approaches it for clarity and depth of treatment. Sorting, line drawing, and laser printing included.

Mastering WordPerfect
Susan Baake Kelly
435pp. Ref. 332-5

Step-by-step training from startup to mastery, featuring practical uses (form letters, newsletters and more), plus advanced topics such as document security and macro creation, sorting and columnar math. Includes Version 4.2.

Advanced Techniques in WordPerfect 5
Kay Yarborough Nelson
500pp. Ref. 511-5

Now updated for Version 5, this invaluable guide to the advanced features of WordPefect provides step-by-step instructions and practical examples covering those specialized techniques which have most perplexed users – indexing, outlining, foreign-language typing, mathematical functions, and more.

Advanced Techniques in WordPerfect
Kay Yarborough Nelson
400pp. Ref. 431-3

Exact details are presented on how to accomplish complex tasks including special sorts, layered indexing, and statistical typing. Includes details on laser printing operations.

WordPerfect Desktop Companion
SYBEX Ready Reference Series
Greg Harvey/Kay Yarbourough Nelson
663pp. Ref. 507-7

This compact encyclopedia offers detailed, cross-referenced entries on every software feature, organized for fast, convenient on-the-job help. Includes self-contained enrichment material with tips, techniques and macros. Special information is included about laser printing using WordPerfect that is not available elsewhere. For Version 4.2.

WordPerfect 5 Desktop Companion
SYBEX Ready Reference Series
Greg Harvey/Kay Yarborough Nelson
700pp. Ref. 522-0

Desktop publishing features have been added to this compact encyclopedia. This title offers more detailed, cross-referenced entries on every software features including page formatting and layout, laser printing and word processing macros. New users of WordPerfect, and those new to Version 5 and desktop publishing will find this easy to use for on-the-job help. For Version 5.

WordPerfect Tips and Tricks (Second Edition)
Alan R. Neibauer
488pp. Ref. 489-5

This new edition is a real timesaver. For

on-the-job guidance and creative new uses for WordPerfect, this title covers all new features of Version 4.2 – including tables of authorities, concordance files, new print enhancements and more.

WordPerfect Instant Reference SYBEX Prompter Series
Greg Harvey/Kay Yarborough Nelson
254pp. Ref. 476-3

When you don't have time to go digging through the manuals, this fingertip guide offers clear, concise answers: command summaries, correct usage, and exact keystroke sequences for on-the-job tasks. Convenient organization reflects the structure of WordPerfect.

Mastering SAMNA
Ann McFarland Draper
503pp. Ref. 376-7

Word-processing professionals learn not just how, but also when and why to use SAMNA's many powerful features. Master the basics, gain power-user skills, return again and again for reference and expert tips.

The ABC's of MicroSoft WORD
Alan R. Neibauer
250pp. Ref. 497-6

Users who want to wordprocess straightforward documents and print elegant reports without wading through reams of documentation will find all they need to know about MicroSoft WORD in this basic guide. Simple editing, formatting, merging, sorting, macros and style sheets are detailed.

Mastering Microsoft WORD (Second Edition)
Matthew Holtz
479pp. Ref. 410-0

This comprehensive, step-by-step guide includes Version 3.1. Hands-on tutorials treat everything from word processing basics to the fundamentals of desktop publishing, stressing business applications throughout.

Advanced Techinques in Microsoft WORD
Alan R. Neibauer
537pp. Ref. 416-X

The book starts with a brief overview, but the main focus is on practical applications using advanced features. Topics include customization, forms, style sheets, columns, tables, financial documents, graphics and data management.

Mastering DisplayWrite 3
Michael E. McCarthy
447pp. Ref. 340-6

Total training, reference and support for users at all levels – in plain, non-technical language. Novices will be up and running in an hour's time; everyone will gain complete word-processing and document-management skills.

Mastering MultiMate Advantage II
Charles Ackerman
407pp. Ref. 482-8

This comprehensive tutorial covers all the capabilities of MultiMate, and highlights the differences between MultiMate Advantage II and previous versions – in pathway support, sorting, math, DOS access, using dBASE III, and more. With many practical examples, and a chapter on the On-File database.

Mastering MultiMate Advantage
Charles Ackerman
349pp. Ref. 380-5

Master much more than simple word processing by making the most of your software. Sample applications include creating expense reports, maintaining customer lists, merge-printing complex documents and more.

The Complete Guide to MultiMate
Carol Holcomb Dreger
208pp. Ref. 229-9

This step-by-step tutorial is also an excellent reference guide to MultiMate features and uses. Topics include search/replace, library and merge functions, repagination, document defaults and more.

Advanced Techniques in MultiMate
Chris Gilbert
275pp. Ref. 412-7
A textbook on efficient use of MultiMate for business applications, in a series of self-contained lessons on such topics as multiple columns, high-speed merging, mailing-list printing and Key Procedures.

The ABC's of WordStar Release 5
Alan Simpson
300pp. Ref. 516-6
This quick guide to getting started on WordStar Release 5's full capabilities covers editing, formatting, printing good-looking documents and more detailed word processing tasks. Ideal for the new user who wants an uncomplicated introduction.

Mastering WordStar Release 5
Greg Harvey
425pp. Ref. 491-7
Harvey's complete tutorial and reference guide covers all the features of WordStar Release 5 from elementary to advanced, and highlights functions new to this release. Better document processing, editing, and printing are emphasized throughout with examples.

Introduction to WordStar (Second Edition)
Arthur Naiman
208pp. Ref. 134-9
This all time bestseller is an engaging first-time introduction to word processing as well as a complete guide to using WordStar – from basic editing to blocks, global searches, formatting, dot commands, SpellStar and MailMerge.

Practical Techniques in WordStar Release 5
Julie Anne Arca
350pp. Ref. 495-X
Arca's classic is fully revised to cover WordStar 5's latest features. Designed to lead readers through step-by-step examples and exercises, this user-friendly title has sold over 100,000 copies in the original edition.

Mastering Wordstar on the IBM PC (Second Edition)
Arthur Naiman
200pp. Ref. 392-9
A specially revised and expanded introduction to Wordstar with SpellStar and MailMerge. Reviewers call it "clearly written, conveniently organized, generously illustrated and definitely designed from the user's point of view."

Practical WordStar Uses
Julie Anne Arca
303pp. Ref. 107-1
A hands-on guide to WordStar and MailMerge applications, with solutions to comon problems and "recipes" for day-to-day tasks. Formatting, merge-printing and much more; plus a quick-reference command chart and notes on CP/M and PC-DOS.

Practical Techniques in WordStar Release 4
Julie Anne Arca
334pp. Ref. 465-8
A task oriented approach to WordStar Release 4 and the DOS operating system. Special applications are covered in detail with summaries of important commands and step-by-step instructions.

WordStar Tips and Traps
Dick Andersen/Cynthia Cooper/Janet McBeen
239pp. Ref. 261-2
A real time-saver. Hundreds of self-contained entries, arranged by topic, cover everything from customization to dealing with the DISK FULL error to keystroke programming. Includes MailMerge and CorrectStar.

Mastering WordStar Release 4
Greg Harvey
413pp. Ref. 399-6
Practical training and reference for the latest WordStar release – from startup to advanced featues. Experienced users will

find new features highlighted and illustrated with hands-on examples. Covers math, macros, laser printers and more.

Introduction to WordStar 2000
David Kolodney/Thomas Blackadar
292pp. Ref. 270-1

This engaging, fast-paced series of tutorials covers everything from moving the cursor to print enhancements, format files, key glossaries, windows and MailMerge. With practical examples, and notes for former WordStar users.

Advanced Techniques in WordStar 2000
John Donovan
350pp. Ref. 418-6

This task-oriented guide to Release 2 builds advanced skills by developing practical applications. Tutorials cover everything from simple printing to macro creation and complex merging. With MailList, StarIndex and TelMerge.

DOS

ABC's of MS-DOS (Second Edition)
Alan R. Miller
233pp. Ref. 493-3

This handy guide to MS-DOS is all many PC users need to manage their computer files, organize floppy and hard disks, use EDLIN, and keep their computers organized. Additional information is given about utilities like Sidekick, and there is a DOS command and program summary. The second edition is fully updated for Version 3.3.

Mastering DOS
Judd Robbins
572pp. Ref. 400-3

"The most useful DOS book." This four-part, in-depth tutorial addresses the needs of users at all levels. Topics range from running applications, to managing files and directories, configuring the system, batch file programming, and techniques for system developers. A major book.

MS-DOS Handbook (Third Edition)
Richard Allen King
362pp. Ref. 492-5

This classic has been fully expanded and revised to include the latest features of MS-DOS Version 3.3. Two reference books in one, this title has separate sections for programmer and user. Multi-DOS partitons, 3 1/2disk format, batch file call and return feature, and comprehensive coverage of MS-DOS commands are included.

MS-DOS Power User's Guide, Volume I (Second Edition)
Jonathan Kamin
482pp. Ref. 473-9

A fully revised, expanded edition of our best-selling guide to high-performance DOS techniques and utilities – with details on Version 3.3. Configuration, I/O, directory structures, hard disks, RAM disks, batch file programming, the ANSI.SYS device driver, more.

MS-DOS Power User's Guide, Volume II
Martin Waterhouse/Jonathan Kamin
350pp, Ref. 411-9

A second volume of high-performance techniques and utilities, with expanded coverage of DOS 3.3, and new material on video modes, Token-Ring and PC Network support, micro-mainframe links, extended and expanded memory, multi-tasking systems, and more.

Performance Programming Under MS-DOS
Michael J. Young
436pp. Ref. 420-8

Practical techniques for maximizing performance in MS-DOS software by making best use of system resources. Topics include functions, interrupts, devices, multi-tasking, memory residency and more, with examples in C and assembler.

SYBEX Computer Books are different.

Here is why . . .

At SYBEX, each book is designed with you in mind. Every manuscript is carefully selected and supervised by our editors, who are themselves computer experts. We publish the best authors, whose technical expertise is matched by an ability to write clearly and to communicate effectively. Programs are thoroughly tested for accuracy by our technical staff. Our computerized production department goes to great lengths to make sure that each book is well-designed.

In the pursuit of timeliness, SYBEX has achieved many publishing firsts. SYBEX was among the first to integrate personal computers used by authors and staff into the publishing process. SYBEX was the first to publish books on the CP/M operating system, microprocessor interfacing techniques, word processing, and many more topics.

Expertise in computers and dedication to the highest quality product have made SYBEX a world leader in computer book publishing. Translated into fourteen languages, SYBEX books have helped millions of people around the world to get the most from their computers. We hope we have helped you, too.

For a complete catalog of our publications:

SYBEX, Inc. 2021 Challenger Drive, #100, Alameda, CA 94501
Tel: (415) 523-8233/(800) 227-2346   Telex: 336311
Fax: (415) 523-2373